D1599156

BOOKS,
MAPS,
AND
POLITICS

BOOKS, MAPS, AND POLITICS

A Cultural History
of the
Library of Congress,
1783–1861

CARL OSTROWSKI

UNIVERSITY OF MASSACHUSETTS PRESS

Amherst and Boston

LC 2003016307
ISBN 1-55849-433-2

Designed by Sally Nichols
Set in Adobe Caslon by Binghamton Valley Composition
Printed and bound by The Maple-Vail Book Manufacturing Group

Library of Congress Cataloging-in-Publication Data

Ostrowski, Carl, 1968–
    Books, maps, and politics : a cultural history of the Library of
Congress, 1783–1861 / Carl Ostrowski.
        p. cm. — (Studies in print culture and the history of the book)

Includes bibliographical references and index.
    ISBN 1-55849-433-2 (alk. paper)
    1. Library of Congress—History—18th century. 2. Library of
Congress—History—19th century. 3. National libraries—Washington
(D.C.)—History—18th century. 4. National libraries—Washington
(D.C.)—History—19th century. I. Title. II. Series.
Z733.U58 O87 2004
027.573—dc22

                                                    2003016307

British Library Cataloguing in Publication data are available.

TO TINA

CONTENTS

vii

ACKNOWLEDGMENTS

It is a pleasure to acknowledge here the many people and institutions who have assisted me in completing this book. My primary debt is to Ezra Greenspan, my adviser at the University of South Carolina, who first suggested to me the possibilities of situating Library of Congress history within the context of the history of the book in America and who then wholeheartedly put his considerable knowledge and experience at my disposal during every stage of composition. Without him, this book simply could not have been written.

No one could expect to make a contribution to Library of Congress history without consulting John Y. Cole of the Center for the Book at the Library. Since I first approached him years ago, as a graduate student in English with little specific training in library history, John has provided intellectual and material resources to the project and has shown continuing interest in my work in the field, for all of which I wish to thank him.

Members of the faculty in American literature and the history of the book in the Department of English at the University of South Carolina have all contributed to my knowledge of the literature and culture of eighteenth- and nineteenth-century America. Among them, I especially thank Joel Myerson, Benjamin Franklin V, Judith James, and Cynthia Davis.

My gratitude is due a number of archivists in the Manuscript Division of the Library of Congress, chief among them Josephus Nelson. I also thank the staffs of the National Archives and the Smithsonian Institution Archives in Washington, D.C., and the Maryland Historical Society in Baltimore.

The Faculty Research and Creative Activities Committee of Middle Tennessee State University (MTSU) made possible a reduced course load as I was revising this manuscript. Thanks to Andie Hudgins of the Interlibrary Loan Department of the MTSU Walker Library, who worked very hard tracking down resources on my behalf.

Paul Wright, my editor at the University of Massachusetts Press, showed unflagging confidence in my work. And I sincerely appreciate the efforts of the anonymous reviewers for the press, who led me down research paths I would never have thought to explore and whose influence on this manuscript has been profound.

A large part of chapter 5 appeared previously as "James Alfred Pearce and the Question of a National Library in Antebellum America" in *Libraries and Culture* 35, 2 (2000): 255–77. Copyright © 2000 by the University of Texas Press. All rights reserved. Thanks to editor Donald G. Davis for granting permission to republish that material here.

INTRODUCTION

The Library and the History
of the Book

The Library of Congress occupies a crossroads in American life where the nation's literary and political cultures intersect. Because of the Library's status as a national, governmental institution devoted to the collection and preservation of books, maps, and other materials, its history provides a revealing lens through which to study American attitudes toward books, literature, and the relationship between the government and the world of letters. This is especially true of the period from the first attempts to found the Library of Congress until the Civil War, when the Library's future was sometimes uncertain and its role in American life was continually redefined and contested by the country's leading political and literary figures, who often entertained widely divergent views about the nature and functions of a congressional library. Though congressmen generally regarded the Library of Congress as merely a small legislative library, because of its location in Washington and official connection with the federal government the Library often loomed much larger than this in the public imagination. In this book I explore conflicting views about the function of the Library of Congress and the larger question of government responsibility for fostering American literature.

By virtue of the range of books on its shelves and the way legislators used them, the Library of Congress was affected by, and in turn sometimes affected, nearly every major intellectual, social, historical and political current in public discourse in the nineteenth-century United States. The cultural nationalism that inspired calls for a national literature; debate over the role of women in American life; the abolitionist movement and sectional animosity; imperialist expansion of the nation's borders; and the transformation of the nation from a republic led by a small group of governing elites into a more raucous and egalitarian democracy— all these familiar themes of nineteenth-century American history find expression in a full treatment of Library of Congress history. The Library of Congress is described in this book as a site where competing visions of the national character met and played out, sometimes in the discourse surrounding the Library and sometimes in its collections. This narrative of the Library's foundation and growth is thereby connected to developments in American society that would escape the view of a more narrowly focused history. Library of Congress historiography has much to gain from such a widened perspective.

The Library of Congress performed certain key functions for its users in the nineteenth century. Primarily, the books in the collection assisted congressmen and highly placed members of the executive and judicial branches of government in the difficult task of crafting legislation for a young and growing nation. A look at successive catalogs of the Library, especially in its earliest years, reveals some of the books that early proponents and administrators of the Library believed were essential for this purpose. Analysis of Library of Congress catalogs and comparison of them with social library catalogs of the era indicate that law, politics, economics, geography, and history were the subjects most assiduously cultivated by members of the Joint Committee on the Library, who selected its books.

The utility of these books is not difficult to discern. For statesmen of the founding era and the early nineteenth century, books about international law provided guidance in diplomacy and foreign relations, while texts on political theory helped legislators to define the principles of classical republicanism on which domestic law was supposed to be based. Up-to-date mercantile information and books on economic theory were necessary as Congress legislated trade and tariff regulations. In his initial proposal on behalf of a congressional library, James Madison had envisioned a collection of books strong in American history and geography that would help legislators to document the nation's territorial boundaries. In subsequent years, particularly during the 1830s and 1840s, the Library did indeed serve as a repository for the books and maps that described the virtues of the West for settlement, argued in favor of American expansion, and helped legislators determine the nation's boundaries with Mexico and Canada.

A secondary function of the Library was providing reading material for the entertainment and instruction of congressmen and their families. Examining this aspect of the Library brings into focus the relationship between the Library of Congress and the nation's evolving literary culture. Acquiring the products of the nation's rapidly expanding publishing industry, the Library participated in this growth. The richness and variety of America's burgeoning literary culture were amply represented on the shelves of the Library, where the major American literary authors of the period were found in the Library's catalogs. The Library of Congress also purchased the works of the leading British writers of the day. In fact, the Library acquired pirated editions of their works even as these same British authors were petitioning and sometimes visiting Congress to lobby for an international copyright law. Providing literary material to congressmen and their families was, in the opinion of its statutory users, one of the Library's most important functions in the early nineteenth century.

Third, the Library was often pressed into service as a symbol. Needless to say, what it symbolized depended on the political slant and immediate purposes of the person writing or speaking about it. To militant supporters of a limited government in the early years of the Republic, for example, the Library of Congress could represent abstruse learning and the useless cultural baggage of the Old World. To cultural nationalists of a later era, the Library was held up as a symbol of either the nation's cultural achievement or the government's failure to do enough to support American writers as they forged a distinctive national literature. These were symbolic functions that writers in the leading literary journals often forced on the Library but were never wholeheartedly endorsed by the legislators who funded it. In its function as a tourist attraction and art gallery for visitors to Washington, the Library also served as a symbol of the progress of American art and architecture.

This history of the Library of Congress is based on the assumption that the Library's eventual development into America's national library was neither inevitable nor straightforward. Political pressures from both the Right and the Left threatened the institution in varying degrees throughout the antebellum period. Indeed, some political commentators expressed the opinion that the young nation had no pressing need for a national library at all, that such an institution was irrelevant or even injurious to the political goals of a republic. The Library's slow rate of growth is particularly notable in comparison with that of the great European national libraries of the period, such as the British Museum Library and the Bibliothèque Nationale. The forces that challenged and inhibited the Library's development warrant at least as much attention as the attitudes that encouraged it in order to gain a comprehensive understanding of the Library's meaning to nineteenth-century Americans.

In this book I devote particular attention to textual aspects of the Library of Congress. Primary sources of evidence include the speeches, newspaper editorials, and letters written about the Library (and about early proposals for a congressional library) between 1783 and 1861. Examining the underlying assumptions of this discourse, one finds that American faith in a dissemination of knowledge through cheap printed media, vaunted by early republican statesmen as the surest way to protect the Republic from tyranny, militated against the collection of valuable books at a central location in Washington. In a related way, the deep suspicion that Americans harbored in the early republican era toward European cultural artifacts, seeing in them emblems of a dissipating and anti-republican luxury, persisted in the American consciousness throughout the nineteenth century with deleterious effects on Library of Congress development.

Most historians of the nineteenth century view the period as one of steady, at times rapid, democratization of America's print culture in which new segments of American society, including women and the middle class, gained access to forms of literature and types of information that previously had been the exclusive province of the social elite. Whether and how these democratizing tendencies influenced administration of the Library of Congress is discussed in the chapters that follow. When the history of the Library is set against the backdrop of changes in the print culture of the era, it becomes clear that for long periods, particularly during the stewardship of the Library by Joint Committee chairman James Alfred Pearce in the 1840s and 1850s, the legislators responded to these changes by retaining a wary, guarded control over the collections of the Library of Congress.

In discussing issues related to American print culture, I employ a methodology indebted to the interdisciplinary field known as the history of the book, defined by Robert Darnton, one of its principal figures, as the attempt "to understand how ideas were transmitted through print and how exposure to the written word affected human thought and behavior" in the five hundred years since the invention of the printing press.[1] As John Feather has argued, library history, to the degree that it moves outside of institutional history to encompass the broader cultural milieu in which a library exists, "has a unique contribution to make to the history of books."[2] This book about the Library of Congress has therefore been influenced by the work of library historians who, in line with Feather's advice, have advanced the field well beyond mere celebratory chronicles into important contributions to the history of the book and to social history. In 1988 Wayne Wiegand suggested that "American library history could benefit substantially by enlisting the interest of scholars now working in related fields like American cultural, literary, social, intellectual, and book history, to name but a few."[3] Wiegand's own works, as well as such books as British library historian Alistair Black's study of the English public library, have turned in this direction, and in writing this book I have regarded their richly contextualized works of library history as models. In the narrower field of Library of Congress history in the past two decades, Charles Goodrum and Helen Dalrymple, Jane Aikin Rosenberg, and in particular John Y. Cole have offered insightful, objective appraisals of the institution's past that have influenced my own approach to the subject.[4] Achieving a more complete understanding of the history of the book in America requires a newly historicized analysis of the Library of Congress and its role in the politics of the nineteenth century.

This account of the history of the Library of Congress is divided into six chapters. In chapter 1, I demonstrate the specific political purposes that statesmen of the founding era expected books to serve, in order to show why James Madison and others believed a library was indispensable to the proper functioning of Congress. This chapter also includes a discussion of the early, failed attempts in 1783 and 1790 to establish a legislative library and explicates some of the attitudes that made such a collection seem undesirable or unnecessary to the political objectives of the young nation. Chapter 2 covers the period 1800–1812, focusing renewed attention on the little-known William Tatham, whose attempts to sell his books and maps to Congress reveal much about the perceived political value of books owned by the government. This chapter also includes a comparison of Library of Congress holdings with social libraries of the era, to show how the books in the Library were peculiarly suited to the purposes of the institution. Chapter 3 opens with discussion of the controversy surrounding purchase of Thomas Jefferson's books to replace the Library destroyed by the British in the War of 1812. In this chapter I also examine the Librarianship (1815–29) of Washington man of letters George Watterston, one of the earliest American literary authors to rely on a government patronage position to further his writing career. Watterston encouraged legislators and other Americans to see the Library of Congress as a fledgling national library on the European model, and although certain members of the Joint Library Committee were sympathetic to this vision, Congress as a whole ignored Watterston's efforts and continued to authorize limited appropriations and a utilitarian conception of the institution.

Chapter 4 covers the election of Andrew Jackson and the effects of the principles associated with Jacksonian democracy on Library of Congress history. While journalists and authors lobbied for an expanded Library of Congress to meet the needs of American literature and scholarship, Congress continued to deny responsibility for the progress of American letters, an attitude embodied in its rejection of international copyright legislation. Chapter 4 also places emphasis on an issue that has not been treated in any of the previous literature on the Library: the question of gender as a factor governing access to the books in the Library. In Chapter 5 I discuss James Alfred Pearce's remarkable influence over governmental involvement in America's literary culture around midcentury, both as chairman of the Joint Committee on the Library and as a member of the Board of Regents of the Smithsonian Institution, which very nearly took on the mantle of the national library in the 1840s and 1850s. This chapter documents the extraordinary influence of a single highly placed, conservative, forceful personality in resisting the democratization of American letters and the demands of the national library proponents. Finally, in chapter 6 I show how congressmen used their Library in the 1840s and 1850s. In its focus on specific book and territorial acquisitions between publication of the 1839 and 1849 catalogs, this chapter shows how deeply the Library was implicated in the expansionist ideology of the age.

CHAPTER ONE

Books, Classical Republicanism, and Proposals for a Congressional Library

The Library of Congress today is an immense institution whose place on the American cultural scene is unquestioned. As of the year 2000, the two hundredth anniversary of its foundation, the Library housed some 119 million items in 460 languages on a universal array of subjects.[1] Copyright deposits and congressional appropriations ensure its continued collection development. And although ministering to the needs of Congress remains an important aspect of its mission, the Library's staff also caters to researchers from around the world as well as to ordinary American citizens. The Library plays an important leadership role in the library world, and through agencies such as its Center for the Book, which promotes the importance of reading and the study of book history, the Library reaches out from Washington to the rest of the country. As a symbol of the nation's commitment to the value of literature and the preservation of knowledge, the Library is an indispensable and seemingly irreplaceable institution. Who could object to such a magnificent institution?[2]

And yet, when the idea for a congressional library—let alone a national library—was first broached, it did meet opposition. The story of the Library of Congress properly begins not with its founding but with failed attempts in the 1780s and 1790s to establish such a library. These failures demonstrate that even a modestly funded governmental library with a strictly circumscribed role was at the time a controversial proposition. For the idea of a congressional library to succeed, it would have to be perceived by frugal legislators as a strictly utilitarian venture. And once this utilitarian rationale for a library took hold, those legislators and cultural critics who envisioned a more grandiose mission for the Library found it difficult to dislodge.

In this chapter, I describe these first attempts to found a congressional library, including the reasons cited in support of and in opposition to such a library. Taking into account the political and cultural context of the era, one finds that books occupied a conflicted place in classical republican ideology of the late eighteenth century. Republican political theorists valued books insofar as they fell under the rubric of useful knowledge and could help solve practical problems. Examination of their published papers shows how the founding fathers relied on a core of books in politics, economics, law, and history in conducting state affairs. On the other hand, books—and by extension, a congressional library— were also potentially regarded as symbols of the corrupting power of luxury to subvert republican institutions. The association of books with luxury, once raised in these initial debates over a federally funded library, recurred persistently through the nineteenth century in discourse surrounding the Library of Congress and its role in American life.

The Madison Proposal of 1783

James Madison and Theodorick Bland, as members of the Second Continental Congress in Philadelphia, were the initial sponsors of a congressional library.[3] Bland, a delegate from Virginia, proposed on 1 July, 1782 that a list of books be imported for the use of Congress. On 21 November, Bland's motion was referred to a committee consisting of James Madison as chair, Hugh Williamson, and Thomas Miflin.[4] Madison's committee reported in favor of Bland's motion in January 1783 and presented a list of 307 titles it recommended for the use of Congress, as well as a set of arguments in favor of the proposal.

Madison's notes from the *Journals of the Continental Congress* on the reasons offered in favor of and against the purchase of books effectively summarize the committee's thoughts on the uses that governmentally owned books would serve. In favor of the report, Madison records, the contention was made that authors on "the law of Nations, treaties, negotiations, etc." were indispensable in order to render proceedings of the Congress "conformable with propriety"; the lack of such authorities was already "manifest in several important acts of Congress." It was also argued that Congress should lose no time in collecting books and tracts related to American history and the affairs of the United States, because they would be necessary "not only as materials for a history of the United States, but might be rendered still more [valuable] by future pretensions against their rights from Spain or other powers which had shared in the discoveries and possessions of the New World." The arguments against the report, "the inconveniency of advancing even a few hundred pounds at this crisis" and "the difference of expense between procuring the books during the war and after a peace," Madison records, "prevailed by a considerable majority." A subsequent motion to confine the purchase to only "the most essential part of the books" also was rejected.[5]

The authors of the report favoring a congressional library urged that books be purchased in order to achieve well-defined political goals. The contention that books on treaties, negotiations, and the law of nations were necessary to Congress obviously conformed to a narrow view of the function of the proposed library. Recognized authorities on international law, such as seventeenth-century Dutch statesman Hugo Grotius and German jurist Samuel Freiherr von Pufendorf, as well as eighteenth-century Swiss jurists Jean Jacques Burlamaqui and Emmerich de Vattel, all of whom appear on Madison's list, were frequently consulted by the founding fathers in the complicated political and legal conflicts of the Revolutionary and post-Revolutionary years. Books by these authors were invoked in arguments concerning the political rights of the colonies with respect to Great Britain, in negotiating alliances with foreign powers such as France, and in justifying or challenging seizures and impoundments of ships.

Madison's report in favor of the library also argued the necessity of collecting the materials required to write the history of the United States. But the collecting and writing of history in this context was by no means a purely belletristic activity, as Madison's comments made clear. The proposed history would serve the purpose of securing the territorial boundaries of the young nation against the claims of foreign powers. In his dissertation on the 1783 list of books, Loren Smith singles out for analysis Madison's intent to collect Americana, grouped together on the list rather than placed in other relevant categories (histories of America were in the "America" section rather than the "History" section), concluding that "Madison wanted all things American in one place [in the list]" because "those materials were the subject matter upon which were based the government's territorial claims. Should those claims produce diplomatic confrontations with Spain, England, or France, the 'America' section would become absolutely crucial to the success of the United States."[6] Books and maps collected in a government library held potentially enormous practical value.

The importance accorded to history in justifying the proposed library is consistent with what H. Trevor Colbourn has observed in regard to the Revolutionary generation, of whom he noted: "To the eighteenth-century colonist, the study of history was a prestigious and a practical pursuit."[7] Histories were of practical use to eighteenth-century legislators because in recording human behavior of the past, it was held by Enlightenment thinkers, histories would allow statesmen to forge a more perfect political state for the future. In other words, the leaders of Madison's generation saw the collecting and writing of history in explicitly political, practical terms. The proposed library, which was heavily weighted toward historical and political titles, would likewise be expected to serve limited, practical ends.

That the congressional library proposed by Madison in 1783, unlike the Library of Congress as it developed much later in its history, did not represent a comprehensive collection of the world's knowledge or a symbol of the nation's cultural standing is evident in the headings under which the books were listed: law of nature and nations, treaties and negotiations, general history, chronology, geography, particular history, politics, law, war, marine, languages (only dictionaries are included), and America.[8] The breadth of knowledge represented in the list extends to the full range of subjects on which legislators might need information to carry out their duties, but no further.

As important to understanding the function of Madison's proposed library is a recognition of what he chose not to include. Two major categories of literature that Madison's committee completely ignored are theology and belles lettres or fiction, mainstays of most other libraries of the period. College libraries were heavily laden with works on theology; in the Harvard library of 1790, for example, "theological works comprised almost half (49 percent) of the collection."[9] Social libraries of the era also stressed holdings in theology. My analysis of six social library catalogs from the early nineteenth century in chapter 2 shows theology holdings ranging from 8 to 22 percent of collections. Although the Library Company of Philadelphia, which the Second Continental Congress was using in 1783 in lieu of a library of its own, did not emphasize theology, it did include a fair number of titles in the belles lettres. About 20 percent of titles in its 1741 catalog were literature, primarily plays and poems. This was typical; catalogs of six social libraries from the early nineteenth century reveal collections in literature or the belles lettres ranging from 12 to 32 percent of holdings. Or to take an example a little closer in time to Madison's 1783 list, the Library Company of Baltimore in 1797 devoted 20 percent of the collection to theology and over 11 percent to novels and romances.[10]

Madison focused on the subjects of America, history, politics, and the law of nature and nations in constructing his list of desiderata for a congressional library. According to an analysis of the list carried out by Tom Glynn and Craig C. Hagensick, the entries in the section of the list titled "America" (103 of 307 entries) actually constituted 42 percent of the total number of volumes.[11] These were mostly histories and travel narratives, many of them concerned with the exploration and settlement of the North American continent by European states. Among the numerous accounts of voyages in the New World (by Martin Frobisher, Henry Hudson, and others), for example, was Jonathan Carver's *Travels through the Interior Parts of North America, in the Years 1766, 1767, and 1768* (1778). Narrating his search for a Northwest passage, Carver offered a glowing account of the settlement and commercial possibilities of the Great Lakes region, complete with exotic animals, abundant natural resources, and romanticized Native Americans. Carver's travel book provided maps and information about a region of the country that American statesmen knew would become more important as settlers continued to move west. Madison presumably hoped that such books as this, along with histories of European settlement, would aid in protecting territorial claims in the West. Also important in this regard would have been the entry in the "America" section for "all treaties entered into with the natives of North America" and the nine titles in the "Geography" section, such as the entry that simply said "Collection of best maps."[12]

Histories of the New World by Spanish, French, and British authors form the other major group of works in the "America" section of Madison's list. In *The History of America* (1777), Scottish historian William

Robertson described the exploration and conquest of the Americas by the Spanish; a distinctive quality of the work was Robertson's description of the cultures of the Aztecs, the Incas, and North American Indians. While Robertson implied that conquest of the New World was an inevitable development in world history, a more critical account of colonialism was embodied in another of the books in this section of the list, Guillaume-Thomas-François de (Abbé) Raynal's *A Philosophical and Political History of the Settlements and Trade of the Europeans in the East and West Indies* (1777, English edition). Describing events from an economic and philosophical perspective, Raynal denounced slavery, mercantilism, and colonization by conquest, earning his book a modern assessment as "the founding work of anti-colonialism."[13]

The high value that Madison and his contemporaries placed on history is clearly reflected in the seventy-nine entries contained in the two categories of the list titled "General History" and "Particular History," a figure that does not include the many histories listed in the section on America. European history was strongly emphasized, with nineteen entries devoted to the history of Great Britain and thirty-seven titles on other nations of Europe. The only non-European nations represented were Turkey (two titles) and China (one title). English history was of particular importance to Americans, whose interpretation of that history was crucial to justifying the Revolution. Madison included works with widely differing perspectives on this subject. In *The History of England* (a revised edition of which was published in 1778), David Hume challenged the Whig interpretation of ancient British constitutionalism, arguing that eighteenth-century British political liberty was not an inheritance from Anglo-Saxon times but an accidental product of seventeenth-century English history. This view made him unpalatable to Thomas Jefferson, who, along with many of his American contemporaries, preferred Paul de Rapin-Thoyras's more radical *Histoire d'Angleterre* (1725–31), which "provided indisputable proof of the theories of all of the radical and anti-establishment writers by demonstrating their validity through a thousand years of English history."[14] Both works appeared on Madison's list. For more contemporary British and European history, Madison included *The Annual Register, or A View of the History, Politics, and Literature for the Year.* This periodical provided a narrative overview of the history of Europe during the past year, a chronicle that listed British and world historical events in calendrical form, a compilation of state papers, and several sections extracting recent publications in various subjects.[15]

Ancient history was also important to Madison and the statesmen of the era. Greek and Roman history was represented by eleven titles on Madison's list, including both ancient and contemporary authors. Edward Gibbon's *The History of the Decline and Fall of the Roman Empire* (1776–88), though controversial for statements perceived as attacks on Christianity, was recognized immediately on publication as a definitive work. Gibbon's combination of antiquarian detail and a broader philosophical perspective integrating social and cultural history made this book the culmination of Enlightenment innovations in historiography. Despite its achievement, though, Gibbon's work did not exercise nearly as great an influence on the founders as the Greek historian Plutarch's *Lives of the Noble Greeks and Romans*. Plutarch paired the biographies of his Greek and Roman subjects to better illustrate their moral character, and his technique of drawing ethical lessons about government and citizenship from the sketches made him extremely popular among statesmen of the early Republic. Plutarch is cited in six of the *Federalist* essays, and Hamilton, Madison, and Jay's collective pseudonym in those papers, Publius, comes from a figure in Plutarch's history.[16]

The next largest section of Madison's list was titled "Politics" (39 of 307 entries). Titles in this division naturally included the authors who influenced the political theories of the founding generation. No author was cited in late-eighteenth-century American political debate more frequently than French political philosopher Charles-Louis de Secondat Montesquieu.[17] In *The Spirit of the Laws* (1748), Montesquieu described the distinguishing features of different types of government (despotism, republics, and monarchies, the last of which he ultimately favored), praised the design of the English constitution, and argued that a people's form of government must be suited to their local culture and climate. His work was "accepted as the authoritative word on the structure of good government" among many American statesmen.[18] Historians continue to debate the extent of John Locke's influence on the founding generation, but it is clear that his *Two Treatises on Government* (1690) provided the terms in which statesmen discussed the social compact, the need for government to protect private property, and the right of oppressed people to rebel against their rulers.[19] Those who found Locke's stand against tyranny too moderate could also find on Madison's list seventeenth-century English Whig Algernon Sidney's *Discourses concerning Government* (1698), a book that Revolutionists in America championed for its strong defense of popular government and its justification of violent rebellion.[20] The "Politics" section also included works that would today be classified under economics, and again Madison's catholicity is evident. Listed were both James Steuart, whose work *An Inquiry into the Principles of Political Economy* (1767) contained his advocacy of vigorous state intervention in economic affairs, and *Wealth of Nations* (1776) by Adam Smith, who took the position that an unregulated free market is the surest path to national prosperity.[21]

Madison's next priorities in drawing up a list of books for the Continental Congress were the law of nature and nations (thirty-one entries) and law (fourteen entries). Books on the law of nations by Grotius, Pufendorf, Burlamaqui, and Vattel were applied in practice to disputes related to international law. They also had a more theoretical appeal, setting forth the principles of the law of nature under which, in part, colonial statesmen had justified their rebellion. The "Law" section included Edward Coke's *Institutes* (1628–44) and William Blackstone's *Commentaries on the Laws of England* (1765–69), works that explained the origin and extent of English common law. The colonists had appealed to these authors when claiming that the Revolution was at heart not a rebellion against but rather a defense of the principles of English law. Finally, Charles-Joseph Panckoucke's edition of Diderot's influential *Encyclopédie Méthodique* (192 volumes, 1782–1832) must not be overlooked; it was the first title on the list.[22]

The Print Culture of Late-Eighteenth-Century American Statesmen

The books that Madison and his committee believed the Continental Congress needed in order to carry out its work effectively were an essential part of the print culture of late-eighteenth-century America. This print culture can be defined as the universe of printed information that Americans of the eighteenth century encountered and referred to frequently, including books, newspapers, broadsides, almanacs, and pamphlets. What is reconstructed in the paragraphs that follow is one specific and vital element of that culture: the books used by statesmen in their public lives. Looking at the published writings and private correspondence of Franklin, Hamilton, Jefferson, Adams, and Washington, one finds not only what books these political figures knew but specifically how they used books to solve practical problems. Books were consulted in justifying the break from Great Britain, fashioning the new nation's form of government, establishing its borders, and responding to its day-to-day crises. The judiciousness of Madison's choices for the proposed congressional library is revealed by the frequency with which his chosen books were employed to serve these ends. These same books were eventually listed in the 1802 catalog of the Library of Congress as well, suggesting the value to statesmen of the era of a select list of standard works on history, geography, politics, economics, and law.

The bookish Benjamin Franklin realized early in the struggle against British authority that citation of pertinent books on legal and political theory played a crucial role in supporting the colonial cause. His writings often show Franklin referring to books that later appeared on Madison's list in defense of the rights of the colonies. In pressing for a repeal of the Townshend Acts in 1770, Franklin, living in England at the time, wrote a series of articles called "The Colonist's Advocate" for the British newspaper the *Public Advertiser*. In the first essay, he quoted from Locke's *Of Civil Government* on the injustice of Parliament taxing the unrepresented colonies, and he concluded the sixth essay by quoting from Sidney's *Discourses concerning Government*. Franklin acknowledged the relevance of books to the American political situation in 1772 when he wrote to his son William, governor of New Jersey, that while in England he (Benjamin) had purchased many books "consisting chiefly of such as contain Knowledge that may hereafter be useful to America."[23]

One of Madison's primary justifications for the proposed library was that books on the subject of American history were useful in protecting the nation's territorial integrity. A striking instance of exactly such a use of history books occurs in the career of Alexander Hamilton. In 1786, Hamilton had been retained by the state of New York as an attorney in its dispute with the state of Massachusetts over western lands. In preparing for the case, Hamilton drew up notes on the history of North and South America that included references to Robertson's *History of America*, Hume's *History of England*, and Antonio de Herrera y Tordesillas's *General History of the Continent and Islands of America*, all three of which appear on Madison's list (and in the 1802 catalog of the Library of Congress). The matter was settled with New York retaining sovereignty of the disputed area but Massachusetts claiming the "right of preemption of the soil from native Indians."²⁴ This deployment of authority drawn from a handful of history books shows how such books, used skillfully, were of immediate practical value.

In their public political writings as well, Hamilton and John Adams often quoted from the established legal and political authorities of the day, writers whose utility Madison had championed in his proposal. In his letters to the *Boston Gazette* in 1773 on the issue of the independence of judges, the books that John Adams found useful to America included Blackstone's *Commentaries*, Coke's *Institutes*, and Hume's *History of England*, from which he quoted at length to support his position that the colonial judiciary needed to be protected from public opinion and the whim of Parliament and the Crown.²⁵ In a 1775 pamphlet called *The Farmer Refuted*, Hamilton supported the revolutionary cause with a wide array of allusions, including Blackstone on the law of nature, David Hume on the need for checks of parliamentary power, and Malachy Postlethwayt on the importance of the colonies to Britain's interests (and the corresponding injustice of Britain's treatment of them). In *Federalist* No. 12, published in 1787, he alluded to French finance minister Jacques Necker's *A Treatise of the Administration of the Finances of France*, while in "Federalist no. 84," from 1788, he cited Blackstone in defending the proposed Constitution against the charge that it had no Bill of Rights. And in his newspaper articles in defense of John Jay's treaty with Great Britain in 1795, Hamilton quoted from or alluded to specific passages from Justinian's *Institutes* and from books by Blackstone, Coke, the French jurist Jean Domat, Grotius, Pufendorf, and Vattel. Every author listed in this paragraph was recommended by Madison and later purchased by the committee that drew up the first book list for the Library of Congress.²⁶ That Franklin, Adams, and Hamilton quoted these writers in newspapers and pamphlets, expecting readers to understand and appreciate the references, testifies to the popularity and weight of authority behind these books.

Madison's list also encompassed the works on finance and economics that Hamilton called upon in his landmark reports as secretary of the treasury. Sources for Hamilton's 1790 *Report on a National Bank* include Smith's *Wealth of Nations*; Wyndham Beawes's *Lex Mercatoria; or, The Merchant's Companion*; Postlethwayt's *Universal Dictionary*, Adam Anderson's *Origin of Commerce*, and the works of John Law. The editors of the Hamilton papers aver that in his 1791 *Report on the Subject of Manu-*

factures, Hamilton leaned heavily on Necker's *Finances of France*, with Smith, Hume, Postlethwayt, Steuart, and Vattel also serving as sources. And in the 1791 *Report on the Establishment of a Mint*, Steuart's *Principles of Political Economy* exercised the most influence, with Anderson, Necker, Postlethwayt, and Smith also contributing ideas.[27] Without exception, all these sources were listed in Madison's 1783 report to Congress.

Jefferson's correspondence also provides an instructive example of the authors and books he considered necessary in the education of a statesman, and not surprisingly, many of these titles were also listed in the report Madison submitted to Congress as well as in early catalogs of the Library of Congress.[28] In recommending books that would aid Thomas Mann Randolph in his study of the law and preparation for public office in 1790, Jefferson called Randolph's attention to Smith's *Wealth of Nations*; Montesquieu's *Spirit of the Laws*; Locke's *Discourses concerning Government*; the *Federalist* papers; Scottish political writer James Burgh's *Political Disquisitions*; eighteenth-century Swiss statesman Jean Louis de Lolme; eighteenth-century French statesman Anne-Robert-Jacques Turgot; a seventeenth-century treatise on parliamentary law called the *Lex Parliamentaria*; and Hume's political essays. Of the nine works or authors listed here, the 1783 proposal to Congress contained six. The *Federalist* papers, of course, had not yet been composed in 1783. Considering that the edition of de Lolme's *Constitution de l'Angleterre* that Jefferson had in mind was probably the one published in London in 1785 and that Jefferson himself acquired the works of Turgot only in 1788, Madison's list was as complete as possible in proposing to supply to Congress exactly those works which Jefferson considered as prerequisites to the practice of statecraft.[29]

Madison's list was designed to stock the proposed congressional library with books that offered a basic education in political science and that provided answers to specific political questions. The books on international law or the law of nature and nations by Vattel, Grotius, Pufendorf, Montesquieu, and Burlamaqui were probably the most frequently invoked by members of the founding generation in negotiating political affairs. William Bradford wrote to Madison in 1774 that the Continental Congress made frequent use of the holdings of the Library Company of Philadelphia: "By what I was told Vattel Burlamaqui Locke & Montesquieu seem to be the standards to which they refer either when settling the rights of the Colonies or when a dispute arises on the justice or propriety of a measure." And Edmund Randolph, attorney general of Virginia in 1782, wrote to Madison that the authority for impounding a British ship had come from one of these works: "this condition was drawn from the 21. cap: [chapter] of the third book of Grotius."[30]

The usefulness of Emmerich de Vattel's *Le droit des gens* (the French title of the book rendered in translation as *The Law of Nations*) was endorsed by Benjamin Franklin as well. As a member of the Continental Congress in Philadelphia in 1775, Franklin wrote to Charles-Guillaume-Frédéric Dumas, who had sent him a copy of his own edition of this book: "Your edition of Vattel . . . came to us in good season, when the circumstances of a rising state make it necessary frequently to consult the law of nations. Accordingly, that copy which I kept . . . has been continually in the hands of the members of our congress." And in 1779 Franklin made good use of this title himself, in his capacity as a diplomat in France working on the new nation's behalf. He wrote from Passy to the foreign minister of Denmark to protest Denmark's seizure of three American ships, quoting in French from "Vattel, in his excellent Treatise entitled *Le Droit des Gens*," to argue the injustice of the Danish action. He quoted from Hugo Grotius in the same letter.[31]

Finally, the utility of this class of books is demonstrated convincingly by reference to two incidents that occurred during Washington's presidency. Apprehensive in late 1790 about the possibility of war between Great Britain and Spain, Washington wrote to John Jay, chief justice of the Supreme Court, and to Treasury secretary Alexander Hamilton soliciting their opinions on whether the United States had the right to refuse to allow British troops to march across American soil from Detroit to the Mississippi River. Deeming a refusal improper, Jay appealed to chapter 7, volume 3 of Vattel's *Law of Nations*. In his own answer Hamilton was more thorough, appealing to Pufendorf, Grotius, and Jean Barbeyrac (a commentary on Grotius) and quoting Vattel at length before arriving at the conclusion that it would be dangerous to refuse passage.[32]

A similar instance of dueling legal authorities occurred in 1793, when Washington consulted Hamilton and Jefferson on the question of whether the United States should preserve treaty relations with the volatile French revolutionary government. As secretary of state, Jefferson decided the question affirmatively in part by citing the authority of Grotius, Vattel, Pufendorf, and the German philosopher Christian von Wolff. In a remarkable display of erudition and of the utilitarian value of these books, Jefferson in his letter quoted side by side the relevant passages from all four authors to demonstrate to Washington that Hamilton's use of a passage from Vattel in arguing the negative side of the question had been spurious.[33] Books of such immediate utility were exactly the titles that Madison had in mind when assembling his proposal for a congressional library. The books on his list constituted an education in the abstract principles on which a republican form of government would be based and provided answers to specific questions of public policy and international law.

Rejection of the Madison and Elbridge Gerry Proposals

Given that books served such eminently practical ends, the rejection of Madison's proposed library requires explanation. The two explicit arguments that prevailed in objection to Madison's report were "the inconveniency of advancing even a few hundred pounds at this crisis" and "the difference of expence between procuring the books during the war & after a peace."[34] Fulmer Mood summarizes them: "The arguments against adoption of the report were grounded entirely on the need for economy. At this moment of serious fiscal crisis, some members urged, no money was available for the purchase of books."[35] Because American publishers constituted little more than a cottage industry, they were unable to supply the legislators with American editions of the relatively expensive volumes that Madison listed. Having to be imported from English book dealers, the books would be cheaper after the war, when normal trade relations had resumed. But imported items, especially of a cultural nature, were subject to a charge of "luxury," meaning that they were perceived as symbols of Old World decadence and aristocratic privilege. As I will discuss later, this charge of luxury is one of a number of elements of American thought about what books and libraries represented for the Republic that may have made the issue of a congressional library more controversial than it at first seems.

Another more concrete reason for the demurral by the Continental Congress is that it already had many of these books on hand. With access to books in the social libraries of Philadelphia (and later New York), most legislators felt little need for a congressional library before the capital moved to Washington, which was devoid of libraries in 1800. In 1774, when the First Continental Congress met in Carpenters' Hall in Philadelphia, the Library Company of Philadelphia ordered that "the Librarian furnish the Gentlemen who are to meet in Congress in this City with the use of such Books as they may have occasion for during their sitting, taking a Receipt for them."[36] Meeting in City Hall in New York City in 1789, the first Congress of the United States acting under the authority of the Constitution was granted use of New York Society Library books. And in 1791, President Washington offered on behalf of Congress, which had relocated again, "his best thanks" to the directors of the Library Company of Philadelphia "for the polite manner in which they have offered him the use of the books in the Library."[37] Until the beginning of the nineteenth century, statesmen gained access to books for official legislative purposes through social libraries, private corporations whose directors supported governmental activities apparently in the spirit of civic responsibility.[38]

Finally, the Continental Congress may have been disinclined to accept Madison's proposal because in addition to social libraries, the legislators had their own (sometimes extensive) personal libraries on which to rely for books. Madison was an avid book collector with a large private library, which he had crated "and sent from Montpelier to New York when the First Federal Congress was in session" and then moved "to Philadelphia and Georgetown as the peripatetic new government took him from Congress to the State House and finally the White House."[39] It seems to have been common for members of Congress to ship parts of their private libraries to the location of the government. Given the utility of books demonstrated in their writings, it is not surprising that members of the founding generation went to such trouble and expense. Statesman Elbridge Gerry, in his own proposal to establish a library for Congress, complained about the members "being obliged at every session to transport to the seat of the General Government a considerable part of their libraries."[40] But with books also available in social libraries, congressmen presented with proposals for a library to be purchased with scarce public funds tended to see the expense as unnecessary.

Serious public opposition surfaced in regard to the next proposal for a legislative library, made by Representative Elbridge Gerry of Massachusetts. Gerry presented a motion on 6 August 1789 recommending that a committee be formed to draw up a list of books necessary for the use of Congress and to estimate the expense of procuring them. On 23 June, 1790 Gerry, as chairman of the committee, submitted his report. He advised that his committee was mindful of the state of the Treasury

and therefore had "confined themselves in great measure to books necessary for the use of the legislative and executive departments, and not
often to be found in private or circulating libraries." He went on to argue
that if provision for a small library was not made, members of the
government would either be forced to do without crucial books or transport their private libraries to the seat of government, "it seldom happen-
ing that they can otherwise command such books when requisite, without trespassing too much on the indulgence of their friends." He
proposed an initial appropriation of one thousand dollars, followed by
annual appropriations of five hundred dollars, to be "applied to the
purpose by the President, Chief Justice, and Secretary of State of the
United States, without confining them to the catalogue reported, until,
in the opinion of Congress, the books provided shall be adequate to the
purpose."[41]

Although it has never been published, Gerry's list of books for the use
of Congress does exist.[42] In contrast to the 307 titles that Madison's
committee had proposed, Gerry's catalog contained (depending on how
entries are counted) between 70 and 80 titles, described accurately by
Loren Smith as "nothing more than a reference shelf for Congress."[43]
The catalog was divided into four sections. The first section listed the
laws and criminal codes of various states and colonies, including the West
Indies, Great Britain, Venice, Switzerland, Geneva, Poland, France,
Canada, and the Russian Empire. Books on the law of nature and
nations, including such well-known authors on the subject as Grotius,
Pufendorf, Burlamaqui, Vattel, and Wolff, were also included in this
section. The second section was headed "Books Relating to Commerce
and Navigation" and included among other works Jacques Necker's *Finances of France*, Sir James Steuart's *Inquiry into the Principles of Political
Economy*, and Adam Smith's *Wealth of Nations*. In the third section,
headed "Parliamentary Books," Gerry and his committee listed the journals and debates of the Houses of Lords and Commons, various books
on elections, and George Petyt's *Lex Parliamentaria, or, A Treatise of the
Law and Custom of the Parliaments of England*. The fourth section,
headed "Common Law," contained only six entries, with Coke's *Institutes*
and Blackstone's *Commentaries* given pride of place.[44]

Though the proposed books were intended to serve both the executive
and legislative branches of government, Gerry's list was less than a third
the size of Madison's. No doubt Gerry's minimalist vision of a govern-

ment library was designed to overcome the objection of expense that Madison's proposal had faced. In confining his list to books on law and politics, ignoring history and Americana, Gerry expressed an even more restrictive, utilitarian vision of the library than had Madison. Its brevity notwithstanding, Gerry's list contained many of the most respected authorities of the time on law and government, including a number of authors and books that appeared on Madison's 1783 list and would later be listed in the 1802 catalog of the Library of Congress. Despite these modest ambitions, though, Gerry's report was laid on the table and not revived.

Gerry's report highlights the status of books as a relatively expensive commodity available in this period mostly to the affluent. The committee confined itself to books "not to be found in private or in circulating libraries," because it assumed that the "gentlemen" who sat in the Congress would either own substantial private libraries or make use of the social libraries at their disposal. Gerry, a graduate of Harvard and a native of Marblehead, Massachusetts, came from a merchant-class family belonging to "the financial, political, and social elite" of the town, whose citizens "continually elected their betters into local political offices because of ingrained habits of subordination."[45] In his report, Gerry appears to have remained true to his genteel upbringing in regarding books as the province of the social elite, as in the way he argued that members who needed them were in the position of "trespassing too much on the indulgence of their friends," also presumably the owners of substantial private libraries. In terms of institutional structure if not collections, Gerry might have had in mind as a model for the proposed library the Harvard College Library, which made books available not only to students and faculty but to "elite members of the community" for whom it "helped to supplement the personal libraries of the clergy and other professionals."[46] This conception of a congressional library as having a very limited range of collections serving at most an elite class of users (if any) in addition to the legislature is worth noting here because of its persistence through the nineteenth century, when more democratic habits of mind led citizens and journalists to lobby—mostly without success—for a much more publicly oriented institution.

Gerry's report occasioned a vehement letter of objection that appeared in the Boston newspaper the *Independent Chronicle* on 31 May 1790. Although the anonymous writer who protested a congressional library with such passion considered himself in direct opposition to Gerry, his letter suggests that the two shared an assumption that it was not in the public interest for the government to amass an extensive library.

> It is supposed that the Members of Congress are acquainted with history; the laws of nations; and possess such political information as is necessary for the management of the affairs of the government. If they are *not*, we have been unfortunate in our choice—or, should they need the assistance of Books upon any particular subject, they are able to furnish themselves *with little expence* at the circulating Library in the city where they reside. But why the States should be at this expence, and the time of Congress taken up in arranging a body of Books for a public Library at this important period, is a piece of policy which no person can reconcile upon any principle of propriety, or expediency.[47]

Like Gerry, this author assumed that the members of Congress already possessed substantial private collections of the books they needed and viewed the proposed library as an extension of these. That the books would represent a piece of public property, the possession of which would contribute in some way to the literary or cultural achievement of the young nation or would meaningfully benefit individual citizens, was not a consideration for either Gerry or his adversary.

In contrast to Gerry, though, the author of the letter to the *Independent Chronicle* was astonished that books should even have been considered as appropriate objects of the time and expense of the states—he considered the suggestion a breach of "propriety." He went on to ask, "What connection has a Library with the public? With our Commerce; or with any other national concern?—How absurd to squander away money for a parcel of Books, when every shilling of the Revenue is wanted for supporting our government and paying our debts." This writer is committed to an idea of frugality on the part of government that he sees as being at odds with the proposal to spend limited funds on a library, no matter how modest. Moreover, books are items that legislators should provide privately rather than use public funds to purchase. The writer continued, "I would ask wherein is a public Library conducive to the purposes mentioned in the preamble of the Constitution? . . . [The members of the government] may with equal propriety charge the public with all the expence of their cloathing, boarding &c. as to touch the Revenue for Books for their own convenience, entertainment or instruction." The analogy between books and the expenses of clothes and boarding is striking because it implies that books are private possessions incompatible with the notion of government ownership or collection in a public space. The problem appears to be the precedent that would be set by governmental support of an institution that had previously been largely consigned to the private sector.

Late-eighteenth-century libraries in the colonies and the early Republic were almost exclusively private ventures, consisting mainly of social libraries and circulating libraries.[48] Following Benjamin Franklin's model for the Library Company of Philadelphia, social libraries drew on the contributions of like-minded individual private citizens, whose payment for shares in a joint-stock company entitled them to use of the books. Circulating libraries, on the other hand, were primarily commercial ventures. Entrepreneurs made books available on the basis of a quarterly or annual membership fee, often renting out titles individually as well. At the time of Gerry's proposal for a congressional library, circulating libraries were a very familiar part of the cultural landscape, with the most successful including John Dabney's Salem Circulating Library founded in 1789 and William P. Blake's establishment in Boston, which he took over in 1792.[49] In contrast to both social and circulating libraries, the idea of a government-supported library, though not unprecedented in the colonies, had not met with much success.[50] In the late eighteenth century, providing legislators with books, much less a library for public access, was not widely accepted as a responsibility of the government, a conclusion borne out not only by the letter in the *Independent Chronicle* but also by the rejection of both Madison's and Gerry's library proposals.

Libraries, Useful Knowledge, and Classical Republican Fear of Luxury

The utilitarian cast of Madison's list of books, Gerry's small library of reference titles, and the Library of Congress itself as it developed in subsequent years can be attributed in part to eighteenth-century beliefs about useful knowledge. Eighteenth-century philosophers and statesmen on the Continent and in America focused their energies on knowledge that they considered practical, excluding the esoteric and the purely theoretical. The Encyclopedists associated with Diderot and the Parisian Enlightenment "found the greatest excitement in the useful arts, engineering, agriculture, and technology. These pursuits were often contrasted with useless speculation in metaphysics and theology."[51] Such ideas resulted in new principles of inclusion and exclusion in regard to library collection development. In an entry on "bibliomanie" in the *Encyclopedie*, Diderot discredited an unduly large library as "a collection of material for the history and infatuation of mankind."[52] The effect on book collecting of Jefferson's well-known impatience with metaphysics is reflected in the list of books he prepared as a guide to starting a private library for his prospective brother-in-law Robert Skipwith. The list included mainly works of philosophy under the heading "Religion," eschewed all but one of the sermon collections that would have been prevalent in most Virginians' private libraries, and provocatively classed in this category the *Essays* of religious skeptic David Hume. Jefferson put the Bible under the rubric "History. Antient."[53] Libraries conceived in the age of liberal Enlightenment thought were of a different character than their seventeenth-century precursors, and the proposals for a congressional library reflected this shift toward the immediately useful.

The library that most closely served as a substitute and eventually a model for the Library of Congress, the Library Company of Philadelphia, provides a case in point. Whereas the libraries of Harvard, Yale, and William and Mary were heavily theological in the eighteenth century, the ambitious tradesmen who joined Benjamin Franklin in his subscription library project in 1731 selected titles primarily in the areas of history, literature, and science. These choices were in line with the purposes for which the library was collected: the self-education, professional advancement, and amusement of the proprietors. Their marked interest in science reflects an age of scientific progress as well as the professional and amateur scientific pursuits of the members, with works on mathematics, astronomy, and natural history. Practical works on medicine and agriculture were also included among the Library Company's early acquisitions. The large proportion of titles in history, nearly a third of the Library Company's first purchases, included "a diversified historical background dealing with uprisings and the mutability of kings and states," such as the *History of England* by Paul de Rapin and *The History of the Revolutions That Happened in the Government of the Roman Republic* by René Aubert de Vertot, both of which were also on Madison's list. These histories fit under the heading of useful knowledge because the situations they sketched out had direct applications to the colonial political situation. Even literature could be considered useful knowledge because, as Franklin would later point out in his *Autobiography*, an acquaintance with the best-known books of the era could help a young man acquire the friendship and patronage of influential people. Because theology was not similarly useful, the Library Company ordered titles in theology "with an extremely light hand," consistent with the secular concerns of the age.[54]

For eighteenth-century intellectuals, books were collected to be put to practical ends. Richard Beale Davis says of colonial southerners that "the planter or professional man or government official or merchant brought and bought books to be used. He was not a collector in any nineteenth- or twentieth-century sense."[55] This is not to say that these colonial-era book owners and supporters of a congressional library were narrow-minded, for their definition of useful knowledge could be quite broad, encompassing any subject, sometimes even theology, that was perceived as leading humanity toward virtue and happiness. But the attitudes toward books described here would not have favored indiscriminate amassing of a library's collections, such as occurs with the policy of copyright deposit, and this is the crucial point. Books that fell outside the range of useful knowledge were not considered by Madison or Gerry as appropriate for the legislative library of a republican government. While these notions of the uses of literature and the practical value of books were challenged and somewhat replaced by new beliefs in the nineteenth century, enough vestiges of them remained to influence policy in regard to the Library of Congress for decades, working against collection development that strayed outside utilitarian bounds.

The influence of Enlightenment beliefs about useful knowledge is evident in the way that both Madison and Jefferson collected and handled their books. Robert Rutland calls Madison "a user, not a collector, of books . . . Madison never purchased a book for its binding or its attractive printing. Madison wanted books for the knowledge they could furnish him."[56] Even Jefferson, one of the most avid book collectors of his generation whose personal collection would become the nucleus of the Library of Congress after the fire of 1814, seems to have held an almost ruthless disregard for the aesthetic or entertainment values placed on books. Jefferson "did not hesitate to take apart a sixteenth-century *editio princeps* of a Greek author, trim its margins to make it the size of a duodecimo instead of a quarto, interleave it with the pages of a seventeenth-century Latin translation, and bind up the whole in a series of small volumes for easier study and handling."[57] Jefferson manipulated these books as if they were tools, literally dismantling what he would have seen as artifacts of aristocratic privilege and social exploitation and refashioning them to make them serviceable in a new republican society. In a catalog for the library of the projected University of Virginia, Jefferson took a similarly utilitarian stance, intoning that "nothing of mere amusement should lumber a public library."[58] Before the advent of Romanticism in Anglo-American culture offered a model for literary production and consumption that championed the spiritual, transcendent value of imaginative literature, in the late eighteenth century books of all kinds were often valued most highly for their ability to serve demonstrably useful ends. When collected in a government institution, books were expected to advance specific political goals.

The emphasis on useful knowledge that informed early attempts to establish a government library also found expression in the Constitution and in the copyright laws that it sanctioned. As early as 1783, the year that Madison presented his library list to the body, the Continental Congress appointed a committee with James Madison and Hugh Williamson as members "to consider the most proper means of cherishing genius and the useful arts through the United States by securing to the authors or publishers of new books their property in such works."[59] The support of the useful arts as the proper justification for copyright law is more forcefully established in article 1, section 8, clause 8 of the Constitution, another document whose authorship is largely attributed to Madison. This clause gives Congress the power "to promote the Progress of Science and useful Arts, by securing for limited Times to Authors and Inventors the exclusive Right to their respective Writings and Discoveries." Authors and inventors are accorded equal status, and their products seen to serve similar ends; the encouragement of "genius" mentioned in the 1783 copyright committee instructions has dropped from consideration. Comparing copyright laws in revolutionary France and America, Jane Ginsburg characterizes American copyright in this way: "The U.S. Constitution authorized Congress to create a copyright system to 'promote the progress' of knowledge. Congress adapted a rather pragmatic view of the kinds of works that achieved that objective: the first U.S. copyright law protected maps, charts, and books—in that order. The great majority of works for which authors or publishers sought copyright protection under that first statute were highly useful productions."[60] In promoting literary culture for strictly practical ends, the justifications for copyright illustrate the same utilitarian rationale for literature expressed in the arguments made on behalf of a library for Congress. As Ginsburg points out, the order in which protected materials are listed in the federal copyright law of 1790 appears to accord primary importance to protection of maps and charts, a highly suggestive point that recalls the connection between literature and territoriality that Madison alluded to as a main justification for a congressional library. An area that is mapped can, providing the maps are disseminated through publication, be settled, defended, and possessed more easily.

Copyright deposit would eventually become one of the primary means by which the Library of Congress developed its collections, but the legislators who passed the 1790 copyright act saw no connection between copyright and libraries. Indeed, when this act was passed on 31 May 1790, a Library of Congress did not yet exist, and the proposal to establish one had been blasted in the press only a short time earlier, on 13 May. John Y. Cole draws a distinction in copyright laws between deposit for record and deposit for use; the 1790 Copyright Act envisioned only the former concept.[61] A single copy of the work to be copyrighted was to be forwarded to the secretary of state in Washington. This remained the law until the Copyright Act of 1831, and it was only in 1846, in a cultural climate somewhat more favorable to the idea of a research library funded and regulated by the federal government, that copyright for use became a means of collection building at the Library of Congress.

The devotion to useful knowledge in late-eighteenth-century America was part of a larger cultural climate in which books and literature were perceived as having ambiguous political connotations. Americans of the Revolutionary War era were shaped by and subscribed to an ideology that historians have come to label as "classical republicanism."[62] Based on the ancient republics of Greece and Rome, republicanism was not merely a form of government; it was equally concerned with the spirit or morality of the people and their leaders. Some of the beliefs associated with republicanism were that citizens would sacrifice their individual interests to the good of society, that habits of deference to social superiors helped to maintain a cohesive society, and that a rough equality of opportunity characterized a just society. Their reading in classical literature convinced leaders of the republican era that the ancient republics had fallen because of the decadent character of their people. This belief, filtered through the various levels of society, instilled in the public consciousness a pervasive fear of luxury.

Luxury might be defined as an inordinate value placed on items such as ostentatious furniture and clothing, usually imported from Europe, that presumably stimulated the passions, encouraged vanity, and thereby corrupted the morals of the people. Luxury was regarded by both statesmen and ordinary citizens as the most significant threat to the continued existence and prosperity of the nation. According to John Sekora, from the ancient world to the first half of the eighteenth century the charge of luxury was invoked as an attack on the presumed idleness of the poor, thereby justifying the social hierarchy. After around 1763, however, liberal English authors redirected the concept into an attack on the excesses of the wealthy. This redirection characterized the American strain of thought on luxury.[63] Some supporters of the Revolutionary cause were even willing to advocate sumptuary laws against luxurious extravagances in dress and diet to guard against the spread of this multifarious vice.[64]

A library for Congress potentially represented an encroachment of luxury into the federal government because the books could be viewed as a frivolous purchase of dubious utility. The charge also applied because the books had to be imported from European book dealers and therefore embodied decadent Old World values. As Neil Harris points out, foreign cultural products were the object of some distrust among Americans: "Art was finally identified with luxury because almost all its products were foreign and required importation, using up much of the precious stock of currency." The fine arts, including literature, were also suspicious because they had been cultivated in the Old World by a small leisured class at the expense of the political liberties of the masses.[65] Gordon Wood agrees that in republican thought, "art and high culture . . . were symptomatic of a degree of luxury and of decadence that had no place in a vital republic."[66] An indictment of the fine arts from John Adams exemplifies the point. Writing to Jefferson late in his life, Adams offered a scathing condemnation of the corruption inherent in the arts: "Every one of the fine Arts from the earliest times has been inlisted in the service of Superstition and Despotism. The whole World at this day Gazes with Astonishment at the grossest fictions because they have been immortalized by the most exquisite Artists, Homer and Milton Phidias and Raphael."[67] Adams's letter, with its blending of authors and painters, suggests that the distrust of the fine arts spilled over into the literary realm. While novels in particular were open to questions of moral indecency, the letter in the *Independent Chronicle* attests that any collection of books purchased by the government was subject to special scrutiny to determine whether legislators were indulging in a luxurious expenditure. The association drawn between books and clothing, which was often singled out for condemnation when it appeared to ape European fashion, particularly suggests that the author's primary concern was with the infiltration of luxury.

The danger of luxury was a prevalent theme in American print culture in the 1780s and 1790s. In the first issue of Mathew Carey's literary and political periodical *The American Museum*, a brief essay "on the fatal consequences of luxury" warned that "there is no greater calamity can befal [*sic*] any people, than when luxury is introduced among them." A second antiluxury tract, "An infallible cure for hard times," appeared in the second issue.[68] Literary authors avoided the charge of luxury by promoting their books as contributing somehow to the social welfare. It was the anxiety about items that served no practical end and corrupted the public morality that led novelists of the period to assert in prefaces and dedications the moral benefits of their work. Inscribing his novel *The Power of Sympathy* to the "young ladies of United Columbia," for example, William Hill Brown defended its social utility by claiming that it would "inspire the female mind with a principle of self complacency" and "promote the economy of human life." Susanna Rowson similarly claimed in the preface to *Charlotte Temple* that she had not written a line "that conveys a wrong idea to the head or a corrupt wish to the heart," holding that saving readers from the errors of vice was more important to her than "the applause which might attend the most elegant finished piece of literature."[69] Civic duty prevailed over elegance or amusement as justification for literary endeavor.

The assumptions underlying Rowson's preface or Adams's letter held serious consequences for the world of letters in the early Republic. Larzer Ziff discusses some of these consequences in his *Writing in the New Nation*, arguing that the ideals of republicanism were unfavorable to the growth of a belletristic literary culture. A new style of literature would be appropriate to this Republic, it was believed, one that devalued works of "genius" in favor of more useful publications such as spelling books and pamphlets. Ziff suggests that "republican enthusiasts were prepared to value [such literature] as characteristic of a society of free and equal men who required printed information for their political well-being and economic growth."[70] In this politico-cultural climate, a Library of Congress that developed on the model or scale of the British Museum Library or the Bibliothèque Nationale would have seemed at best irrelevant to the goals of a republic and at worst dangerous in its corrupting influence, for both these institutions had their origins in monarchical book collections, exactly the kind of unjustifiable accumulation of wealth based on social exploitation that classical republicans deplored.

After the Constitutional debate of the late 1780s, American consensus on the values represented by republicanism began to give way to a more contentious political culture split between two parties, Republicans and Federalists. Because the values of government frugality, public virtue, and fear of luxury fit more neatly into Jefferson's vision of a republic of yeoman farmers, it would seem that the views of the Federalist Party held more promise toward the expansion of literary culture beyond utilitarian limits and to the eventual foundation of a congressional (and perhaps someday a national) library. Ziff reads the early Republic in this way, writing that "political culture followed a predominantly liberal course while literary culture . . . followed a predominantly conservative course."[71] Federalists such as Fisher Ames scoffed at the profusion of spelling books and the dearth of more serious literature in America. In his often quoted essay "American literature," Ames wrote that "there is no scarcity of spelling-book makers, and authors of twelve-cent pamphlets . . . nobody will deny that we justly boast of many able men, and exceedingly useful publications. But has our country produced one great original work of genius?" Unlike his republican contemporaries, Ames insisted that the cultural maturity of a nation depended on production of works of genius, not on the literacy or political awareness of the general populace, of whose judgment he was deeply suspicious. That the cultivation of the national genius as recommended by Ames would involve collection of scholarly books on a large scale, in something like a national library, is beyond doubt. Ames is the source of the assertion that "all of our universities would not suffice to supply [materials and authorities] for such a work as Gibbon's."[72] Ames argued unapologetically in favor of a greater collection of expensive and rare books by appealing to the needs of the serious scholar.

Changing political realities, however, could affect these attitudes about books and scholarship in a notably brief span of time. With Thomas Jefferson's election to the presidency in 1800, anti-intellectualism and a distrust of high culture reversed fields and become a weapon that the Federalists cynically turned against his administration. Richard Hofstadter considers Thomas Jefferson "the first notable victim of a distinctively anti-intellectualist broadside . . . and his assailants were Federalist leaders and members of the established clergy of New England."[73] One attack on Jefferson from this period recalls the letter from the *Independent Chronicle*. Fisher Ames argued that Jefferson "like most men of genius . . . has been carried away by systems, and the everlasting zeal to generalize, instead of proceeding, like common men of practical sense, on the low, but sure foundation of matter of fact."[74] This passage reveals the distinction between abstract political theory and the more practical application of politics that the *Independent Chronicle* correspondent raised when he argued, in opposition to a library for Congress, that "the people look for *practical politicks*, as they presume the Theory is obtained previous to the members taking their seats in Congress."[75] One more distinction, then, that was working against the foundation of a congressional library at the end of the eighteenth century was that between theory, which was associated with effete intellectualism (and with the kind of books Gerry proposed purchasing for Congress), and practice, which was associated with the more plebeian discourse of the common person and the more ephemeral literature of the day.

Diffusion of Knowledge in the Early Republic

A book collection funded by the government faced a certain resistance in the new nation because, by its very nature, such a library would not achieve one of the most important ends that literary culture could serve: the diffusion of knowledge, a theme that Michael Warner calls "one of the most prominent in the discourse of early national America."[76] According to this influential belief, the future of the Republic depended on a relatively educated citizenry able to use reason to defend itself against despotism. Merrill Peterson explains Jefferson's understanding of the concept of diffusion as securing individual freedom and social harmony: "Without the diffusion of knowledge through all the ranks of society, adapted to its different degrees and conditions, individuals could neither attend to their own happiness nor, as citizens, secure the freedom and the welfare of the state."[77] Along these lines, Jefferson wrote to George

Wythe, "I think by far the most important bill in our whole code is that for the diffusion of knowledge among the people. No other sure foundation can be devised for the preservation of freedom, and happiness."[78] Jefferson was referring to his Bill for the Diffusion of Knowledge in Virginia (1778), which would have provided for a statewide system of public education to ensure that Virginians would have an adequate level of education to secure their political rights.

The notion of a diffusion of knowledge accorded easily with the spread of print discourse in newspapers and magazines for a general reading audience, as well as with distribution of basic educational books, but in the minds of citizens of the United States it was not consistent with the accumulation in a single location of literary classics, books on abstruse or highly specialized subjects, or other expensive or rare books imported from the Old World. Despite the size of his own private collections, when it came to the value of libraries, Jefferson seems to have thought mainly in terms of diffusion of a few useful books for the general education of the lower classes. He wrote to John Wyche: "I have often thought that nothing would do more extensive good at small expense than the establishment of a small circulating library in every county, to consist of a few well-chosen books, to be lent to the people of the county . . . These should be such as would give them a general view of other history, and particular view of that of their own country, a tolerable knowledge of Geography, the elements of Natural Philosophy, of Agriculture and Mechanics."[79] The cultural value assigned to the diffusion of knowledge reinforced the American preference for a few cheap, useful books dispersed across a wide geographic area as opposed to the collection of a large number of expensive volumes in a central location.

Newspapers and other cheap, widely disseminated periodicals were regarded as a means of securing protection against despotism and of raising the level of public morality. In a 1788 issue of the *American Museum*, a contributor styling himself "Crazy Jonathan" argued that "it may be doubted whether tyranny can rear his iron sceptre over a people, where a free press is enjoyed, and a frequent circulation of newspapers takes place among all orders and ranks of society." And in an issue from later that year, Carey reprinted a letter in which George Washington asserted that "easy vehicles of knowledge" such as the *American Museum* were "more happily calculated than any other, to preserve the liberty, stimulate the industry, and meliorate the morals of an enlightened and free people."[80] Whereas fiction and other fine arts stimulated vice, newspapers and magazines filled with useful knowledge promoted virtue and strengthened the Republic.

Historians and literary scholars have for some time recognized a uniquely symbiotic relationship between the dissemination of printed discourse and the political foundations of the United States.[81] Discussing the importance of pamphlets in spreading the political ideas that led to the Revolution, Bernard Bailyn asserts that they were "the distinctive literature of the Revolution," because they were flexible, cheap, and widely available throughout the colonies.[82] Warner extends Bailyn's discussion of the importance of the printed word to the new nation, arguing that by the time of the Revolution, printed discourse in the colonies had engendered a public sphere that served as a forum for the disinterested debate of political issues, and "print had come to be seen as indispensable to political life."[83]

To determine the impact of this value attached to printed works on the establishment of a congressional library, however, a distinction must be drawn between the proliferation of print discourse in the form of pamphlets and newspapers and the more narrowly circumscribed limits of book culture in the new nation. Whereas pamphlets and newspapers were cheap and widely available and therefore consistent with the republican goal of an informed populace, books were more expensive, did not reach as broad an array of readers, and therefore did not have the same political connotations as more ephemeral forms. Novels were perhaps most readily associated with the immorality or antirepublican values of European life, but books in general were not considered a primary means of diffusing information. Generally speaking, their very format seems not to have fit with the concept of diffusion of knowledge. Postal rates furnish an illustration of this principle. In its 1792 postal act, the federal government drew a significant distinction between the uses of books and periodicals. Newspapers were accorded cheap postal rates because of their utility in disseminating political information to the country. The law did not acknowledge bound books, which were "virtually excluded . . . from the mail until the mid-1800s," because they were not perceived as disseminating useful knowledge in the same way as did newspapers.[84]

The theme of diffusion of knowledge and a consequent distrust of national cultural institutions were characteristic not only of the leaders of the early Republic but also of the less educated ranks of society, at least those aligned against the political right. These themes were central, for example, to the writings of William Manning, a Massachusetts farmer with a rudimentary education who wrote about the interests of the common citizen in a republic. A devoted critic of the Federalist Party in the 1790s, Manning was a regular reader of Boston's Republican-leaning *Independent Chronicle* and, it seems likely, would have seconded the sentiments of the correspondent quoted in the *Chronicle* who objected to Gerry's library proposal. His 1798 manuscript "The Key of Liberty" included his theories about how "the Many" have oppressed "the Few" throughout history and how these mistakes could be avoided in the new nation. Manning, like Jefferson, believed that knowledge was the key to liberty. But a diffusion of knowledge did not by any means require national cultural or educational institutions, as Manning made clear in his remarks on how the Few have used education to their advantage: "Instead of promoting cheap schools and woman schools for children to read and write while they are so young as to be spared from labor, they are continually crying up the great advantages of costly colleges, national academies, and grammar schools." Although not in principle opposed to all higher institutions of learning, Manning believed that the preservation of liberty more immediately required a diffusion of knowledge among the Many. To achieve this, he proposed publication of a magazine devoted to the interests of the Many, to be published by "a good republican printer [who] would deliver one in every town in the state for a dollar a year large enough for a laborer to peruse."[85] Manning's text reproduces a number of the factors that worked against establishment of a congressional library: distrust of high culture; the value accorded to a diffusion of knowledge; and the link between the theory of diffusion and the proliferation of such literary forms as pamphlets or magazines that made knowledge widely available to the average citizen.

These ideas about diffusion of knowledge and distrust of luxury were entertained not only by the leaders of the early Republic and by a few disaffected farmers such as Manning. They were widespread enough to find ample expression in the print culture at large, such as in magazines of the 1790s. David Paul Nord's analysis of the *New-York Magazine*, which began publication in 1790 and lasted for eight years, turned up three major themes in the magazine's content: the importance of public virtue, suspicion of luxury, and the power and democracy of knowledge. The latter two, at least, have direct implications in regard to attempts to found a government library. On the question of diffusion of knowledge, Nord summarizes arguments on this subject as "stress[ing] the broadest possible diffusion of knowledge through universal participation in public schools."[86] A library in the nation's capital did not easily accord with this principle.

Similar ideas were expressed in New York's *Monthly Magazine and American Review* by a pair of writers who espoused the value of newspapers and almanacs in disseminating information widely and cheaply. Even these useful mediums, they believed, could be tweaked more rigorously into shape to produce the maximum social benefit. The pseudonymous "Looker-On" reported a fictionalized dialogue he had with a friend who had complained that newspapers were filled with factional sniping and quotes of mercantile prices. What a waste, the friend had argued, considering that "of all the forms of publication, that of a large sheet, filled with small type, and printed and dispersed daily, is the most to be admired . . . How might the knowledge diffused through costly, or inaccessible, or widely scattered volumes, be compressed, with new forms, arrangements and illustrations, into this easy and current vehicle!"[87] Another correspondent to the magazine observed that almanacs, present in almost every home in the country, were filled with zodiacal signs, saints' days, and in general "an abundance of useless and unintelligible learning . . . abstruse and remote from vulgar apprehension." Yet these almanacs, being thoroughly dispersed, provided "an opportunity of imparting wholesome truths to thousands, whose audience he could never hope to obtain in any other way." Indeed, he went on to argue, the duty of an enlightened person should lie not "in advancing the various branches of physical and moral knowledge" but rather "in contriving and executing schemes for making simple, intelligible, and concise, the sciences in their present state of improvement . . . making cheaper and more commodious, in cloathing in more popular and attractive forms, and putting into the possession of a greater number the knowledge already ascertained."[88]

These articles reveal much about American beliefs regarding the uses of print. The authors proposed that it was incumbent on enlightened people to absorb and then condense and popularize knowledge to reach the widest number of readers, presuming a filtration of knowledge from the more educated class of Americans downward to the many households whose reading consisted mainly of newspapers and almanacs. The goal was to take advantage of widespread habits of reading to give even the laboring classes the ability to participate in government. Abstruse learning and the advancement of the sciences were accorded a measure of distrust in these articles; though not in themselves dishonorable pursuits, they were not the most pressing tasks faced by the new nation. Both correspondents to the *Monthly Magazine* proposed changes in already useful and widely diffused forms of print to make them even more so. In their zeal to improve the moral character and intelligence of the average reader, writers looked for every opportunity to reshape American print culture along lines appropriate to a republic of readers. Such an atmosphere was not nearly as politically favorable to government patronage of a congressional library as it was to support of cheap publishing forms that diffused information to the widest possible audience.

James Madison and Elbridge Gerry realized in the 1780s and 1790s that a legislative body, to function well, required a library. In 1783, Madison proposed that the Second Continental Congress acquire a relatively ambitious list of books on subjects ranging from American history and geography to world history, political theory, economics, common law, and international law. Though his proposal was rejected, ostensibly for economic reasons but probably for cultural reasons as well, these were the subjects that would come to dominate a congressional library once it was established. Gerry proposed a much more modest list in 1790 to the first Congress acting under the authority of the Constitution, but his reference shelf of books, mostly on law and commerce, not only was tabled but met with a decidedly hostile reception in the press. Establishing a congressional library was not an uncomplicated proposition.

Madison's and Gerry's proposals, and the responses they received, should be interpreted in the light of a set of shifting, contradictory attitudes toward books and literature in the early Republic. The dominant ideology of classical republicanism encouraged a utilitarian conception of the value of literature. Statesmen of the era such as Madison, Jefferson, Adams, Franklin, and Hamilton frequently had recourse to books to solve practical political problems, as their correspondence and public writings amply attest. Consequently, both Madison and Gerry defended their propositions on the basis of utility. But the utilitarian view of letters was accompanied by other beliefs less favorable to federal library development. The ideology of classical republicanism entailed a fear of luxury corrupting the morals of the populace and undermining the political health of the nation. And an association of higher learning with the decadence and oppression of the Old World helped to place books under suspicion of luxury. These concerns created a discernible distrust of an institution of letters connected with the federal government and financed at public expense, factors that worked against the collection of a government library on any but the most limited and frugal grounds. These ideas about books must be kept in mind when analyzing the history of the Library of Congress in the years after its founding in 1800, because their influence continued for decades.

Americans of the eighteenth century held a radically different conception of the relationships among government, books, and the public than that which came to prevail within a few generations. This is most strikingly evident in the reliance of Congress on social libraries for its books. In the late eighteenth century, private citizens provided books to the government to promote the social welfare. By the middle of the nineteenth century, with proposals in state legislatures and in the press for municipally supported libraries and a national library in Washington, many believed that the government should provide books to private citizens. Put another way, a certain class of books representative of higher learning went from being conceived as mostly the province of the social elite to becoming a public commodity, appropriate for collection in a municipal space and accessible to a much larger segment of the population, within about half a century. This shift is obviously connected with larger changes in the democratic character of American society as well as with the growth of the reading public and the rise of the American publishing industry between the beginning and middle of the nineteenth century. It remains to be seen, however, how much the Library of Congress actually participated in these changes. To a surprising extent, until the era of the Civil War, it maintained its status as a private social library for a small cadre of users. How the Library of Congress developed late in the nineteenth century and into the twentieth had little to do with the atmosphere in which such an institution was originally debated at the end of the eighteenth century.

CHAPTER TWO

Madison's Vision Realized,
1800–1812

Once the Library of Congress had been founded in 1800, it followed along the developmental lines sketched out by James Madison in 1783. Congress collected books in a few well defined subject areas to assist it in carrying out its official duties. Under the continuing influence of the tenets of classical republicanism, utility was the rationale for the Library, which meant that luxury, conversely, had to be avoided. This view of the Library of Congress, exemplified by Joint Library Committee member John Randolph and written into the petitions for patronage submitted to the federal government by engineer William Tatham, was also reflected in Library of Congress catalogs of 1802 and 1812. These catalogs show that the areas of history, law, politics, and geography tended to be the most heavily collected. In marked ways, Library of Congress holdings were less catholic than those of the typical social library of the era, in accordance with its legislative orientation.

In other ways, the Library did resemble the social libraries from which congressmen had taken books before they created a library of their own. In its institutional structure and architecture, the Library of Congress drew from existing social library models. And by 1812, the Library of Congress had also begun to spend more of its appropriations budget on titles in the belles lettres, a subject which Madison had eschewed completely and which was not emphasized in the 1802 initial purchase. This allowed the Library to serve a social and recreational purpose for legislators and their families, a role that would become more pronounced as the century progressed. Aside from this function, the Library of Congress in the years preceding the War of 1812 was fashioned as a working library for government officials, and its collections consequently reflected some of the important historical events of the period.

Establishment of the Library

Despite the failure of Elbridge Gerry's 1790 proposal for a library, legislators in subsequent years nonetheless quietly went about collecting the books they deemed essential. No record survives to document exactly how or where Congress procured them, but William Dawson Johnston reports that either before or immediately after the removal of the legislature to Washington, but separately from the later acquisitions approved by statute, Congress amassed some 243 volumes.[1] Apparently wary of public scrutiny into the matter of a government-funded library, legislators acquired without fanfare the books that they had not authorized purchasing through direct legislation. These books are listed separately in the 1802 catalog, so it is possible to identify the fifty-five titles (not many fewer than the seventy to eighty that Elbridge Gerry had proposed as the basis of a congressional library) collected some time in the 1790s. Among these, many are familiar from Madison's 1783 list, including the *Annual Register*, Adam Anderson's *A Historical and Chronological Deduction of the Origin of Commerce*, Blackstone's *Commentaries*, Hume's *History of England*, Jacques Necker's *Finances of France*, and Vattel's *Law of Nations*. In addition, a number of books published after Madison drew up his list—John Adams's *Defense of the Constitutions of Government of the United States of America* (1787); John Baker Holroyd, Earl of Sheffield's *Observations on the Commerce of the American States with Europe and the West Indies* (1783); Tench Coxe's *Brief Examination of Lord Sheffield's "Observations"* (1791); Jeremy Belknap's *American Biography* (1794); and Jedidiah Morse's *American Geography* (1789)—dealt with U.S. history, commerce, politics, and geography, subjects that Madison had identified as central to the government's interests. Controversial or not, books were too essential to be done without entirely, even with the Library Company of Philadelphia at the legislature's disposal.

With the relocation of the capital in 1800 to Washington, D.C., where the legislators would no longer have access to the collections of a well-stocked social library, a congressional library for reference purposes became a justifiable expenditure in the minds of congressmen. The legislature established the Library of Congress in a single paragraph of the "Act to make provision for the removal and accommodation of the Government of the United States." The fifth section of this act, approved on 24 April 1800, resolved "that for the purchase of such books as may be necessary for the use of Congress at the said city of Washington, and for fitting up a suitable apartment for containing them and placing them therein the sum of five thousand dollars shall be, and hereby is, appropriated."[2] The strictly circumscribed role of the congressional library is notable in this piece of legislation; as David Mearns points out, the bill "studiously refrained from referring to [the books] as a library."[3] The legislators were apparently mindful of the resistance to the idea of a government-funded library that had accompanied Elbridge Gerry's 1790 proposal. As it had done in the 1790s, Congress discreetly allocated money for books without announcing the creation of a library in a separate piece of legislation. On the other hand, an appropriation of five thousand dollars was an unprecedented step in regard to a congressional library. Congress further resolved that a committee be appointed to draw up a catalog of desiderata, resulting in the purchase, made under the direction of Senator William Bingham and Congressman Robert Waln, of 155 titles from the London bookselling firm of Cadell and Davies.

After the arrival of the books in Washington, legislation was required to regulate their use. As Johnston describes the debate on this question begun in December 1801, points of contention between the House and Senate versions of a bill organizing the library included the extent of borrowing privileges and the amount of appropriations. The Senate bill provided for an annual appropriation but limited use of the Library to Congress alone, while the House lobbied against the annual appropriation but favored a wider pool of users, including other branches of government such as the justices of the Supreme Court and members of the cabinet.[4] Congress approved a compromise, *An Act Concerning the Library for the use of both Houses of Congress*, on 26 January 1802. Based largely on a report drafted by Representative John Randolph of Virginia, this act stipulated a limited pool of borrowers including only "the President and Vice President of the United States, and members of the Senate and House of Representatives, for the time being."[5] The act also created a joint committee of Congress to direct the library and spend the balance of the original appropriation of five thousand dollars. No annual appropriation was mentioned.

In its institutional structure, the Library of Congress created in this bill resembled the social libraries of the period. As we have seen, when the government was headquartered in New York and Philadelphia, members of Congress had consulted the New York Society Library and the Library Company of Philadelphia, and Representative Waln and Senator Bingham were in 1802 past and present directors, respectively, of the Library Company of Philadelphia. In designing its own library, Congress not surprisingly created something similar to the joint-stock corporation on which the proprietary library was based. Proprietary libraries occupied one level in the complex world of eighteenth-century library forms. Proprietary and subscription libraries, also known as social libraries, were private corporations; privilege to withdraw the books required either stock in the company or payment of an annual subscription fee, though the collections were sometimes open to members of the public who simply wanted to use them on the premises. College libraries, obviously, were collected for the use of students, faculty, and alumni, but the books were not always easily available even to members of this constituency. Circulating libraries were the most democratic and inexpensive of library types in the period, requiring either payment of an annual fee or sometimes a rental fee per book withdrawn, but they also tended to shelve current periodicals and a more ephemeral class of books.[6] In contrast, proprietary libraries served a wealthier, more exclusive clientele with more substantive books.[7]

The proximity and availability of proprietary libraries reinforced in legislators' minds the notion of libraries as private corporations serving a limited group of users with a collection of somewhat learned and expensive books. Comparing the structure of the proprietary library with that of the Library of Congress, Mearns concludes that "it is possible to assume that the founding fathers conceived of their prospective books as constituting a proprietary library. . . . Now, however, there would be this difference: Membership would be limited to the Members of the Congress, the joint committee would perform the function of directors, and stock in the corporation would be purchased from the public purse."[8] The model of a joint-stock company was not entirely suited to the creation of a federal government library. Congressmen had the usage privileges of stockholders, though the money was put up by the public treasury. Members of the public were not written into the legislation as having any interest in or access to the Library, which meant that the Joint Committee on the Library could always choose to restrict or set conditions on public access. Although the membership of proprietary libraries was drawn mainly from the wealthier segments of society, these institutions sometimes extended access beyond the stockholders to "any civil Gentleman" who wished to peruse the collections; this was the policy at the Library Company of Philadelphia.[9] Therefore it is probable that legislators had in mind some limited form of public use similar to the custom in the social libraries of the period.

This institutional form of the early Library of Congress is consistent with the late-eighteenth-century ideology of classical republicanism discussed in the previous chapter, particularly in regard to the idea of a diffusion of knowledge. Classical republicanism involved the enlightened leadership of a corps of representatives, a meritocracy that guided the masses toward self-government. In these terms, a well-selected library needed to be accessible only to those leaders as a source of the political, legal, and historical knowledge that would allow them to craft judicious laws. Whatever useful knowledge that the leaders then wished to impart to constituents could be diffused to the public in a digested, popularized form—for example, through the medium of pamphlets or periodical publication. Congress clung to this genteel, hierarchical conception of its Library even when, by the middle of the nineteenth century, democratic habits of mind had replaced the deferential tone of classical republicanism, leading commentators in the press to call for a more democratic orientation of the Library.

The character of the Library of Congress during this period is reflected in the architecture of the Capitol building as well as in the reactions of visitors to the Library space. The original plan for a capitol made no provision for a library, so that when Benjamin Latrobe took over as architect of the Capitol in 1803, he was given the task of designing rooms for the congressional library. Like the legislators who had established the Library a few years earlier, Latrobe relied on the models that he had at hand. A congressional report of 1981 concludes that "there were only two types of English libraries from which [Latrobe] could derive designs— the institutional library [university library] and the gentleman's library." Latrobe combined the two library types, designing an "apsed main library with its gallery and bookshelves ranged along the walls of a long hall" in the style of a university library and a reading room "modeled after the country house library."[10] The architectural space in which the books were housed supported a conception of the Library's role not far removed from aristocratic models of book ownership inherited from England.

These were the terms under which visitors to the Library seem to have viewed its collections, judging by Charles Wilson Peale's description of the Library in its first quarters in the Capitol (preceding the move to the library that Latrobe would later design) in June 1804. Peale wrote, "The Library is a spacious and handsome Room, and although lately organized, already contained a number of valuable books in the best taste of binding."[11] Because he was a painter, Peale might be expected to focus on the aesthetic impact of the Library. Nonetheless, his praise of the collection on the basis of the elegance of the room and quality of the book bindings, as if he were indeed looking at a country gentleman's library, strikes an odd note. If Peale's aesthetically oriented and class-inflected evaluation appears to contradict the utilitarian purpose of the Library that is implied by the limited scope of collections in the early catalogs, the paradox brings to light the conflicted status of books in republican ideology, as both bearers of useful knowledge and potential vehicles of a corrupting luxury.

The 1802 Catalog

The list of books ordered by Waln and Bingham shows that Congress purchased a statesman's library much along the lines originally suggested by Madison. This initial foray into collection development at the Library of Congress was made up of 155 titles in 728 volumes, costing $2,200 of the $5,000 appropriation. History was the largest category of works, with 59 titles in general, European, and classical history. The next largest category included works on America, with 27 titles, including histories and travels in various regions; Madison's list had been much richer in this area, with 103 separate titles. The purchase from Cadell and Davies also included 24 works on the law, including standard reference books and treatises on the law of nature and nations; 15 titles on politics and economics; and 12 on geography and travel.[12] The committee that authorized these purchases thus adhered fairly strictly to a narrow view of the subjects suitable for collection at the Library of Congress, spending less than half the money appropriated for the purpose.

As the library historian Tom Glynn points out, a few significant differences separate Madison's 1783 list of books from the ones purchased in 1800. Most notably, books on America constituted more than a third of Madison's list but less than 20 percent of the 1800 purchase. Glynn's explanation is that Madison and his committee were concerned with forging a strong sense of nationalism among legislators in the volatile period of 1783, a concern that was less urgent by 1800. The 1800 list includes no books on war or languages, "reflect[ing] the fact that few of the powers delegated to the Congress under the new federal Constitution involved foreign affairs." In contrast, under the Articles of Confederation in 1783, Congress had responsibility for conducting foreign affairs. Finally, as Glynn points out, a significant difference between the two lists is that the later one includes a small number of books in the belles lettres, including James Boswell's *Journal*, Hugh Blair's *Lectures on Rhetoric and Belles-Lettres*, and four literary periodicals: the *Rambler*, the *Spectator*, the *Adventurer*, and the *Tattler*. Glynn classes these titles as "less practical, more recreational," highlighting the role that the Library of Congress would come to play as a source of amusement in a new city sorely lacking in cultural events or resources.[13]

In 1802, Congress published the first printed catalog of the Library of Congress.[14] This catalog was simply a list arranged by size (folio, octavo, duodecimo) of the works that Congress had amassed before 1800, combined with the Cadell and Davies purchase and a few other recently acquired works. Such a list of works with no subject classifications or alphabetical list of authors was not the usual cataloging method of the time. Catalogs customarily followed either broad subject groupings or provided an alphabetical list of authors' names. But the lack of organization in the 1802 catalog probably did not much hinder Library of Congress users, given a library of such limited size that the entire seven-page catalog could be easily perused in a matter of minutes. The prices of books were included in the catalog, because congressmen wishing to take books out of the Library had to leave a note promising to either return them or pay for replacements.

Finding titles common to Madison's 1783 list and the Library of Congress catalog of 1802 is highly instructive. The books present on both lists are presumably works that statesmen of the era considered indispensable for a legislative library, regardless of the body's specific Constitutional functions. In other words, books found on both lists on subjects such as law, government, economics, politics, and history form an essential part of the print culture that late-eighteenth-and early-nineteenth-century statesmen moved through in their professional lives. A look at the 1802 Library of Congress catalog reveals just under sixty titles in common with Madison's list. Blackstone's *Commentaries on the Laws of England* and Coke's *Institutes* were important enough to have been acquired before Congress had explicit statutory authorization to collect a library; once this authorization was made, Congress purchased additional copies. Other law books common to both lists include Justinian's *Institutes*, French author Jean Domat's *Civil Law in Its Natural Order*, and the *Lex Parliamentaria*. On the law of nature and nations, books by Montesquieu, Emmerich de Vattel, Jean Jacques Burlamaqui, Hugh Grotius, and Samuel Pufendorf are common to both lists. On government and political theory, the works of Machiavelli, David Hume, John Locke, and Algernon Sidney are found on both lists, as are a number of books on economics, trade, and commerce: Adam Anderson's *Origin of Commerce*, Whyndham Beawes's *Lex Mercatoria Rediviva: Or, the Merchant's Dictionary*, Charles Molloy's *De Jure Maritimo*, Jacques Necker's *Finances of France*, Malachy Postlethwayt's *Universal Dictionary of Trade and Commerce*, Adam Smith's *Wealth of Nations*, and James Steuart's *Political Economy*.

History titles form a significant portion of the overlap between the two lists. Histories common to both Madison's list and the 1802 Library of Congress catalog include Edward Gibbon's *History of the Decline and Fall of the Roman Empire*, Antonio de Herrera y Tordesillas's *General History of the Vast Continent and Islands of America*, David Hume's *History of England*, Paul de Rapin's *History of England*, Abbé Raynal's *A Philosophical and Political History of the Settlements and Trade of the Europeans in the East and West Indies*, William Robertson's *History of America*, and multiple works by Voltaire. Standard histories of individual states and reference works also appear on both lists. The 1802 catalog was not particularly strong in geography, voyages, and travels, probably for the reason Glynn states, though it did include William Guthrie's *A New Geographical, Historical, and Commercial Grammar* and Jonathan Carver's *Travels through the Interior Parts of North America*, two works from the 1770s that had also appeared on Madison's list.

The 1802 catalog was notably strong in classical literature. Intellectual historians have often noted the contribution of classical writers to the political thought of the late eighteenth and early nineteenth centuries. George H. Nash mentions Herodotus, Thucydides, Plutarch, Tacitus, Sallust, and Cicero as major influences on the founding fathers, to which could be added the names of Aristotle, Demosthenes, Livy, and Polybius.[15] These classical writers could be invoked in questions of immediate political importance with the assumption that most educated men were familiar with them, at least in translation. Although Madison overlooked many of these writers, including only Plato, Aristotle, and Plutarch's *Lives* in his 1783 list, the 1802 Library of Congress catalog stressed classical literature. Senator Bingham and Representative Waln ordered English translations of the works of Greek authors Demosthenes, Arrian, Diodorus Siculus, Dionysius Halicarnassus, Herodotus, Polybius, Plutarch, Thucydides, and Xenophon, as well as Roman writers Tacitus and Cicero. These holdings furnished members of each successive Congress, should they wish to consult them in this way, with the materials for a basic course in classical literature, which would have been useful given the frequency with which Greek and Latin authors were quoted in political discourse. Moreover, the historians on the list provided the lessons in human behavior and morality that eighteenth-century social theorists thought statesmen should have in mind when writing laws and instituting government policies. Therefore, these classical works, too, support an interpretation of early Library of Congress history that stresses its essentially utilitarian character.

Cultural Authority and the Librarian of Congress

Legislation gave the president power to appoint a Librarian of Congress. In the first years of the institution, the position was not in practice a separate post but rather a responsibility that devolved upon the clerk of the House of Representatives, a political patronage position.[16] Jefferson asked John James Beckley, a political ally from Virginia who was already serving as clerk of the House of Representatives, to assume duties as Librarian of Congress in 1802; the extra work entailed an additional salary of two dollars per day of attendance. Beckley had come to Virginia as an indentured servant in 1769, became a scribe and clerical assistant to his master, John Clayton, and then after Clayton's death studied law, probably under Edmund Randolph, attorney general of Virginia. Beckley and Jefferson had been acquainted since at least 1779, the year in which Beckley took over as clerk of the House of Delegates in Virginia and

Jefferson was elected governor. Beckley took advantage of his connections with Virginia's ruling elite (including John Randolph, Thomas Jefferson, and James Madison) in securing his election to the post of clerk of the House of Representatives in 1789. Although he was ousted from the clerkship for political reasons with the election of John Adams in 1796, he regained the position in 1801 when the Jefferson administration came to power, no doubt in part as a reward for his work in support of the party.[17]

Although Beckley was not chosen to serve as Librarian of Congress on the basis of his literary attainments, he was a frequent essayist on behalf of the Republican Party and knew some of the important literary figures of the era. Beckley contributed political pieces to a number of periodicals, including the *Argus, or Greenleaf's New Daily Advertiser* of New York and the *National Gazette*, published by Philip Freneau, whom Madison and Henry Lee had persuaded to move to Philadelphia in 1791 to counter the efforts of Federalist publisher John Fenno.[18] Beckley also knew Philadelphia publisher Mathew Carey, who printed two thousand copies of Beckley's election-year campaign biography of Jefferson. The extent of Beckley's propagandistic efforts is revealed in a letter he wrote to James Madison in August 1800: "The packet [accompanying the letter] contains 1 doz. copies of an Epitome of the life of Mr. Jefferson to be distributed as you see proper . . . 1000 copies were struck for me, 1000 more by the printer—1000 at New York, 1000 in Connecticut & 1000 in Maryland, have since been struck, and imperfect as it is, it will I trust do some good. The author need not be named. You will see my reply to ['Serious Considerations on the Election of a president &c.'] in a series of numbers in the Aurora, disguised in stile & manner from the Epitome."[19] Able to appropriate various writing styles in the service of the party, Beckley recognized the political effectiveness of wide dissemination of printed forms. On the whole, though, Beckley took pains to conceal his authorship, confined himself to short works of a polemical character, and clearly considered himself a writer only in subordination to his efforts as a party organizer, as he was a librarian only subordinately to his duties as clerk of the House.

The post of Librarian of Congress was not in these years what it would later become, a patronage position for a literary author (as in the case of George Watterston) or a position imparting to its holder some amount of cultural authority as an arbiter of what constitutes worthwhile literature. It was instead merely a bureaucratic duty involving just enough remuneration to spur a few applicants to compete for the post. These applicants were not literary figures but lawyers and clerks looking to supplement their income. Nonetheless, John Beckley took a few steps in his brief tenure toward increasing the national visibility of the institution and endowing it with cultural significance. Sending Jefferson a letter in July 1802 clarifying the amount of the unexpended initial appropriation for books, Beckley suggested the acquisition of works by naturalist Georges-Louis Buffon and Mark Catesby. This is the first instance of a Librarian offering acquisitions advice, a responsibility that some later Librarians would reject as outside their expertise. He asked his friend Benjamin Rush to forward copies of Rush's publications to the Library, and he prompted Samuel Harrison Smith to insert a notice in the *National Intelligencer* in 1806 encouraging authors and publishers to send copies of their work to the Library, where "they will be seen and perused by gentlemen of distinction from all parts of the United States," an action that would constitute "a publication of them to all the states and territories."[20] This is an early statement of the idea that the Library was a central point from which a hierarchical diffusion of knowledge by congressmen down to their respective constituencies would occur, as these leaders read the latest publications deposited (voluntarily, not as a matter of securing copyright) at the Library. Beckley's efforts to place the Library at the center of the nation's literary life, however, would not be continued by his successor.

After Beckley's death in April 1807, Jefferson continued the tradition of appointing the clerk of the House of Representatives to the post of Librarian of Congress when on 6 November 1807 he notified the new House clerk, Patrick Magruder, that he could also begin serving as Librarian. Like Beckley, Magruder was a member of the Republican Party; he had been a lawyer, a member of the Maryland House of Delegates, and a circuit court judge and had served one term as a member of the Ninth Congress. In a biographical essay on Magruder, Martin K. Gordon asserts that "Magruder was not much involved in the routine of the Library of Congress. This, of course, was based on the normal practice in libraries at the time. Librarians were regarded as custodial employees whose main tasks were to shelve and to circulate books; selection and procurement was left to a committee of the governing board of the institution involved."[21] No evidence exists to suggest that Magruder followed Beckley's lead in trying to shape the collections or promote the Library in the press. Magruder's undistinguished term as Librarian was tainted by scandal after the burning of the Capitol in 1814, when he was held responsible for failing to prevent the loss of important financial records and was unable to account for almost twenty thousand dollars in expenditures. He resigned on 28 January 1815.

The unexceptional tenures of Beckley and Magruder as Librarians of Congress highlight both the limited symbolic importance of the Library of Congress and the immaturity of American literary culture at the beginning of the nineteenth century. Caring for the Library was, in the years 1802–14, merely a secondary function of the clerk of the House of Representatives, and consequently, the Librarian of Congress was a figure of little significance in the world of letters. Whatever cultural authority Beckley had tried to attach to the Library itself or the post of Librarian of Congress appears to have been squandered by Magruder. It would remain for a strong personality, that of the third Librarian of Congress, novelist George Watterston, to attempt to restore some of this authority to the position. Before the War of 1812, the cause of American letters and the character of the Library of Congress were not closely linked either in the public consciousness or in the minds of legislators, as they would come to be within a generation.

The Joint Committee on the Library

The lack of a guiding role for the Librarian of Congress in this period meant that various members of the Joint Committee on the Library, whose membership shifted from year to year with each new congress, determined the extent and direction of the Library's development. The Joint Committee was responsible for selecting and purchasing books, drawing up catalogs, writing rules and regulations for Library use, and writing annual reports on the Library. One important early member of the Library Committee was Samuel Latham Mitchill. A physician from New York and professor of natural history, agriculture, and chemistry at Columbia College, Mitchill served as both a member of the House and a senator from New York in the years 1801–13. A prolific author and promoter of the sciences, Mitchill founded and edited a journal of natural history, the *Medical Repository*, to which he was also a contributor. Mitchill's erudition suited him well to serve on and at times chair the Joint Library Committee during the Ninth, Tenth, and Twelfth Congresses.

His most important contribution to Library of Congress history was his authorship of the 1806 Joint Committee report on the Library. Mitchill lamented a lack of "geographical illustration" that he considered "truly distressing" and wrote that "the deficiency of historical and political works is scarcely less severely felt."[22] His arguments convinced Congress to appropriate five thousand dollars over five years to the Library, the first legislation authorizing an annual appropriation. Mitchill, John Quincy Adams, and Joseph Clay used this money during book-buying expeditions to New York, Boston, and Philadelphia in the summer of 1806.[23] Mitchill also supported the Library directly through donation. The 1812 catalog shows that the Library held thirteen volumes of the *Medical Repository* and a copy of Mitchill's *Picture of New York*, a statistical manual and traveler's guide (and, incidentally, the work that Washington Irving initially intended to parody as he conceived *A History of New York*). A number of other volumes, including the *Collections of the New York Historical Society, for the year 1809*, DeWitt Clinton's *Address to the Benefactors and Friends of the Free School Society of New York*, Joshua Gee's *Trade and Navigation of Great Britain*, and Albert Gallatin's *Report on the Subject of Public Roads and Canals*, are denoted as "Presented by Dr. Mitchill" in the 1812 catalog. Mitchill was the type of broadly learned, bookish member that the Joint Committee was not always able to draw from the ranks of Congress in subsequent decades.

Probably the most influential and intriguing member of the Joint Committee during this period, however, an individual whom Library of Congress historian William Dawson Johnston holds up as "one of the earliest friends and supporters of the Library, [who] always took pains to secure liberal appropriations for it," was the quixotic, fractious John Randolph of Virginia. After the arrival of the shipment of books from Cadell and Davies, Randolph, as a member of the committee, wrote a report dated 18 December 1801, which Johnston considers "one of the most notable documents relating to the early history of the Library" because it became the basis of the legislative act of 26 January 1802, establishing the Library's regulations.[24] Randolph was responsible in some measure for the character of the Library in its early years, including its institutional structure and the rules regarding access to the collections. In certain ways, the Library was shaped in accordance with Randolph's complex understanding of the relationship between books and republicanism.

Coming from the aristocratic Randolph clan of Virginia and having as an uncle Theodorick Bland, who was involved with Madison in the initial proposal for a legislative library in 1782–83, Randolph was raised in an atmosphere favorable to an appreciation of books. A letter that he wrote to his niece amply attests to his love of literature:

> Shakespeare, and Milton, and Chaucer, and Spenser, and Plutarch, and the Arabian Nights' Entertainments, and Don Quixote, and Gil Blas, and Robinson Crusoe, and "the tale of Troy divine," have made up more than half of my worldly enjoyment. To these ought to be added Ovid's Metamorphoses, Ariosto, Dryden, Beaumont and Fletcher, Southern, Otway, Congreve, Pope's Rape and Eliosa, Sheridan, Addison, Young, Thomson, Gay, Goldsmith, Gray, Collins, Cowper, Byron, Aesop, La Fontaine, Voltaire, (Charles XII., Mahomed, and Zaire;) Rousseau (Julie,) Schiller, Madame de Stael—but, above all, Burke.[25]

As a further testament to Randolph's wide-ranging literary tastes, Hugh B. Grigsby, writing in the *Southern Literary Messenger* in 1854, asserted that Randolph's reading "embraced all the finest productions of genius in every department of literature" and that his private library "in the number and rarity of its books, in its richness in the department of history, and that of Virginia especially, and in old English literature, nearly equaled . . . that of Col. Byrd of Westover." Not only was Randolph widely read and appreciative of the fine arts, states Grigsby, but he also "had the true bibliographic love of a fine copy of the best edition."[26] Nathan Sargent reports that Randolph was an "enthusiastic admirer of the British government, British aristocracy, English horses, and English books,—everything, indeed, English. He would not have in his possession an American book, not even an American Bible."[27] It would seem that as an avid reader and as a collector of valuable and rare books encompassing the broadest range of subjects, John Randolph would be the ideal booster for a Library of Congress that could begin to transcend the utilitarian acquisitions principles under which it had been founded.

In contrast to his personal love of expensive books, however, Randolph was the fiercest congressional defender of the Republican Party platform of the late 1790s emphasizing states' rights and a frugal, limited national government. David Carson summarizes this platform as including "a low national budget, a conservative interpretation of the Constitution, elimination of the national debt, and more direct action by the state and local agencies than the Federal government." According to Carson, Randolph "considered it his mission to help Jefferson's party reverse the perceived trend toward centralization of government authority. . . . His understanding of the principles was fixed and literal. Any deviation was flirtation with the corruption of the American government."[28] When Randolph believed that Jefferson had departed from these principles, particularly in regard to the Yazoo Land issue, for example, he sharply criticized the president and fell out of favor with the leaders of his party, becoming a perpetual outsider to both parties for the rest of his career. Randolph keenly distrusted the federal government and, like another Republican Party purist, William Manning, would have considered a comprehensively collected national library irrelevant to the goals of a republic and contrary to the values of fiscal restraint and decentralized power associated with Jeffersonian republicanism. Randolph's anxiety about corruption in the government exemplifies the classical republican fear that indulgence of luxury constituted a threat to the virtue of the citizenry. While a well-stocked private library was a marker of membership in the ranks of American gentility, to create such a library under the auspices of the federal government, in Randolph's view, invited an encroachment of luxury dangerous to the moral character of the nation.

Randolph's vision of the Library of Congress did not extend beyond certain well-defined limits. The Washington newspaper the *National Intelligencer* reported on 4 January 1802 how Randolph "moved to strike out that part [of the Library Bill] which gave permission to the Heads of Departments, Judges of the Supreme Court, and foreign ministers to take out books," and Johnston writes that "the Republicans opposed any considerable appropriation for what would evidently become a national library, Mr. Randolph thinking it better, he said, to save money than to spend it."[29] Limited access to the books, even among government officials, and a collection restricted to utilitarian purposes were the legacies of Randolph's involvement with the Library. The contrast between Randolph's staunch defense of frugality in regard to Library appropriations and the accumulation of rare and expensive books in his private library seems an odd paradox. But it is emblematic of the conflicted place that books and the fine arts occupied in classical republican ideology. As the self-appointed watchdog of the Republican Party and guardian of the nation's morals, Randolph supported spending limits to prevent this federal institution from growing beyond the bounds of a narrowly defined expediency.

John Randolph deviated only once from what Republicans called the "principles of 1798" to support a major expenditure by the federal government—he stood by Jefferson in advocating the Louisiana Purchase.[30] During this period when the country's population grew and expanded to the west and the government negotiated with European empires attempting to retain their holdings in the New World, as well as with Native Americans asserting their rights to land on the frontier, the importance of land acquisition and the protection of territorial boundaries at times superseded other political or philosophical differences. In regard to a congressional library, this concern with territorial integrity was recorded in the way Madison had justified his proposal for a legislative library in 1783 by referring to its value in securing the national borders, in the way the legislation for the Library of Congress always carefully stipulated that its regulations applied to the "books and maps" in the collection, and in Samuel Latham Mitchill's concern over geographic description expressed in his 1806 report. The importance of geography is also manifest in the Library of Congress catalog of 1812, where books on geography and maps combined to make up over 16 percent of the collection. The maps and accounts of Zebulon Pike, Lewis and Clark, and others in regard to the territory gained through the Louisiana Purchase were important new additions to the catalog between 1802 and 1812. Previous Library of Congress historians may not have recognized how vital and politically useful the maps in the Library would have been to Congress; this value is evident, however, in the remarkable career of William Tatham and the history of his attempts to sell his collection of books and maps to the United States.

William Tatham and the Library

William Dawson Johnston introduces Tatham as "the first to define the functions of a national library of the United States," an attribution that has been repeated somewhat carelessly by Tatham's biographers.[31] Before I examine the document on which Johnston based this judgment, some description of the course of Tatham's career is necessary. Tatham was born in England in 1752, came to America in 1769 to seek his fortune, and served the patriot cause sporadically during the Revolutionary War. He became acquainted with Thomas Jefferson in 1780, a friendship that Tatham later tried to exploit to advance his pleas for government patronage. He worked at various times as an engineer, surveyor, and topographer and also authored books and essays on these subjects, but more important here, he tried intermittently for decades to interest the governments of the United States and Spain in purchasing his collection of books and maps. Biographer George Herndon asserts that Tatham "probably collected and possessed at one time or another more books, maps and manuscript material than any other individual in the country."[32]

In February 1806, Tatham proposed to Congress the establishment of a Department of Works and Public Economy, creation of which would involve the purchase of his collection. This plan was virtually identical to one he had sent directly to President Jefferson in the summer of 1805 and only one of his seemingly endless petitions to presidents, United States department heads, state councils, governors, and foreign countries for some form of patronage, either through creation of a job or purchase of his books and maps. This was the proposal that Johnston referred to in suggesting that Tatham had "define[d] the function of a national library," but Tatham's letter of 10 February 1806 to the Speaker of the House in regard to the proposal makes it clear that purchase of his collection of books and maps was incidental to the establishment of a department of public economy in which Tatham would presumably occupy a major post. In the letter, Tatham states a desire "that my collection should form the basis of a practical public institution, under control of the executive branch of the Government."[33] The institution in question was not to be primarily a library, nor did the congressional committee assigned to evaluate Tatham's proposal take it as such. The committee, whose report on Tatham's proposition is dated 1 April 1806, looked somewhat favorably on Tatham's collection, noting:

> His collection of papers includes, besides many manuscript maps of parts of the United States, and the adjacent countries . . . draughts and plans of different military posts on the American continent, of barracks, magazines, storehouses and other buildings, and of the forts and fortifications formerly erected, or intended to be erected, not only within the neighborhood of the United States, but within the actual territory of the Union. . . . A knowledge of the places selected by other Governments as sites of military stations either for invasion or defence, must essentially assist the inquiries which may be hereafter conducted for similar purposes by officers of our own. . . . The southern frontier is an object of peculiar importance,

and the charts of the different parts of the Floridas attracted the attention of your committee.[34]

The language of its report suggests that the committee considered strategically useful books and maps a crucial element in the national defense and for this reason recommended that "a sum not exceeding___dollars [the amount was left unspecified] be appropriated as a part of the fund for the purchase of books, maps, and charts, for the Department of War, to enable the Secretary of War to purchase from William Tatham such parts of his collection as may be . . . of public use."[35] Material on Florida would have been especially useful around 1806 because the Spanish possession was both a place of refuge for escaping American slaves and a base from which Indians launched raids (in 1810 West Florida would be annexed by President Madison). The committee demurred on creating a department of public economy and was far from purchasing what could in any way be construed as the nucleus of a national library, if this is defined as a comprehensive collection of books involving some degree of service or access to the public. Tatham's books, if purchased, would have functioned much like Madison's proposed library as a small but politically valuable collection of documents intended to promote the defense, maintenance, and perhaps eventual expansion of the country's borders. Tatham shrewdly understood the value that maps could serve both in prosecuting wars and in making legal claims to a given parcel of land; as early as 1790 he had tried to sell some maps to the state of Virginia by arguing that "as Maps have a tendency to beget prejudice, which often turns the scale of Fact on intricate and distant matter, there can be nothing amiss, I suppose in such peaceable assertion of our *future expectations*."[36] Tatham no doubt had an eye on the nation's future expectations in trying to sell to the government his maps of the southern and western frontiers in 1806. The timing suggests that his petition was a response to Mitchill's report of 20 January 1806 lamenting a lack of geographic resources in the Library of Congress.

Tatham also understood the objections his audience of legislators might raise against purchase of the collection and the larger ideological issues surrounding government ownership of books. His proposal to Congress consisted of a schedule of the documents he offered for sale, broken down into the following sections: manuscripts, surveys, plans and drawings, maps and charts, engravings, books, models, instruments and apparatus, tools, implements and utensils, and patent rights. Obviously,

books formed only a small part of Tatham's collection, an element properly subordinated to the materials whose utilitarian value might be more
immediately apparent. The section labeled "Books" also includes the following curiously overwrought description of the volumes in his library:

> They are wholly scientific and useful; it having been an invariable rule
> with the selector to reject plays, farces, novels, romances, fabulous stories,
> and all that trash and fashionable nonsense which tends to give a contam-
> inated tone to the popular morals and habits; to disseminate indolence,
> dissipation, immorality, vice, artificial wants, false luxury, envy, hatred,
> ambition, mental inquietude, individual strife, and the more lamentable
> mania of foreign wars, bloodshed, and contention, too often about a mere
> definition of words and terms, which both parties would construe alike
> under the governance of reason.[37]

Tatham went to great lengths—at first glance, verging on irrelevancy—
to separate his books from any charge of immorality that might be raised
against them, assuring Congress that books which promote "false luxury,"
or any of the other related vices into which the wrong kind of book led
unsuspecting readers, were studiously excluded from his collection.
Tatham's fear of being perceived as peddling morally questionable books
indicates his awareness of how books could be implicated in the charge
of luxury associated with classical republicanism. Works of fiction were
considered particularly dangerous because of their pernicious effect on
the morality of readers. Books were doubly vulnerable to charges of
corruption because their danger could lie either in terms of form, as
unnecessarily luxurious and expensive physical objects, or on the grounds
of morally questionable content.

Astutely, Tatham recognized that books in general and fiction in
particular were the site of significant cultural apprehension in the early
Republic. Perhaps he had divined what Cathy Davidson pointed out
much later: the potentially revolutionary social and political implications
of fiction. On the subject of fiction's ideological impact, Davidson concludes that "the pervasive censure of fiction eloquently attests to the force
fiction itself was perceived to have as an ideology (or as an agent of
ideology). . . . Might not the American novel by addressing those unpri-
vileged in the emerging society persuade them that they had a voice in
that society and thus serve as the literary equivalent of a Daniel Shays by
leading its followers to riot and ruin?"[38] Given his earnest attempt to
reassure Congress that his collection would not challenge but uphold the

social hierarchy, Tatham was clearly attuned to the broader social implications of fiction and the controversy that might attend a governmental purchase of books.

But as Tatham was aware, the world of letters could also be associated, in other forms, with the diffusion of useful knowledge and improvement of public virtue. In another section of the proposal, Tatham described in detail his collections in American history, this time focusing not on the dangers of letters but on their potential benefits:

> All new materials, ancient works, tracts, &c. should be . . . published in neat, cheap, periodical numbers, accessible to the great bulk of the people, for the popular information, and more particularly for your rising youth, who should be thus taught to know and respect the most distant parts of the Union as one common people, linked together by the ties of reciprocity, mutual affection and general interest; and who should be kept to more useful employments than they meet with in taverns, cards, dice, theatres, cock-fights, and horse-races, which, being once rendered unfashionable, would soon become odious.[39]

If some books were dangerous agents of corruption, other printed forms, more likely to be issued as periodicals, had an ameliorative effect on public morality. Periodicals full of useful knowledge could be cheaply disseminated to people who would otherwise spend their time at cock-fights and horse races; the attack Tatham mounts here is not against the luxury of the upper classes but the restless and undirected energy of the lower ones. Skillfully playing on class anxieties in two directions, Tatham's proposal to Congress registered the contradictory attitudes toward books and literature inherent in republican ideology, which championed the diffusion of knowledge but feared the introduction of luxury.

Tatham clearly was not proposing that Congress establish a national library that would be liberal in its acquisition policy. Throughout his career, Tatham understood that he would more likely receive government support for a project that involved diffusion of useful knowledge through periodicals than for one that advocated collection of a large number of books in a central location. This understanding was evident in another of Tatham's moneymaking schemes outlined in 1813 in the *National Intelligencer* and addressed to the booksellers of the United States. Tatham contrasted the capitals of European nations, where the "means of promoting manufactures, commerce, arts and sciences" were concentrated in one place and led to the support of public improvement, with the capital of the United States, where "we collect to this spot, (but as a mere dead letter) all the *news*, all the knowledge, all the science, all the improvements in agriculture, arts, manufactures and commerce; but, unfortunately, and indolently, save the gleanings of a few casual curious persons, *and the annual reverberations of legislative convention*, we neglect to use competent and practicable exertions to return their benefits to the remotely sequestered citizen." Tatham appears to be referring to the Library of Congress and its failure to accomplish the diffusion of knowledge that would make it more useful to the Republic. He suggested that if the members of the book trade would pool their resources to publish some of the manuscripts that were at the time collected in the capital, "that much valuable matter will be distributed from this central repository, which is now lying useless." He went on to call for "immediate access to the public archives" so that the trade could use its resources, as well as the works in Tatham's own collection, to publish "an *improved Gazetteer*, applying to the Canadian war" and "progressive of improvement of our *national* Gazetteer; in, at least, three pocket volumes."[40] The proposal this time is for a private association of booksellers to publish a gazetteer, a geographic dictionary, a project that would assist the government in prosecuting the war against Britain. Putting this proposal next to his earlier interest in selling maps of the frontier to Congress, it is apparent that the connection between literature and territoriality and the value of diffusion of knowledge are ideas that Tatham perceptively identified as most likely to receive a sympathetic hearing from legislators of the period.

Johnston could not have been unaware of the nature of Tatham's proposal to Congress, including his explicit characterization of the kinds of books unfit for collection by a government agency; Johnston quotes from Tatham's attack on fiction at some length. Why he still considered Tatham "the first to define the functions of a national library of the United States" is difficult to say, but the reason might be traceable to Johnston's own association with the institution. When Johnston was writing at the beginning of the twentieth century, after the Librarianship of Ainsworth Rand Spofford and during the long tenure of Herbert Putnam, the Library had grown into the most important collection of books in the nation. It is conceivable that Johnston wished to extend the institution's image as a national library as far back into the nineteenth century as possible. While Tatham was not attempting, as Johnston claimed, to theorize the nature of a national library in America, his conception of what books represented to Americans was nonetheless telling. Because Tatham was well traveled, an avid reader, and very observant, his "ideas, proposals, and projects . . . were always in tune with the times."[41] Tatham's carefully crafted proposals offer a glimpse into the complicated, paradoxical attitudes that members of Congress (and their constituents) were likely to hold about the value of books and the propriety of expending public funds for them.

The 1812 Catalog

Although Congress chose not to acquire William Tatham's books and maps, the Joint Library Committee, under the leadership of Mitchill, slowly continued the work of collection development, assisted by the annual appropriation for books that Mitchill's Library Committee report had made possible in 1806. The 1812 catalog shows the results of these efforts and is probably a much more accurate indicator of the committee's (and Congress's) perception of the collections needed for the Library than is the 1815 catalog of the library soon to be acquired from Jefferson.[42] The books cataloged in 1812 represent the specific acquisitions wishes of the Joint Library Committee over the course of a decade, whereas Jefferson's entire library had to be purchased or rejected in one lot, with no opportunity for legislators to distinguish the useful from the unnecessary. The 1812 catalog shows that the Library had grown from 971 volumes in 1802 to 3,076 volumes (941 titles) in 1812, to form a collection aptly described by Robert Rutland as "a working members' library, containing mainly references that a country lawyer might need if he moved into the complicated business of maritime or international law."[43]

The most striking feature of the 1812 catalog is its division of the collections into sixteen subject and two format categories. The 1802, 1804, and 1808 catalogs had all been arranged by size, thus the subject classification of the 1812 catalog was an innovation in Library of Congress cataloging. This particular subject classification was derived from the 1789 catalog of the Library Company of Philadelphia, which itself had been modeled on the classification of knowledge sketched out by Diderot and D'Alembert in the preliminary discourse to the *Encyclopédie*.[44] Diderot and D'Alembert developed their classificatory scheme from Francis Bacon's division of knowledge into the three major classes of history, philosophy, and the fine arts based on his ideas about the three faculties of the mind: memory, reason, and imagination. This conception of the faculties of the mind is visible in the arrangement of subjects in the 1812 catalog. Memory encompasses the following four classes: (1) Sacred History; (2) Ecclesiastical History; (3) Civil History, including Chronology, Biography, Antiquities, etc, and (4) Geography and Topography, Voyages, and Travels. The faculty of reason yields ten categories: (1) Law; (2) Ethics, or the Moral System in General, Theology, and Mythology; (3) Logic, Rhetoric, and Criticism; (4) Dictionaries, Grammars, and Treatises on Education; (5) General and Local Politics, Political Economy, etc., (6) Trade and Commerce; (7) Military and Naval Tactics; (8) Agriculture; Rural Economy, etc., (9) Natural History, Natural and Experimental Philosophy, etc., and (10) Medicine, Surgery, and Chemistry. The faculty of imagination is represented by two categories: (1) Poetry and the Drama, Works of Fiction, Wit, etc., and (2) Arts and Sciences and Miscellaneous Literature. The two format categories are gazettes (newspapers) and maps, charts, and plans.

In line with the acquisitions decisions made by Waln and Bingham as reflected in the 1802 catalog, history was quite the largest category in the 1812 catalog with 248 titles and 1,053 volumes. The next largest section, counting by title, was law, with 170 titles in over 500 volumes. Reminiscent of Madison's 1783 list of books necessary for the use of Congress, the third largest division of the 1812 catalog was the section on geography and topography, with 106 titles (197 volumes) and an additional 53 maps, charts, and plans. Twenty-one of the 27 maps displayed North America. The subject classification of general and local politics and political economy was the third largest single chapter, with 70 titles in 118 volumes. The four areas of history, geography, law, and politics (which included economics) together accounted for 647 titles, or about 69 percent of the entire library. For members of the Joint Library Committee in the first twelve years of the Library's history, acquisitions priorities favored these subjects.

The appearance of the subject classification in the 1812 catalog allows one to read the catalog to recover assumptions legislators held about the value of certain classes of knowledge. Statesmen of the period continued to believe that study of history was crucial to their work. Interestingly, though, the 1812 catalog began not with the important area of civil history (which had 248 titles) but with sacred history, a class that held a single title: a 1798 Philadelphia edition of the Bible. This pride of place given to the Bible appears to indicate that this book outranks the others; it is perhaps a gesture of adherence to the mainstream Protestant values of the age. And the choice of a Philadelphia imprint blended piety with patriotism. Other libraries of the era, those which followed the Diderot and D'Alembert classification scheme, also sometimes opened their catalogs with theology, but they did not put the Bible in a chapter of its own. This arrangement would come to an end with the acquisition of the Jefferson library.

The classification called "Civil History, Including Chronology, Biography, Antiquities, etc." united a number of works that would find their way into various classifications in a modern library. Organized within the classification by size, this section of the Library included works of ancient history such as Plutarch's *Lives* and the works of Herodotus in English translations. It also encompassed the major historians of the eighteenth century including Robertson, Voltaire, Raynal, Rapin, and Hume, as well as more-recent works on American history such as Mercy Otis Warren's *History of the Rise, Progress, and Termination of the American Revolution* (1805). Political documents such as the debates of the American Congress and the English Parliament were also classed under civil history. The promiscuous mingling of ancient and modern history illustrates the belief held by these early-nineteenth-century statesmen, still the inheritors of Enlightenment tradition, that study of the past need not be divided by geography or chronology because all of history together provided the clues to the principles of human behavior that would guide legislators in their decisions.

Another revealing classification is the large section on arts and sciences and miscellaneous literature (only 64 titles but 631 volumes), which was swelled by the inclusion of a number of multivolume works. Counting by volumes instead of titles, this would be the second largest section of the catalog, representing about a fifth of the collection. One of the most important of these was a thirty-five-volume set of Diderot's *Encyclopédie*, a title frequently borrowed by congressmen and a work that embodies the emphasis placed on useful knowledge by thinkers of the age. The *Encyclopédie* devoted much attention to the mechanical arts, which Diderot, the son of a cutler, felt had been degraded and ignored by previous historians of the arts and sciences. This section of the catalog, which also included a seventy-volume set of Voltaire's works in French and a thirty-six-volume set of his works translated into English, might be contrasted with the opening two sections of the catalog, sacred and ecclesiastical history, which contained a total of three titles and only eight volumes. In the contest between religious and secular authority, placement of the Bible at the head of the catalog appears to signal a certain preeminence given to this book, but the number of volumes in the arts and sciences classification shows that the true weight of the collection heavily favored the secular. The 1812 Library of Congress was much more a product of the Enlightenment than many other libraries of the age. The small portion of the collection devoted to theology was unique to the Library of Congress, as most college and social libraries of the era maintained large collections of sermons and theological tracts, but it serves to confirm Rutland's characterization of the Library in this era as a workshop for members of Congress.

Many of the titles in the 1812 catalog reflected congressional interest in recent historical events. For example, the slave revolt in Santo Domingo (Haiti) in the West Indies led by Toussaint-Louverture in 1791 aroused much interest in the United States, particularly in the South. The evolving relations between the United States and France, which wanted to reassert its authority over the island, meant that the government had a reason to monitor developments there. The catalog of 1804 shows that the Library had by then acquired Moreau de Saint-Méry's *Description . . . de l'Isle Saint-Domingue* (1797), which detailed the state of St. Domingo before the slave insurrection of 1791, and by 1812 it had also purchased a more-recent account of the island after the revolution, Marcus Rainsford's *Historical Account of the Black Empire of Hayti* (1805).[45]

Also in regard to foreign affairs, Congress desired information on Napoléon's reign and the Napoleonic Wars, which it found in numerous titles in the 1812 catalog, mostly under the classification of civil history. The Library held Stewarton's *Picture of the Empire of Buonaparte . . . or, the Belgian Traveller* (1807); Jacques Peuchet's *Campaigns of the Armies of France, in Prussia, Saxon, and Poland* (1808); and William Lodewyk Van-Ess's *Life of Napoleon Buonaparte* (1809). The Library Committee showed an interest as well in the Spanish colonies of South America, several of which were agitating for independence in the early nineteenth century. Some relevant titles in this area include Joseph Skinner's compilation titled *The Present State of Peru* (1805); François Raymond Joseph de Pons's *Travels in Parts of South America during the Years 1801, 1802, 1803, and*

1804 (1807); and John H. Sherman's *General Account of Miranda's Expedition* (1808). Francisco de Miranda was the Venezuelan revolutionary whose 1806 invasion of the country was repulsed but who returned in 1810 as general of the revolutionary army that liberated the country from Spanish control.

Reflecting events closer to home, the law section of the 1812 catalog included *Report of the Committee Appointed to Inquire into the Official Conduct of Samuel Chase* (1804) and *Trial of Samuel Chase* (1805). Chase was the Supreme Court justice whom Jefferson tried to have impeached in his efforts to weaken the Federalist hold on the judiciary; John Randolph of the Library Committee was the impeachment manager. The law classification also had the transcript of Aaron Burr's trial for treason after his apparent conspiracy to establish an empire of his own in the Southwest. And a notable accession in the politics classification was a State Department publication titled *State Papers for 1808–9*, which contained correspondence related to the Chesapeake-Leonard affair of 1807, in which officers of a British ship boarded a United States Navy frigate and impressed four sailors, to the outrage of the American public.

The geography section continued to grow, with a number of literary and scientific works on America such as William Bartram's *Travels through North and South Carolina* (which was published in 1793 but first appeared in the 1808 catalog) and Count Volney's *View of the Soil and Climate of the United States of America* (1804).[46] But the most politically valuable geography accessions were probably the ones that dealt with the Southwest, where Spain, France, and the United States were engaged in complex maneuverings for territory from Florida to the Mississippi. One title from the 1812 catalog relevant to this region is Andrew Ellicott's *Journal of Andrew Ellicott . . . for Determining the Boundary between the United States and the Possessions of His Catholic Majesty in America* (1803), about the boundary between the United States and Spain's colony of Florida. After Spain ceded the territory known as Louisiana to France, which then sold it to the United States in 1803, information on the Southwest became even more essential. The treaty that Robert Livingston and James Monroe signed with France failed to define the boundaries of Louisiana, so it was in the interest of Congress, the Department of State (the secretary of state gained borrowing privileges at the Library of Congress in 1806), and the president to obtain as much information as possible to defend the United States claim against any protestations from

Spain. When Mitchill complained about a lack of geographic information in the Library in 1806, he probably had this region in mind.

Many of the titles in the 1812 catalog dealt with the Louisiana Purchase, most notably Zebulon Pike's *Account of Expeditions to the Sources of the Mississippi: And through the Western Parts of Louisiana to the Sources of the Arkansaw, Kans, La Platte, and Pierre Jaun Rivers* (1810), which was the first account published in America about the trans-Mississippi Louisiana Territory. Other titles that Congress consulted for information about the area included *An Account of Louisiana, Being an Abstract of Documents, in the Offices of the Departments of State and of the Treasury* (undated); George Heriot's *History of Canada . . . Comprehending an Account of the Original Establishment of the Colony of Louisiana* (1804); and Alexander Humboldt's *Political Essay on the Kingdom of New Spain . . . with a Separate Volume of Maps* (1811). Finally, the section "Maps, Charts, and Plans" included maps titled *The Western Part of North America* (1805) by Meriwether Lewis; the *Southern Mail Route, from Washington, to New Orleans* (1807); and the *Orleans Territory* (1807), documents whose value had been anticipated in James Madison's original proposal for a congressional library.[47] From its comparative neglect in the catalog of 1802, the subject area of geography had begun to assume critical importance to Congress and the expanding nation by 1812.

The class of books labeled "Poetry and the Drama, Works of Fiction, Wit, etc." was modest (43 titles, 164 volumes) but probably important nonetheless to legislators who would have found little in the way of entertainment in Washington. Notable among the collections were a twenty-five-volume set titled *British Theater*, which Rutland explains as "a treat for Congressmen who liked plays and found the playbill fare sparse to nonexistent in the 'city' of Washington," and a forty-nine-volume set of *The Works of the British Poets*. Congressmen looking for literary amusement or instruction could also find works by Aeschylus, Virgil, Cervantes, and Shakespeare, as well as British periodicals including the *Gentleman's Magazine* (sixty-two volumes), along with the eighteen-volume set of issues of the *Spectator, Rambler, Adventurer,* and *Tattler* and the other literary titles purchased in 1802. Among English poets, the works of Americans Joel Barlow and Philip Freneau stood alongside volumes by Robert Burns, Erasmus Darwin, and Alexander Pope. Rutland speculates that because it was open until 7:00 P.M. on days when the legislature was in session, "the Library of Congress probably served as a social gathering place."[48] The class of books on natural history in the 1812 catalog included several works with attractive plates and drawings such as Alexander Wilson's *American Ornithology* (1808); Alexander Anderson's *General History of Quadrupeds* (1804); and William Nicholson's *Journal of Natural Philosophy* (1797), the kind of books that would draw curious and bored members of Washington's social circles into the Library in subsequent decades to converse and look at innovations in book illustration. Combining the section on "poetry, drama, fiction, and wit" with the one on "logic, rhetoric, and criticism" yields 64 titles, or about 7 percent of the collection, a marked expansion in the belles lettres from the catalog of 1802.

Comparison of Library Holdings and Social Library Holdings

Perhaps the best way to get a sense of the collection priorities of the Joint Library Committee is to contrast the catalog of the 1812 Library of Congress with catalogs from a number of social libraries of the period. In light of what was being collected at these other libraries whose institutional structure served as the model for the Library of Congress, the priorities of the Joint Committees on the Library stand out more sharply. For this purpose, I analyzed the catalogs of six library companies that also used subject classification in their catalogs. The catalogs, in chronological order, are those of the Library Company of Burlington, New Jersey, of 1807 (1,055 titles); the Library Company of Baltimore of 1809 (3,706 titles); the Charleston Library Society of 1811 (2,984 titles); the New York Society Library of 1813 (4,593 titles); the Alexandria, Virginia, Library Company of 1815 (996 titles); and the Hartford Library Company of 1818 (1,149 titles).[49] The 1812 catalog of the Library listed 941 titles. Table 1 in the appendix provides a breakdown of selected subject holdings at all seven libraries.

The civil history section of the 1812 Library of Congress catalog accounted for over 25 percent of the collection. This is an area on which members of the Joint Committees put somewhat more emphasis than did their social library counterparts. The four catalogs whose subject classifications make comparisons possible reveal that history books were well collected in social libraries. As indicated in table 1, history collections at the Burlington, Baltimore, Charleston, and New York libraries ranged from 13.8 percent to 19.3 percent of the catalog. While these proportions are substantial, they are nonetheless significantly smaller than the percentage at the Library of Congress. Enlightenment interest in historical experience as a guide to political practice exercised a strong influence over collections decisions at the Library in its early years.

It might be expected that the hallmark of a legislative library would be law holdings. This was true for the Library of Congress in 1812. Acquisitions in this classification tended to center on international law, the laws and constitutions of the various states, and decisions of state supreme courts. Counting by number of titles, the law section of the 1812 catalog represented 18.1 percent of holdings, which far exceeded the proportion at the other five libraries with comparable classifications. As table 1 indicates, the proportion of law holdings in the catalogs of the other libraries ranged from 1.2 percent at Hartford to 7.5 percent at Alexandria. The Charleston (5.9 percent) and Alexandria figures, however, are inflated because their classifications also included books on such other subjects as politics, agriculture, and commerce. The collective average of law books (without trying to separate the law books embedded in classifications that included other books) in these libraries was 4.0 percent of holdings, which means that by a conservative estimate, the Library of Congress held over four times the proportion of law books as did social libraries of the era.

The importance that the Joint Library Committees accorded to geography has been discussed. At the Library of Congress in 1812, the two classifications of (1) geography and topography, voyages and travels, and (2) maps, charts, and plans accounted for 16.9 percent of the collection. Comparisons with the other libraries are complicated by differing subject classification schemes but are nonetheless telling. At the four libraries with distinct classifications for geography, topography, or voyages and travels, table 1 shows that the proportion of geography books ranged from 8.1 percent (New York) to 9.6 percent (Burlington) of the catalog, about half of the proportion at the Library of Congress. Comparisons are more difficult in the cases of the Alexandria Library Company and the Hartford Library Company, whose catalogs devoted a single classification to geography and history. The capacious geography and history classifications represented 32.1 percent of holdings in the Alexandria library and 22.2 percent in Hartford. Adding history and geography titles from the 1812 Library of Congress catalog, in contrast, yields about 43 percent of the entire collection, again demonstrating the emphasis placed on these subjects by the Joint Library Committee.

Politics and economics, often classified together in libraries of the period, form another subject area in which Library of Congress holdings exceeded those at other social libraries. At the Library of Congress, 96 titles accounted for 10.2 percent of the collection. Two of the six library company catalogs, Hartford and Burlington, did not even include classifications that mentioned politics, political economy, or commerce. In the Charleston Library Society and Alexandria Library Company catalogs, books on politics were subordinated under a classification on law and are not included here. At both the New York Society Library and the Library Company of Baltimore, classifications that included politics, political economy, and commerce represented 8.1 percent of collections, only slightly less than the proportion at the Library of Congress.

On close inspection of the Library Company of Baltimore catalog, however, one finds that many of the books classified under politics and political economy would have been classified elsewhere at the Library of Congress. For example, in the Baltimore catalog, books on the law of nature and nations, such as Pufendorf's *Law of Nature and Nations*, Montesquieu's *Spirit of the Laws*, and Vattel's *Law of Nations*, were all classed under politics. At the Library of Congress, these books were classified under law. At other libraries under study, the issue does not come up because of classifications that blended law and politics.[50] The relative poverty of the law division of the Baltimore library (87 titles, 2.3 percent of the collection) seems to be due to this peculiarity of classification. Public documents, too, such as *Journals of the U.S. House of Representatives* and *Debates of the House of Lords and House of Commons*, were classed under politics at the Baltimore library, whereas at the Library of Congress such documents would have been classed under civil history. Thus the 8.1 percent of collections ostensibly devoted to works on politics and political economy in the Library Company of Baltimore is actually a significant overestimate in comparison with the Library of Congress. Given that the subject was not important enough to merit its own classification at four of the libraries, politics was clearly a higher priority at the Library of Congress than at most social libraries of the period.

Aside from the irregularity in classification of certain books on legal and political subjects at the Library Company of Baltimore, classification of individual works at the various libraries was reliably consistent. Standard law books such as Blackstone's *Commentaries*, Justinian's *Institu-*

tions, Jean Domat's *Civil Law in Its Natural Order*, and Charles Molloy's *De Jure Maritimo* were classified under "Law" or "Legislation" in all the libraries that held them. Algernon Sidney's *Discourses concerning Government* was always placed in the classification that included the word "politics," while Adam Smith's *Wealth of Nations* was consistently categorized under "Political Economy" (where such classifications existed), including at the Library Company of Baltimore.[51] Books on history were easily and consistently classified. David Hume's *History of England*, William Robertson's *History of America*, and Edward Gibbon's *History of the Decline and Fall of the Roman Empire* were present in all seven libraries, always placed in the classification that included the word "history." Books of travel or geography, too, were classified uniformly across libraries. Jonathan Carver's *Travels through the Interior Parts of North America* and Jedidiah Morse's *American Geography* were always placed in classifications that included the terms "geography," "voyages and travel," or both. Count Volney's *View of the Soil and Climate of the United States of America*, a book whose title did not necessarily lend itself to classification as easily as Carver's and Morse's works, also was classified under geography or voyages and travels in all five libraries that held it. In short, classification was certainly consistent enough to make comparisons across the seven libraries valid.[52]

Comparing the Library of Congress with other libraries in terms of imaginative literature, one finds that this class of works was much better represented at the social libraries, even though Library of Congress holdings had increased noticeably between 1802 and 1812. The 1812 Library of Congress catalog devoted one subject classification to poetry, drama, fiction, and wit, in which 43 titles accounted for 4.6 percent of the Library's collections. Adding the section on dictionaries, grammars, and treatises on education, some of which were classified with literature in other catalogs, brings the figure to 8.2 percent. This figure was significantly higher at all the other libraries under consideration, ranging from 12.2 percent (Burlington) to 32.7 % (Alexandria). Librarian and novelist George Watterston would influence acquisitions in these categories during his tenure from 1815 to 1829, and the Joint Committee would continue to add modestly to literature collections until midcentury, generally keeping up with the most popular or critically acclaimed fiction of the day for the amusement of congressmen and their families. By the time of the

1839 and 1849 catalogs, under new subject classifications, literature would account for between 7 and 8 percent of holdings. But in the years from the founding of the Library until 1812, literature was not a priority.

Finally, the Library held a very small proportion of theology volumes by comparison with other libraries of the period, where theology accounted for anywhere from 8.3 percent (Charleston) to 22.2 percent (Hartford) of titles. At the Library of Congress, in stark contrast, the two categories of sacred history and ecclesiastical history accounted for only three titles, a scant 0.3 percent of the collection. Adding the eight titles that had something to do with theology from the classification on ethics brings the total to 1.2 percent. Whether these other libraries amassed such collections in theology by donation, as was often the case, out of a sense of moral responsibility for members' souls, or through a perceived desire for such books, the Library of Congress Joint Committee saw no legislative, moral, or entertainment value in the subject. Incidentally, two of the six catalogs (Burlington and New York) listed theology first among subject classifications, but neither did so because it was following the Diderot and D'Alembert divisions of knowledge, and neither devoted a classification exclusively to the Bible.

The pattern of acquisitions set by the Library of Congress in its first decade, favoring the subjects of history, geography, law, and politics, was well suited to its function as a legislative library. This point is further emphasized by a quick look at the State Library of New York, established in Albany in 1819. In that year the Assembly of the State of New York published a catalog of the first purchase of books for its legislative library, which shelved a mere 600 volumes in about 170 titles. The same subjects that were collected at the Library of Congress were deemed useful by the legislature of New York. A third of the books were devoted to a single broad subject classification including law, parliamentary proceedings, and political economy. The rest of the catalog was simply arranged alphabetically, but slightly less than a third of the collection was devoted to history. Geography was also important, represented by seventeen titles on geographic subjects and eight maps, including three maps of New York State and maps of the city of Albany, Connecticut, Maine, the United States, and the world. The library had a small collection of titles (a dozen) in literature and belles lettres and a few reference books on the arts and sciences. Theology was almost completely ignored (four titles).[53]

Founded in 1800 with the removal of the federal government to Washington but not formally organized until 1802, the Library of Congress was a very modest institution in its first decade. In accordance with classical republican ideology, the Library collected books that would be of use to members of Congress in carrying out their official duties. Subjects most assiduously collected were law, politics, economics, history, and geography, with certain purchases reflecting the impact of important historical events, such as the Napoleonic Wars and the Louisiana Purchase. A small number of titles in imaginative literature were also collected in this decade, providing legislators with entertainment for their leisure hours, a role that would expand in years to come. But for the most part a frugal Congress avoided purchases that could be associated with an enervating luxury. In its institutional structure and its architecture, the Library resembled the social libraries of New York and Philadelphia on which Congress had previously relied for books. In its holdings, it deviated from their model through its relative neglect of theology and belles lettres.

The post of Librarian of Congress in this period was a mere bureaucratic duty. John Beckley, considered the first Librarian of Congress, made a few efforts to enhance the public visibility of the Library and enrich its collections; these tentative moves were not followed up by his successor, Patrick Magruder. Much more important to its history were Joint Committee on the Library members, who helped shape the Library in these early years. Samuel Latham Mitchill contributed books and lobbied for increased appropriations, while John Randolph's paradoxical union of a genteel love of books with an ideological distrust of their implications seems to have been imprinted to some extent onto the Library whose regulations he helped write. This conflicted attitude toward books was also evident in the petitions of William Tatham for government purchase of his collection of books and maps. Like Madison in his 1783 proposal for a congressional library, Tatham recognized the value that books and maps could have in boundary disputes with foreign countries. Congressional interest in Tatham's books about the frontier in 1806 foreshadows collection decisions of the 1840s, the decade of the annexations of Texas and Oregon and the Mexican-American War.

The Library of Congress experienced important milestones in the period from its founding to the War of 1812. Library privileges in this period were extended to the secretary of state, secretary of the treasury, secretary of war, secretary of the navy, and the attorney general of the United States (1806); to the agent of the Joint Library Committee (1810); and to the justices of the Supreme Court (1812), extensions that also implied a broadened function, as the Library now served all three branches of government.[54] An equally significant milestone in these years was the precedent set for an annual appropriation, which allowed Congress, in the absence of a copyright deposit provision, to acquire the books it needed. Appropriations before the 1814 destruction of the Library averaged about a thousand dollars per year. With the purchases made possible by these appropriations, the Library fulfilled the utilitarian function that had been traced out for it, nearly two decades before its actual foundation, by James Madison. Ironically, it would be during Madison's presidency that the Library of Congress began to accrue symbolic significance well beyond anything he comprehended in his initial vision of the role of a congressional library in American life.

CHAPTER THREE

Thomas Jefferson,
George Watterston,
and the Library,
1814–1829

An attack on the Capitol in Washington by British troops in 1814 resulted in the nearly complete destruction of the Library of Congress. The subsequent purchase of Thomas Jefferson's library to become a new Library of Congress in 1815 has been treated by Library of Congress historians as the start of a new era for the institution, which in some ways it was. The suggestion that the Library should function as something like a national library emerged after this purchase, and collections in the new Library were more comprehensive than in its predecessor. But debate over the purchase also revived arguments against government ownership of a library which were inherited from an earlier age. Moreover, the expenditure of so much money for books in 1815 was a convenient excuse for Congress not to spend much money on Library appropriations in the years that followed. For these reasons, the effect of the purchase was not unequivocal and should not be overestimated.

The Library of Congress became linked in a new way with the nation's literary culture through the appointment of author George Watterston to the Librarianship in 1815. Putting a novelist instead of a clerk in charge of the Library set a precedent for later patronage positions for professional authors in the United States. It also imbued the post with a cultural authority it had not before possessed. Watterston's appointment and the purchase of Jefferson's library suggested to some commentators that the Library would step into a new role, as a symbol of American literary achievement. But these observers—as well as like-minded members of the Joint Library Committee—found that although congressmen enjoyed the opportunities for light reading and social interaction that the Library and its rooms in the Capitol provided, Congress continued to hold a limited conception of the function of its Library and had little interest in promoting the cause of American arts and letters. Despite the expansion and democratization of the print culture of the 1820s and 1830s, which opened up new avenues of information and expanded access to books for most people, Congress held to a narrow view of the Library consistent with the classical republican ideology that had shaped its foundation and its growth since 1800.

Purchase of Jefferson's Library

British soldiers marched into Washington on 24, August 1814 and, in retaliation for a similar attack on public buildings by Americans in York (Toronto), set fire to the Capitol building. The conflagration destroyed most of the books in the Library of Congress. On hearing of the destruction, Thomas Jefferson, who had fostered development of the Library during his presidency by recommending book purchases, wrote from Monticello to his friend Samuel Harrison Smith in Washington and offered to sell his private collection to Congress as a replacement.[1] This offer was read by the Joint Committee on the Library to the Senate and accepted there immediately, in October 1814. But Jefferson's wide learning and instinct for book collecting made his library somewhat different in its collections from the one Congress had lost. Jefferson's library held six thousand volumes, about twice the size of the library it was being offered to replace, and covered subjects that had not previously been collected by Congress. Debate over the purchase ensued, therefore, both in the House of Representatives and in the press.

When the debate began in the House in October, amendments were offered to give the Joint Committee authority to exclude certain books from the library or to impose a price ceiling. These were rejected, however, and the committee was instructed to negotiate the purchase. Appraisal of the books at $24,000 was reported in November to the Senate, which approved the purchase and again passed the issue to the House. Here it was taken up anew and vigorously debated in January 1815.

Despite objections, the Republican majority carried the day, and the final vote in the House was eighty-one to seventy-one in favor. On 30 January 1815 an act authorizing the purchase at a cost of $23,950 was approved. While it is true that the final vote fell largely along party lines, the episode is not, as it has been described, "little more than a lesson in partisan politics."[2] The arguments available to both parties in formulating their position speak to the changing cultural significance of books in the second decade of the nineteenth century.

The speeches made by Cyrus King and Timothy Pickering of Massachusetts, Thomas Peabody Grosvenor of New York, and others against congressional acquisition of Jefferson's library reprise a number of the antiluxury and anti-intellectual charges that had been raised against Jefferson in the presidential campaign of 1800. These charges were characteristic of classical republican discomfort with the political implications of the fine arts. For example, a correspondent reporting the 26 January debate for the *New York Evening Post* wrote: "it was urged by those who opposed it . . . [that] the library was not such as Congress wanted, being almost entirely literary, containing comparatively little of law or history, that it abounded with productions of an atheistical, irreligious and immoral character,—a fourth of the books were in foreign languages, and many in the dead languages, such as romances, tracts on architecture, farriery, cookery and the like."[3] Federalists had for twenty years associated Jefferson with atheism, immorality, effete intellectualism, and an infatuation with France. They predictably transferred these qualities from Jefferson to his library to carry the weight of their argument against purchase. Cyrus King, the congressman most vocally opposed to purchasing the entire library and the one who offered amendments that would have authorized the Joint Committee to reject individual books, opined that the collection was probably rich in "works of the French philosophers" and that he opposed "a general dissemination of that infidel philosophy."[4] As Neil Harris summarizes Federalist opposition to the purchase, the main arguments employed described the books as "dangerous [to morality], useless, abstruse, expensive, and low on the agenda of public needs."[5] In short, charges of luxury continued to be deployed against government ownership of books, as they had been in 1790 after Elbridge Gerry broached the subject of a congressional library.

A parody of the proposed purchase appeared in the Federalist *Georgetown Daily Federal Republican* on 18, October 1814. Its writer satirically addressed Jefferson as a fellow private citizen also hoping to dupe the government into purchasing his library. The pseudonymous "Johannes Vonderpuff," whose attack is more witty and engaging than the pro-purchase articles, describes his own library as "rare" and "elegant," claims that the collection was made "with a particular view to the promotion of genuine republicanism, and the true orthodoxy in matters of faith of regenerated France," and notes that "four-fifths of this library are in foreign languages." All these are familiar Federalist criticisms of Jefferson's character, but the letter ends, a bit awkwardly, with a comment on U.S. imperialism: "The enlightened philosopher looks to the present war, which we have so wisely and righteously waged, as terminating . . . in the conquest of immeasurable regions to the north, west and south, and to the day when the representatives of this country will be composed 'of all people, nations and languages under the whole Heavens.'" Vonderpuff's closing attack on American land acquisition at first seems curiously out of place in a letter ostensibly on the subject of Jefferson's library. But the comment makes sense in the historical context of the War of 1812. The war was strongly opposed in the Northeast by Federalists (and by some Republicans, including Virginian and former Library Committee member John Randolph), who believed it was motivated primarily by American interest in the conquest of Canada. This link between a library purchase and aggressive American expansionism recalls how both Madison and William Tatham had presumed a library capable, through preservation of documents and maps, of securing and extending a nation's territorial claims. Without putting too fine a point on the apparent connection between library acquisitions and land acquisition, this broad satirical attack marks the extent to which a government library served as a focal point for ideological controversy.

The arguments made in favor of the purchase illuminate an emergent cultural nationalism in which the Library of Congress became a symbol of American arts and letters. The burning of the Library by the British allowed patriotic Americans to align themselves with the forces of civilization and culture in opposition to an act of barbarism committed by a European nation (notwithstanding the attack at York). Jefferson made use of this trope in the message he sent to Congress by way of Samuel Harrison Smith, lamenting the way the British had engaged in "acts of barbarism which does [sic] not belong to a civilized age."[6] A newfound cultural self-consciousness manifested itself in the House debate of 26

January as well, during which advocates of purchase, who included Robert Wright of Maryland, James Fisk of Vermont, and John Rhea of Tennessee, "contended that so valuable a library, one so admirably calculated for the substratum of a national library, was not to be obtained in the United States," an argument that was seconded in the pages of the *National Intelligencer*, which, as the mouthpiece for the Republican Madison administration, supported the purchase.[7]

The designation by members of Congress of the Library of Congress as a national library, a term that was used but not precisely defined, is a striking development in light of the Library's modest history to that point. But the idea resonated with new Librarian of Congress George Watterston, who tried to nurture it through the title he invented for the 1815 catalog of the newly acquired library: *Catalogue of the Library of the United States*.[8] Because these statements mark the first time in official or unofficial discourse that the Library of Congress was denoted as a national library, it seems that through this debate the institution was—at least symbolically—becoming something more than a social or reference library for congressmen. For advocates of the purchase, for Watterston, and perhaps for segments of the U.S. public, the Library might serve as a symbol of the nation's cultural maturity on the order (if not nearly the scale) of the great monarchical libraries of Europe. Evidence of national, public interest in the Library is suggested by the appearance of articles about the purchase in newspapers around the country.[9]

Two years after the purchase, an editorialist in *Walsh's American Register* looked back over the debate and praised the acquisition in terms that indicate a conception of the political implications of books well removed from the classical republican ideology of the late eighteenth century. The writer defended the purchase in part by pointing out that "the collection is exuberant in the ancient classics" and that "when we advert to the *real* condition of the *Fine Arts* in the United States,—whatever may be the pretensions advanced,—we cannot attach too much importance to the contents of the chapters under that title in Mr. Jefferson's catalogue." With this comment, the editorialist linked the fortunes of the fine arts in the United States and the contents of the Library of Congress, a notable connection given the Library's utilitarian history and one that would be repeated in years to come. This writer went on to argue that the new Library of Congress held "in the most attractive and splendid form, all that could be desired,—especially in architecture, where we are most lame,—for the diffusion of technical knowledge and the improvement of the public taste."[10] This comment combines two ideas about books that seemed mutually exclusive under classical republican ideology: books are expensive physical objets d'art, and they also serve to diffuse knowledge. In this text the "attractive and splendid books" are taken to symbolize a noble devotion to culture instead of an enervating luxury.

The writer went on to predict that the Library "will be one day duly appreciated, without looking to the time when the Bibliomania may rage in the United States; a period which may be descried, although at the end of a long vista."[11] While the expansion of American print culture in the early nineteenth century discussed later in this chapter might not have constituted an outbreak of bibliomania, it did help to change the way that Americans thought about books. The embrace of high culture and enthusiasm about a congressional library in this editorial mark the emergence of new opinions about the potential value of a government-funded library. These sentiments are in sharp contrast to the utilitarianism and parsimony that were characteristic of Madison's and, especially, Gerry's initial proposals for a congressional library.[12] With the controversy over purchase of the Jefferson library, the Library of Congress took on a new visibility in American life, becoming recognized by some as a national possession of some cultural significance, whose mission was a subject for national debate. The question became whether the United States Congress would also embrace this symbolism.

Librarian George Watterston and the History of Authorship in the United States

Early in 1815, with the resignation of Patrick Magruder and the impending arrival of Jefferson's library from Monticello, President Madison required a new custodian for the Library of Congress, and he appointed for this purpose Washington's resident man of letters, George Watterston. Unlike his predecessors, Watterston did not act simultaneously as the clerk of the House of Representatives. Perhaps Madison, the earliest proponent of a congressional library, intended to make a statement about the Library's importance by designating a separate appointee. His specific reason for appointing George Watterston was novel: the latter's career as a poet, novelist, and journalist. Beckley and Magruder had been chiefly political figures who assumed the duties of Librarian with few if any literary qualifications to recommend them, but Watterston prided himself on his identity as a man of letters. He wrote in an autobiographical memoir present among his papers that he was "appointed by Mr. Madison in consequence of his [Watterston's] literary attainments," and historians of the Library have further speculated that the appointment had something to do with Watterston's dedication of a poem called *The Wanderer in Jamaica* (1810) to Dolley Madison in the following words: "Madam, I have presumed to address this poetical effusion to you, from the reputation you have acquired of being desirous to promote the cause of general literature."[13]

Watterston's literary career spanned four decades and included forays into a number of genres, including drama, poetry, epistolary and psychological novels, guide books to Washington, reviews, statistical manuals, scientific essays, and political journalism. Before his appointment as Librarian of Congress he had published the novel *The Lawyer, or Man as He Ought Not to Be* (1808); a play, *The Child of Feeling* (1809); *The Wanderer in Jamaica*; the novel *Glencarn; or, The Disappointments of Youth* (1810); and another poem, *The Scenes of Youth* (1813); he had also edited the *Washington City Gazette*, an organ of the Republican Party. He continued to write during his tenure as Librarian, publishing the novels *The L.... Family at Washington* (1822) and *The Wanderer in Washington* (1827), both of which include telling fictional portraits of the Library. While his achievements have not recommended him highly to twentieth-century literary historians (one characterizes his novels as "pretentious and ridiculous"), the fact of his authorship of belles lettres serving in some measure as the rationale for appointment to a government post (his journalism on behalf of the Republican Party also helped his case) appears to signify a change from the political climate of the pre–War of 1812 era in which purveyors of fiction had been seen as morally questionable.[14]

Watterston was trying to establish himself as a man of letters during a period when the figure of professional author was only beginning to be defined in America, and his career illustrates the challenges and inconsistencies that attend the transition from a gentlemanly to a professional model of authorship. He had been trained in the law, a profession that had sometimes provided a point of departure for aspiring writers in the early republic, as in the cases of Joseph Dennie and Charles Brockden Brown, writers with literary inclinations who found that authorship as a career was neither wholly reputable nor profitable. Unlike these authors, however, Watterston appears to have been able to live by the productions of his pen for a considerable period of his life, although his seeking a government post as a tax collector as early as 1813 and his unsuccessful twenty-year campaign to reclaim the Librarianship after he was dismissed both suggest that a patronage position was a more secure way of supporting a family than was writing.[15] If his ability to forge a career as a literary man marks Watterston as at least a semiprofessional author at a very early period in American literary history (Irving published *A History of New York* in 1809; Cooper's first novel would not be published until 1820), in other respects he subscribed to a view of writing as a gentlemanly avocation. Watterston published his novels anonymously, a convention that recalled an aristocratic, Old World model of authorship in which a stigma was attached to writing for profit. Anonymous publication early in the nineteenth century in the United States also ensured that a writer's name would not be associated with the morally questionable realm of fiction.[16]

Watterston's appointment as Librarian of Congress looks forward to the time when authors such as Bancroft, Lowell, Paulding, Irving, Hawthorne, and Melville would rely on various levels of government support to provide income while they continued to pursue literary careers. Watterston was particularly canny about the advantages of his position, which gave him access to books and apparently time to write as well. While acting as Librarian, Watterston coauthored with Nicholas B. Van Zandt a work titled *Tabular Statistical Views of the Population, Commerce, Navigation, Public Lands, etc. of the United States*, published in 1829. He wrote numerous letters to Edward Everett, chairman of the Joint Library Committee, requesting that Congress purchase the work, and an act of 3 April 1828 authorized a fifteen-hundred-dollar subscription.[17] This patronage was doubly remunerative—while collecting a salary as a government employee, Watterston penned a book that he then sold to the government. Patronage of works of demonstrable utility to Congress was not uncommon, and no one would have been in a better position to know this than Watterston, who refers in one of his letters to "the usual patronage extended to works of this kind by the government." Capitalizing on his acquaintance with one of America's leading literary figures of the period, Watterston even asked Everett to "confer an additional favour on us by noticing [the book] in the North American, when you have received the work complete, if you think it merits such a notice."[18] After he had been dismissed as Librarian, Watterston would continue to write to Everett, still acting as chairman of the Joint Committee on the Library, regarding congressional purchase of a continuation of the statistical work in the years 1832–34.[19] George Watterston's career as a literary figure who relied on government support for almost twenty years was a significant moment in the history of authorship in America. The precedent set by a patronage position being awarded to a novelist was one of the federal government's few contributions to the growth of literary culture in America in the two decades following the War of 1812.

Several times in his career, usually through anonymous articles in the *National Intelligencer*, Watterston expressed an interest in expanding the Library of Congress beyond its legislative function.[20] Watterston made a significant statement with the title he gave to the 1815 *Catalogue of the Library of the United States*. Watterston also lobbied for a form of copyright deposit in a brief notice he inserted into the *National Intelligencer* on 15 September 1815, suggesting that Congress "no doubt" intended to make the Library "the great national repository of literature and science, and in some instances of the arts also," and advising "American Authors, Engravers, and Painters who are solicitous to preserve their respective productions as *mementos* of the taste of the times" to "transmit to the Library a copy of such work as they may design for the public eye—this will serve not only as a literary history of this now interesting country, but will also tend to exhibit the progress and improvement of the arts." This early appeal for voluntary copyright deposit, however, does not seem to have had much effect.

The 1815 Catalog

George Watterston presided over a Library that was significantly different from the one that had been destroyed. These differences were embodied not only in the books themselves but also in the classification scheme by which they were cataloged. Among his other talents, Thomas Jefferson was an innovator in the area of library cataloging. While many libraries in the eighteenth and early nineteenth centuries were relatively small and could be cataloged simply by size, Jefferson cataloged his books according to an elaborate subject classification system that Watterston retained in preparing the 1815 catalog. Like the 1812 Library of Congress catalog, the Jefferson catalog made use of subject classifications derived from the division of the mind into the three faculties of memory, reason, and imagination. Jefferson went significantly beyond his predecessors

Diderot and D'Alembert, however, rearranging the Encyclopedists' categories to suit both his intellectual convictions and the specific nature of his library holdings. Jefferson's catalog divided the library into forty-four classes or "chapters," in contrast to the eighteen divisions of the 1812 Library of Congress catalog. Jefferson devoted fifteen chapters to history, fourteen to philosophy, and fourteen to the fine arts. The forty-fourth chapter, headed "Polygraphical," was for works that covered multiple subjects, such as encyclopedia, magazines, or complete works by multidisciplinary writers such as Locke, Milton, Bacon, and Voltaire. Whereas Jefferson had carefully arranged the books within chapters in a system he described as "sometimes analytical, sometimes chronological, & sometimes a combination of both," Librarian Watterston, to Jefferson's chagrin, rearranged the entries into alphabetical order within each chapter.[21] Aside from this modification, Jefferson's classification system proved serviceable to the Library and was carried over into the 1830, 1839, 1849, and 1861 catalogs with only minor emendations.

Jefferson's innovative catalog (and by extension the 1815 Library of Congress catalog derived from it) can be read for what it reveals about his underlying assumptions concerning the nature of knowledge. Perhaps Jefferson's most famous alteration to the classifying schemes of his predecessors came in the area of theology. Bacon had divided knowledge into revealed theology and human knowledge; Diderot and D'Alembert, in their system of knowledge, had also included a class devoted to God that split into natural and revealed theology. Jefferson characteristically had little use for revelation or metaphysics, writing in his catalog of books for the University of Virginia that "metaphysics have been incorporated with Ethics, and little extention [sic] given to them" because "prolonged investigations of a faculty unamenable to the test of our senses, is an expense of time too unprofitable to be worthy of indulgence."[22] In the library that he sold to Congress, Jefferson included a chapter on religion, under the larger divisions of "Philosophy: Moral: Jurisprudence." The chapter was well stocked with 191 titles (compare the three titles and eight volumes on sacred and ecclesiastical history in the 1812 catalog) but reflected Jefferson's skepticism in according the Bible no more sacred status than the Koran. This conception of revealed knowledge differed greatly from that in the 1812 Library of Congress catalog, which had prominently displayed the Bible as the first entry.

Analysis of the 1815 catalog of the library acquired from Jefferson brings debate over the purchase more sharply into focus.[23] Jefferson's library was perhaps the most comprehensive and carefully collected in America, reflecting its owner's range of intellectual interests. Indeed, it was this catholicity of Jefferson's library that congressional critics—who had been able to inspect Jefferson's catalog before debating the purchase— found objectionable. The library of 3,392 titles in some 6,487 volumes (replacing a library of 3,076 volumes) had chapters devoted to subjects that had hardly been touched on in the previous library, such as architecture (42 titles), gardening, painting, and sculpture (25 titles), and music (9 titles). Comprising less than 3 percent of the library, though, these subjects hardly dominated (table 2 in the appendix presents an analysis of each major subject area as a percentage of the entire catalog). Another criticism, perhaps more accurate, was that many of Jefferson's books were in foreign languages, whereas the Library of Congress up to 1812 had acquired almost all its books in English.

On the other hand, the newly acquired library was not as different as its critics implied from the library it was replacing. The new library was stronger than the old one in the very subjects that the Joint Committee on the Library had previously been most diligent about collecting. Like the 1812 Library of Congress, the one purchased from Jefferson was heavily stocked in history. The first five chapters of the 1815 catalog, on ancient, foreign, British, American, and ecclesiastical history, correspond to the civil history section of the 1812 library. The new Library of Congress held 524 titles in history (compared with around 250 in the destroyed library), an area that had traditionally been a high priority. Jefferson's library was also strong in law, with six and a half chapters on the law of nature and nations, equity, common law, merchant law, maritime law, ecclesiastical law, and foreign law, yielding 512 titles altogether (170 titles were in the 1812 Library of Congress catalog). The new catalog's chapter on politics included 454 titles (70 titles in 1812), many related to theories of government, a vein of information that congressmen could profitably mine for years. The geography chapter of the new catalog had 301 titles (159 in the 1812 catalog), with 174 titles devoted to American geography. This concentration brings to mind the importance accorded Americana in the 1783 list compiled by Madison, likely with some advice from Jefferson. Jefferson had spent many hours in Paris combing through booksellers' stores for works on America, and in 1815 Congress became the beneficiary of his thoroughness. The four sections of history, geography, law and politics (which also included books on economics) accounted for about 53 percent of Jefferson's library. Although this figure had been considerably higher, around 69 percent, in the 1812 Library catalog, all four areas were strengthened by the purchase.

In addition, Jefferson's library was also well stocked with books on science and technical arts. With separate chapters on physics, agriculture, chemistry, surgery, medicine, anatomy, zoology, botany, mineralogy, physicomathematics, astronomy, and the occupations of man, the Jefferson library offered Congress a wealth of technical and scientific information. These twelve chapters together accounted for 529 titles, or some 15.6 percent of the collection. Adding two more chapters on mathematics and geometry brings the total to 583 titles, or 17.2 percent. The other strength of the new library was belles lettres. Jefferson's library devoted separate chapters to various genres of poetry (epic occupied one chapter; pastorals, odes, and elegies another). Didactic, tragic, comic, and epistolary literature each had a chapter; one chapter collected together logic, rhetoric, and orations; and three others were devoted to theory, bibliography, and languages. These chapters together added up to some 568 titles, or 16.7 percent of the library. Rounding out the library were the chapters on fine arts (76 titles, 2.2 percent); religion (191 titles, 5.6 percent); and moral philosophy (140 titles, 4.1 percent), as well as works on multiple subjects (43 titles, 1.3 percent).

Commentators have often pointed out that the linguistic and intellectual catholicity of Jefferson's library differentiated the Library of Congress after 1815 from its predecessors and provided an acquisitions model that would allow the Library of Congress to grow into its position as a national library aspiring to universality. While it is true that Jefferson's library provided such a model, Joint Committee members of the antebellum era were not always committed to following it. Purchase of the Jefferson library was a milestone for the Library of Congress in that it brought the Library a new visibility and doubled its size, but claims about its setting the trend for growth and expansion into the kind of library it would become after the Civil War should not be exaggerated. In the pre–Civil War era, the Library remained largely utilitarian in function. Moreover, what has not received enough stress is the importance of the arguments that were brought up against purchase. Debate over the purchase allowed for the articulation of anti-intellectual positions that would be revisited by opponents each time a substantial expansion of the institution was proposed, such as when large European libraries came on the market and were offered to Congress in the 1830s or in debates over the disposition of James Smithson's bequest. For this reason, the vocal opposition to the purchase reveals as much as the purchase itself about American attitudes toward government ownership of books.

The Joint Library Committee and Collection Development

Once the newly purchased books arrived in Washington, the Joint Committee on the Library held responsibility for deciding how to develop the collection. The terms in which successive incarnations of the Joint Committee framed their requests for appropriations and the way Congress responded show the body returning to a fairly utilitarian view of the Library's function rather than expanding on the catholicity of Jefferson's collection. Senator Eligius Fromentin took over the Joint Committee in 1815, during the first session of the Fourteenth Congress. Fromentin, an immigrant from France, former Catholic priest, and Republican senator from Louisiana, found that he had some three to four thousand dollars in unexpended funds available, left over from the annual appropriation of one thousand dollars that had been authorized in 1811.[24] In his view, this amount was insufficient to shore up weak points in the Library's holdings.

In the 1816 report of the Joint Committee, Fromentin drew attention to gaps in the collections and urged Congress not to squander opportunities to fill them. He observed that some departments of arts and sciences in the Library were "swelled to a prodigious size" and others were deficient, an inconsistency that, the report stated, "is not to be wondered at, if we consider that the inconsiderable sums put from time to time at the disposal of the joint committee precluded the possibility of their availing themselves of the many opportunities which, for twenty-five years past, were daily offering in Europe of purchasing large collections of very valuable books on reasonable terms." The refugee from the Reign of Terror probably had much firsthand knowledge of the bargains available on the European book market. Fromentin apparently objected to the size of certain chapters in the recent catalog, though his attribution of the gaps to the Joint Committee, and not to Jefferson, is a bit puzzling—historians have always believed that all but a handful of books from the original library were destroyed in the British attack.[25] Fromentin did not specify which chapters were so overdeveloped, but one can speculate that he had in mind such areas as religion and the belles lettres, on which Congress had never previously expended much of its small acquisitions budget. Fromentin's committee recommended a single appropriation of ten thousand dollars in addition to the annual appropriation of one thousand dollars, making the argument that with libraries going on the market in Europe "the convulsions of the eastern might, in a literary view, be made conducive to the interests of the western world" in correcting the "lamentable deficiency" of the Library in certain unspecified departments.[26]

Congress chose not to honor Fromentin's request. Considering the strength with which the purchase of Jefferson's library had been opposed just a year earlier, on the grounds that many of the books had been procured in Europe and were morally objectionable in content, it is not surprising that legislators rejected the committee's proposal. The decision not to purchase books described as originating from declining European aristocracies should be seen in light of a history of classical republican fear of luxury and distrust of foreign cultural products. The unexpended sums at the disposal of the committee, as well as Congress's recent outlay of an unprecedented $23,950 for the Jefferson books, must also have worked against Fromentin's appeal.

In the next annual report, submitted in January 1817, Fromentin appears to have given up the struggle to round out the collections through large appropriations. He also shifted the terms of the argument in order to downplay the wealth of European book markets, appealing instead to a narrower definition of the Library's acquisitions policy. He first detailed a number of proposals that would allow the committee to expend the balance of remaining appropriations, including the purchase of literary and political periodicals and of transactions of learned societies. Next, in a short paragraph he alluded briefly to subscribing "occasionally" to European catalogs of "works of merit," purchase of which would "require a disposable fund to be used on the emergencies created by the publication of such works, either in this country or in Europe." Having deemphasized the importance of European accessions with this cautious phrasing, Fromentin then invited "the chairmen of the several committees in both Houses, to furnish the Library Committee with a list of such books or maps, as may be deemed by them more particularly to refer to the business devolving upon each respective committee," in the hopes that such a process would "stamp the Congressional Library with that degree of usefulness contemplated in its establishment."[27] Phrasing the request in this way linked the books to be purchased directly with the legislative process and allowed legislators to request individual titles rather than requiring Congress to sift through books acquired in lots at auction. Fromentin then requested a five-year extension of the one-thousand-dollar annual appropriation and an appropriation of three thousand dollars for law books. The bill that accompanied this report, though passed by the Senate, languished in the House and was forgotten.[28] It seems evident that Fromentin was attentive to the failure of his 1816 request while writing the 1817 Joint Committee report, scrupulously avoiding any suggestion that he had designs on the Library that exceeded the will of his peers in Congress and stepping back from acquisitions policies that would seem to have been a logical development after the purchase of Jefferson's books. Nonetheless, he met with frustration, an emotion that would plague Joint Committee chairman Edward Everett about a decade later.

Another overture to expand Library of Congress collections came from a former member of the Joint Committee, John Quincy Adams. In 1817, Secretary of State Adams considered procuring the library of German historian Christopher Daniel Ebeling for Congress. This collection has since been described as "the finest library of materials on American history which had ever been amassed."[29] Adams wrote to his former law student Alexander Hill Everett, Edward Everett's brother and secretary of the U.S. legation at the Hague, asking him to get Edward (then studying in Germany) to buy the books on behalf of Adams: "My object is at all events to secure the books; and the public Library of Congress shall have them at their cost to me, if Congress think proper to make the purchase."[30] Adams later learned, however, that President Monroe was of the opinion that "150 volumes would comprise all the books relating to America worth having in the Library of Congress, and probably three-fourths of them are already there."[31] This information held much sway with Adams, who then feared that he would indeed get the books only to find himself unable to afford them. The volumes were eventually purchased by Joseph G. Cogswell on behalf of Harvard University, which pleased Adams. The next time Adams tried to acquire a rare item on behalf of the government, a map of Louisiana, it was instead to deposit it in the library of the Department of State—a library that Adams assiduously cultivated during his secretaryship.[32] This was the first of several lost opportunities pursued by U.S. diplomats in Europe to obtain libraries on behalf of the Library of Congress.

When the appropriation for book purchases did increase significantly in 1824, the argument that swayed the legislature, like Fromentin's 1817 report, appealed strongly to the limited conception of a legislative library that had traditionally informed congressional purchases. The House Ways and Means Committee reported in February 1824 that the small expenditures for books to that date had resulted in a Library "defective in all the principal branches of literature." The committee, perhaps mindful of past failures to increase the collections, deemed it "of the first necessity that this deficiency should be speedily supplied, at least in the important branches of law, politics, commerce, history, and geography, as most useful to the members of Congress," and finished the report by again invoking "not only the utility, but the absolute necessity of an extensive and judiciously selected library for the use of Congress." This argument— coming from the powerful Ways and Means Committee—that books in the subjects Congress had traditionally stressed for its Library were needed for the immediate use of the legislators was apparently persuasive, as Congress approved an expenditure of five thousand dollars.[33] It might also have helped that the Ways and Means Committee admitted that although French books would be cheaper, "the committee are of opinion that it would be better to purchase English books and English transla- tions of foreign books in all cases where such translations have been made." This resolution marked a return to the pre-1814 buying policy of the Joint Committee and a decided move away from the precedent set by purchase of Jefferson's books, many of which were in foreign languages. In its report the committee further alluded to "purposes as well of amuse- ment as instruction," appealing to the role the Library played in providing light reading to members and their families.[34] Finally, a distance of almost a decade since the heated debate over purchasing the Jefferson library might have contributed to a more liberal view of the expediency of spending public funds for books. Not only had the controversy over the purchase begun to fade from memory, but the passage of a decade also meant that some of the books purchased from Jefferson had become superseded by more recent publications, which needed to be acquired.

The appointment of Edward Everett, one of America's leading literary figures, to the Joint Committee on the Library in 1825 could have marked a milestone in the Library's history. But the most persistent trait of

Everett's tenure on the committee was his frustration over the reluctance of Congress to spend money for books. Educated in the Harvard Divinity School and at the University of Göttingen, a former professor of Greek at Harvard, and at the time of his appointment editor of the *North American Review*, America's most influential literary periodical, Everett held an optimistic view of the progress of letters in the United States, a subject on which he had delivered a Phi Beta Kappa address at Harvard in 1824. He must also have been aware of an article by Harvard president John T. Kirkland in the *North American Review* in December 1818 (Everett took over as editor in 1820) calling for a large library to support the work of U.S. scholars. Moreover, according to a biographer, Everett held a liberal view of the role of the "central government as the agency that would . . . enable the republic to put the many contemporary advances in science, technology and learning to use in creating a model republic."[35] And perhaps most germane to the Library of Congress, Everett would later become one of the prime movers behind the first major municipally funded free public library in America, in Boston. The Library of Congress could not have found a more suitable figure to work on behalf of both expanded collections and a more public role for the institution.

Everett worked enthusiastically to improve the Library in the first year of his membership on the Joint Library Committee, frequently writing to Librarian Watterston from Boston to find out if the Library possessed certain volumes that he wished to purchase for it.[36] He asked Watterston to "prepare and keep on hand a catalogue of works most wanted in every department, to which new books could be added as they appear. In no other way can the appropriations be expended to the best advantage."[37] Despite conscientious efforts, however, Everett was thwarted by the Joint Committee's reluctance to incur the expense that an ambitious acquisitions program would require. His frustration is apparent in a diary entry of 4 January 1827: "At a meeting of the Library Committee I proposed the purchase of Humboldt's large work on America. No one gentleman cordially seconded me. Most opposed me & the most I c'd get them to consent to was to buy it, if on consulting several members they would approve it."[38] The large work that Everett had in mind was Alexander von Humboldt's *Voyage de Humboldt et Bonpland*, which was published in Paris in 23 volumes from 1805 to 1834 and republished in translation as new volumes came out, both in England and America. In this case, a work published by the premier naturalist and explorer of his day, one that fell within the bounds of Americana (traditionally strong at the Library) and in an area in which Jefferson's collection was strong—natural history—did not meet with the approval of the Library Committee.[39] Everett also proposed the purchase of a collection of books and manuscripts relating to America from Obadiah Rich, a collector and bookseller living in England who would later become the Library's main supplier. According to George Matheson, in 1828 Everett convinced the Library Committee to sanction an appropriation of five thousand dollars for the purpose, but the purchase finally fell through.[40]

Everett also met with resistance from Librarian Watterston. Though of a literary turn and generally a promoter of the Library, Watterston was no bibliophile, and he expressed reluctance when asked to take a more active role in guiding acquisitions. Everett wrote to Watterston on 31 October 1826 that "it would be desirable that somewhere there be an authority to sell imperfect or duplicate sets and inferior works & in short any books which may by accident have found their way into the library & are not wanted there," to which Watterston responded: "Perhaps it may not be improper to suggest that it may be leaving too much to the taste & discretion of the Librarian to select such books as he may deem imperfect or defective from any cause, for the purpose of excluding them from the Library." Watterston appears to have had little ambition and perhaps little time to take on responsibility in book selection (or exclusion), except in the one field he considered his area of expertise, literature. On 3 November 1826, Watterston suggested to Everett that if the committee had not already ordered them, the novels of Charles Brockden Brown and James Fenimore Cooper would be worthy acquisitions. In this period before the era of mandatory copyright deposit, the Library could have granted a privileged status to individual American authors such as Brown or Cooper, sanctioning their works through purchase as officially approved representatives of American literary production. Everett, however, was not interested in making fine distinctions. He had expressed the opinion to Watterston that "American Works (tho' not excellent) ought to be in the library to furnish, I trust to after times the means of proving the ratio of advancement."[41] This attitude was in line with the Library's function, at least implicit in Madison's initial proposal for a congressional library, of acquiring Americana as a way of defining the character of the nation; it also anticipated the goal of copyright deposit, instituted successfully only after the Civil War, as a means of effecting a comprehensive collection of American publications.

Despite Everett's strenuous efforts, Congress did not significantly expand its conception of the function of the Library after the purchase of Jefferson's books. Just how precarious the Library's situation was during the period is evident in a letter from Watterston to Everett dated 2 July 1825, in which the Librarian complains that "the Chairman of the Comm[ittee] of Ways & Means, has omitted altogether both the Lib[rary] & Librarian & has made no provision in the general appropriation bill for the salary of the one or the expenses of the other."[42] The quality of the collections in 1826 can be inferred from a comment made by historian Jared Sparks, who judged that "on American history the library is exceedingly meagre, containing nothing but a few of the commonest books; but on American politics it is full, particularly to the year 1808, when Mr. Jefferson left the government."[43] And history was a subject area that had always been cultivated at the Library. The Joint Library Committee was doing well if it could merely prod Congress into maintaining a consistent, if limited, supply of funding for books in subject areas that had always been stressed in Library acquisitions. Proposals to expand the collections of the Library of Congress in the directions that were apparently implied by congressional approval of the Jefferson purchase—books in foreign languages or important contributions to the natural history of America, for example—met with little success in this period.

The Physical Space of the Library

As a physical space, the earliest Library quarters had been nothing more than a storage facility, a cramped and leaky committee room in the Capitol. Following the British attack, while the Capitol was being rebuilt, the Library purchased from Jefferson was housed in Blodgett's Hotel, at some distance from the temporary quarters of Congress. This arrangement lasted until 1818, when, after complaints about inconvenience, the books were removed to rooms in the north wing of the Capitol. The lack of space in these crowded rooms was cited by the Library Committee in 1820 as a reason for suspending "any considerable purchase of books" until the situation was remedied.[44] When Charles Bulfinch succeeded Benjamin Latrobe as architect of the Capitol in 1818, he designed new accommodations for the Library in the center building, to which the books were removed in 1824. A fire threatened the Library on the night of 22 December 1825, but it was put out without serious damage to the books, and the Library remained uneventfully in these rooms until the disastrous fire of 1851.

Spurred by the inconvenience that attended getting to the Library at its quarters in the hotel during the winter of 1816–17, the Joint Committee proposed that a separate building be constructed. Joint Committee chairman Fromentin submitted a brief resolution to the Senate in February 1817 that the commissioner of public buildings should erect a structure for the Library (no dimensions or architectural plans were mentioned), but Congress showed no interest in this first proposal for a separate Library building.[45] The idea of a separate building resonated with Librarian Watterston, however, who took to the pages of the *National Intelligencer* to offer his vision of proper accommodations for the Library.

Watterston's architectural vision was consistent with his general intent to promote the Library and elevate its status as a literary and cultural icon. He complained that "in all other countries, this is an object of national pride, and edifices are erected for the accommodation of national libraries, not only admirable for their convenience, but distinguished for the taste, beauty, and excellence of their architecture." Given that the Library was at the time housed in what the *Washington Gazette* referred to as "a garret," the grandeur of Watterston's proposal for a separate building, which he said came from "an elegant and splendid design for a national library at Paris," is notable, if not absurd:

An immense gallery of 266 feet long by 47 breadth, and 6 vast halls, which are contiguous, constitute principally the interior of the library. . . . This gallery is terminated by a temple of Apollo surrounded by the muses. . . . The elevation presents a peristyle of 8 corinthian columns, bearing a front decorated with basso relievos which represent Parnassus, other basso relievos and statues placed in niches enrich the walls of the edifice. Such a building as this would indeed be a national ornament, and contribute essentially to the beauty of the Capital of the United States. . . . A governmental munificence extended to literary subjects, is at all times commendable, and tends to the promotion of human knowledge and the advancement of genius.[46]

The space Watterston envisioned for the Library was as grandiose as it was improbable, given the history of congressional appropriations for its library—the $23,950 spent on the books in the Jefferson collection had been expended only under conditions of dire need and had nonetheless been strongly contested. With Fromentin's motion for a building of any scale summarily rejected in the Senate a month earlier, Watterston's proposed design quite obviously exceeded congressional interest in the physical plant of the Library. Despite its impracticality, the proposal can and should be read as a symbol of Watterston's optimism—shared by boosters of American culture—about the future of the arts and letters in the country. Yet the grandeur of the design also glaringly exposes the inadequacy of the Library of Congress as a national library in comparison with European collections. In 1818 the Library held around ten thousand volumes, while the Bibliothèque Nationale in Paris housed more than a million.[47]

Though the Library quarters in the north wing of the Capitol fell far short of Watterston's ambitions, they were large enough to accommodate the occasional visitor. The Library's role as a site of social interactions would increase after 1824, but it was first noted by Watterston in his novel *The L.... Family at Washington; or, A Winter in the Metropolis*, published in 1822. This was a satirical epistolary novel about a provincial Connecticut family that comes to Washington hoping to secure an ambassadorial position for the father and eligible members of Congress as husbands for the daughters. The scene in the Library has the son, Richard L.... wandering into an unmarked door during his tour of the Capitol building and finding "a region of learning, where like the Alps, books on books arose." These were the rooms in the north wing of the Capitol, where space was a problem. Richard is immediately struck by the social purposes of the library and by the presence of women there: "The room was filled with honourable members and their ladies, more intent, I thought, on gazing at pictures, than on feasting their reason." He next intrudes upon two members "engaged in some political discussions," who rebuff him, and a third reading by the fire, who also chastises him for his "impertinent curiosity," before being cast a dirty look by Watterston, who inserts himself into the novel merely to glare at Richard: "I met a man that I thought looked devilish sour at me: this was the librarian, but I passed on."[48] The next two gentlemen he encounters, presumably congressmen, are discussing not politics but the merits of the English poets Scott, Byron, Moore, and Campbell and the Lake school; they go on for several pages apparently acting as mouthpieces for Watterston's own literary opinions. One irony of the scene is that Watterston, whose aspirations for American culture were encoded in his architectural proposal for the Library, has his congressmen discussing British rather than American literature. A second is that the library that Joint Committees assembled by emphasizing its utility is here shown to serve a recreational function.

After 1824, with the completion of the rooms designed by Architect Bulfinch, the Library was more than ever appropriated for social and recreational purposes by members of Congress and by residents of Washington with sufficient social clout to gain admittance. The spacious architecture and lavish furnishing of the rooms significantly affected the way congressmen and visitors interacted in the Library. A contemporary account provides a visual description of the space: "The room for the permanent accommodation of the Library of Congress . . . occupies nearly the whole west front of the center building, is 90 feet in length, 30 in width, and about 35 in height. It is divided into 12 arched alcoves, ornamented with fluted pilasters, copied from the pillars in the celebrated Octagon Tower at Athens. . . . Those pillars . . . support two galleries, extending nearly the whole length of the room . . . and divided into the same number of shelved recesses as the lower apartment." Adjacent to the long principal gallery, in which the books were stored, were reading rooms "handsomely furnished with sofas, mahogany tables, desks, Brussels carpeting, etc." The walls of the rooms were decorated with bronze medals and busts of figures from American history.[49] The elegance of the quarters invited visitors to linger in the Library as they took in its architectural beauty, while the comfortable furnishings encouraged them to sit and converse.

After the opening of its new rooms, the Library developed rapidly into a premier and apparently somewhat exclusive Washington social haunt. Watterston described this aspect of the Library in his 1827 novel *Wanderer in Washington*. The narrator of the novel, the wanderer, is brought to the Library of Congress by his boardinghouse roommate Marion, whose "intimate acquaintance with Washington, and the distinguished personages who have figured and now figure in it," gives him access to all levels of Washington society. The wanderer observes that the "splendid" and "elegant" Library rooms are "the resort of the literary, as well as the fashionable lounger, for we found it almost crowded with ladies and gentlemen, who were engaged in different parts of the room, some in conversation, some in reading, and others in looking over the volumes of plates, with which the library abounds. Among the ladies I recognized many of those I had seen at the different parties I had attended, and as gay and thoughtless, and fashionable here, as I had seen them elsewhere." The guide Marion describes the Library as the place not where congressmen do their work but where they escape from it: "It is undoubtedly an invaluable privilege, and he must, indeed, be happy who can retire from the agitating scenes of political strife, to lounge in this splendid repository of wisdom and learning. . . . But I fear it is not so often resorted to as might be expected, by those who have free admission into its recesses."[50] Interestingly, Marion does not take for granted that anyone can gain admission to the Library rooms. Although it has been a fixture of Library of Congress history that the public had access to collections from the founding of the institution, it seems instead that such access was sometimes restricted, depending on the decisions of the Joint Library Committee.

The passage from Watterston's novel emphasizes how the Library had become a lounge that provided opportunities for socializing between congressmen and their acquaintances. Indeed, the "volumes of plates" that patrons are looking over, books with no discernible political utility, were used by them as conversation pieces that enhanced social interactions. The artwork that decorated the Library walls, in addition to the impressive architecture itself, invited the admiration and commentary of viewers, further encouraging casual visitors of the Library to engage in social activities rather than silent reading and research. It is clear that between its founding and the 1820s, the rooms inhabited by the Library had evolved considerably. Initially a mere storage room for books, the Library eventually occupied an elegant suite of rooms in which the books and architecture together facilitated social interactions among Washington gentility. This important addition to the developing identity of the Library had not been envisioned in the initial legislation enabling the purchase of books that legislators needed to carry out their official duties.

The Library and the Public

The view of a library that emerges from Watterston's fiction, as a genteel institution offering books and a social space to a select group of users—congressmen, their families, and acquaintances—though common in the world of nineteenth-century libraries, lagged behind the plans that more progressive, ambitious observers had in mind for the Library of Congress. Purchase of Jefferson's library stimulated new ways of thinking about the Library, at least in the public mind, if not among congressmen themselves. For example, on hearing of Jefferson's plan to sell his books to Congress, Georgetown bookseller Joseph Milligan wrote to Jefferson, "If Congress should purchase it, to literary men it would be a great privilege to be permitted at all times of the year to have free access, not to take away the books, but to read in the Library and make extracts."[51] Similar plans for the Library proliferated once the purchase was accomplished.

One such plan is found in an article from the *National Intelligencer* of 31 July 1815 that focused on expanding the collections and making them available to the public. The author of this article, presumably either Joseph Gales Jr. or William Seaton, the two proprietors of the newspaper, argued for an increase in the annual appropriation for the Library (from one to two thousand dollars) with the following reasoning: "In a country of such general intelligence as this, so laudable an example [as the national libraries of Europe] should by all means be imitated, and the Congressional or National Library of the United States become the great repository of the literature of the world—the medium of information and the source of improvement and gratification to all whom inclination may prompt or whom curiosity may lead to literature." The author then discussed some of the literary treasures already in the Library's possession as well as the areas in which the collections needed expanding and ended with the observation that "the Librarian attends every day, which will render an examination of this fine collection of books easy to the curious and the Literati."

A month and a half later in the same venue Watterston struck a similar note, asking American authors, engravers, and painters to "transmit to the Library a copy of such work as they may design for the public eye."[52] And in the editorial quoted earlier from *Walsh's American Register*, it was argued that "there is an absolute obligation on the part of the federal government to provide, in the metropolis, in shape of a library, a great reservoir of instruction in all the departments of human knowledge, for the use of the public as well as the use of its own members, and the library [of Congress], certainly, may be so administered as to be open to the one, without at all interfering with the studies or researches of the other."[53] With the new visibility of the Library of Congress fostered by purchase of the Jefferson collection came new ideas about the federal government's responsibility for providing library resources to the public.

Gales and Seaton continued to campaign for a larger and more publicly oriented Library of Congress throughout Watterston's years as Librarian. An editorial of 28 August 1823 was prompted by King George IV's gift of his father's library to the British Museum, which expanded that library's collections from 150,000 to 215,000 volumes. The piece also included a reference to the Bibliothèque Nationale's collection of 450,000 volumes (which the authors underestimated). Gales and Seaton appealed to national pride in urging Congress to purchase books more liberally for the institution, but they also proposed a change in the public's relationship to the institution. After mentioning the two thousand visitors a day to the British Museum Library, Gales and Seaton asked of the Library of Congress, "Why should it not be accessible every day, at proper hours between sun-rise and sun-set, to every citizen who may wish to avail himself of the use of such treasures of wisdom as may be collected there for the public benefit?" Acknowledging the possible cost of employing a larger staff for the Library, they suggested that "if the nation felt interested in accumulating and maintaining such a monument of its literary taste, it would not begrudge the small appropriation necessary to render it a constantly increasing source of pleasure and profit, not only to Congress, nor the reading part of the population of Washington, but to all our countrymen, and even foreigners who pass through, or who occasionally reside in, the Metropolis."[54]

These pleas in the *Intelligencer* and elsewhere had little if any effect on congressional action in regard to the Library. Although the idea was proposed that the government was responsible for cultivating well-stocked libraries for public use, Congress was not interested in accepting this responsibility. Evidence suggests that literary figures or other learned members of the public were allowed to consult the books in the Library for research and reference purposes, and the Library was open three days a week when Congress was in recess, apparently for these users as well as for the Librarian to attend to work such as cataloging acquisitions.[55] But Congress generally refrained from changing the statute that granted borrowing privileges almost exclusively to members.[56] As long as these rules remained in place, access by the public to consult the books on the premises was an uncodified privilege that could be revoked or selectively curtailed.

Even Watterston, who generally had high ambitions for the Library of Congress, sometimes demurred at the prospect of a library open widely to the public. While it seems likely that, as a self-identified man of letters, Watterston would have been sympathetic to authors who needed to use the collections for their research, his liberality in regard to the public's ownership of the books in the Library finally did not stretch very much further than that of the Congress he served. The tone of much of Watterston's writing on the Library—notwithstanding his 1815 comments about artifacts in the Library coming under the scrutiny of the public eye—implies that he unenthusiastically suffered visitors to the Library. It is clear, for example, in the passages quoted earlier from *The L…. Family at Washington* that his naïve narrator is an interloper trying to force his way "unceremoniously" into Washington society. Richard L….'s presumptuousness in speaking to members of Congress and wandering around the Library is signaled by Watterston's displeased glare and by the way Richard is chastised as "impertinent."

Impertinence, in fact, is a recurring theme in Watterston's writings about public visitors. He wrote to Edward Everett in 1828 to remind the Joint Committee to pay his assistant, whose "duties this winter have been very arduous & they seem to increase every year, both from the increased demand for books & the great influx of strangers into the City who visit the Library."[57] Watterston looked with no great approval on the "strangers" who were making his duties as Librarian more arduous. He expressed a similar opinion even more indignantly during the small newspaper war that he initiated after his dismissal by President Jackson. Taking on the charge made by the *United States Telegraph* that he was supercilious in manner, Watterston fired back: "If my manners were at any time 'supercilious,' it was found necessary to assume them to get rid of such impertinent and vulgar intruders as he and his satellites, and to save the books from being purloined."[58] And he wrote to Edward Everett in 1830, after the Joint Committee questioned him about some books that were not present in the Library when the new Librarian took over: "In consequence of these frequent removals and the free ingress of strangers of all classes it must be a matter of surprise that more books were not purloined than appear to have been."[59]

On the whole, Watterston appears to have regarded strangers of unknown provenance in the Library as "vulgar intruders" and potential thieves. His attitude probably arose in part from his own social pretensions (he was a master builder's son who cherished his ability to hobnob with Washington's most important political figures) and from personal financial concern: he had been given a bond for the security of the government property placed under his care.[60] But the tone of Watterston's comments about strangers in the Library, combined with the satire he had leveled at the uneducated "L...." family in his novel, when viewed in light of the social and political context of the 1820s, suggests that larger cultural trends were involved. Developments in the American publishing industry and the growth of libraries in the country made books available in increasing numbers to broader segments of society in the 1820s. Meanwhile, changes in the national political culture offered the common person a new voice in the nation's affairs. These democratic tendencies may have sparked a less egalitarian backlash. Watterston's complaints about the movement of "strangers of all classes" in the Library appear to be symptomatic of a larger cultural concern about both new groups of readers participating in the hitherto relatively exclusive and genteel world of letters and new groups of citizens playing a direct role in politics. His fear of strangers stealing books from the Library of Congress betrayed a larger concern that a new class of readers was about to assert claims to ownership of knowledge and political power, both of which were symbolized by access to the Library of Congress.

The Library and Print Culture in the United States

The trend in American print culture following the War of 1812 was toward dramatically expanded public access to information. In the period between 1815 and 1829, the literary culture of the United States began to reflect the "democratization of mind" that Gordon Wood sees as the hallmark of American culture in the late eighteenth century and the "democratization of the written word" that Cathy Davidson ascribes to American literary history from the Revolution into the middle of the nineteenth century. In the expanding print environment of the 1810s and 1820s, a marketplace of information began to develop in which consumers had a wider variety of choices among competing sources of instruction and entertainment, as documented by Richard D. Brown in *Knowledge Is Power*. Citing statistics on the distribution of printing presses, the number of newspapers, the development of the postal system, and the spread of voluntary associations in America, Brown concludes that "at the end of 1819, the information systems that Americans employed had passed several critical milestones and what may be called the information revolution was well underway." According to William J. Gilmore, New England experienced a "vast explosion of printed and written means of communication" in the period 1780–1835, exemplified in part by the wide circulation of numerous print vehicles including almanacs, books, broadsides, pamphlets, newspapers, and periodicals; by 1830, 62 percent of families in the Upper Connecticut River Valley with probate inventories owned private libraries.[61]

Access to books in America in these years was facilitated through a variety of library forms, some of which were the precursors to a public library system, providing a growing percentage of the population with books and periodicals. Jesse Shera writes that "during the twenty-five years between 1790 and 1815 the social library experienced unprecedented growth," and he characterizes the period as the "golden age" of the social library in New England. In the 1820s, mechanics' libraries made books available more broadly than ever across the middle classes, as well as geographically throughout and beyond New England to cities across the country, including Philadelphia, New York, Albany, New Orleans, Cincinnati, and Washington.[62] The first few decades of the nineteenth century saw a marked increase in the number of commercial circulating libraries as well, which were also beginning to provide new services to the public. These libraries supplied newspapers to users, maintained extended hours of operation, and provided on-site reading facilities, all services that "did much to create the expectation in the public mind that other kinds of libraries in the community ought to be able to serve similarly."[63] Such changes in the character of libraries and the introduction of a culture of books into a larger segment of the population created an environment favorable to the growth of a public institution devoted to collecting books.

These developments were visible in 1820s Washington, where people interested in books consulted several nongovernmental sources: a Georgetown circulating library; the Davis and Force Washington Circulating Library, whose catalogs from 1820 and 1821 still exist; and the Washington Library, the most enduring of the three institutions. The Washington Library was a social library founded in 1814. Shares were initially twelve dollars, eventually reduced to six dollars, and patrons could also use the library by merely contributing a three-dollar annual fee. The 1815 catalog of the library listed 371 titles in some 902 volumes, a very modest collection but one that would grow to 6,000 volumes by the 1850s.[64] The library in its early years emphasized history, geography, and literary holdings. Like the Library of Congress, the Washington Library held works by the major eighteenth-century historians, including Gibbon, Hume, Macaulay, Raynal, Robertson, and Voltaire; such popular works in geography, voyages, and travels as Morse's *American Geography*, Jonathan Carver's *Travels through the Interior Parts of North America*, and an account of the Lewis and Clark expedition; a judicious selection of literary titles, including the *American Museum*, the *Spectator*, Shakespeare's plays, Johnson's works, and a number of Scott's romances; and poetry by Wordsworth and Coleridge, Robert Burns, Alexander Pope, Lord Byron, and Joel Barlow. Existence of this institution demonstrated to Congress the growing popularity and utility of libraries, as the legislature formally recognized when it made the library an annual recipient of federal government publications in 1823.[65] On the other hand, the presence of a social library in the city might have led legislators to believe that they need not try to facilitate public use of their own collection, since other resources were available.

Another notable element of American print culture in this period with implications for the Library of Congress was widespread commentary on the state of the arts and literature in the United States. The two decades following the War of 1812 were a time of intense self-consciousness and boosterism regarding the arts in America. This cultural nationalism was part of a larger trend toward U.S. nationalism manifested in a number of events, such as the celebration of Andrew Jackson's military victory at the Battle of New Orleans in 1815; President Monroe's 1823 message to Congress defying European influence in the Western hemisphere (later dubbed the Monroe Doctrine); the enthusiastic reception of Revolutionary War hero General Lafayette in nationwide celebrations in 1824–25; and the expressions of patriotism that surrounded the fiftieth anniversary of the Declaration of Independence, including the response to news of the deaths on 4 July 1826 of both Thomas Jefferson and John Adams.

The national pride inspired by these events led to reflections about the state of American letters. Some commentators expressed disappointment that the confident predictions about the rising glory of the United States from the 1780s and 1790s had not come to fruition in its literary production. In the pages of the *North American Review* in 1815, Walter Channing took the skeptical position in two essays titled "Essay on American Language and Literature" and "Reflections on the Literary Delinquency of America," in the latter of which he wrote: "The title of this paper . . . implies that this country wants literary distinction; that we have not entered the service of literature; that we want the results of intellectual labour; . . . that the whole elements of our literature, were they collected into one mass, would amount merely to accidental efforts of a very few adventurous individuals."[66] American writers felt challenged to respond to the problem of the country's literary deficiencies, especially in light of European criticism. The European evaluation of American literature was famously voiced by Sydney Smith, who asked his readers in the *Edinburgh Review* in 1820, "In all the four corners of the globe, who reads an American book?"

Some Americans realized that a principal impediment to the development of American letters was the small number of books available to serious researchers. John T. Kirkland, president of Harvard, made an eloquent plea in the *North American Review* in 1819 for a systematic effort to compile a single great library for the use of scholars in the United States. Reminding readers of Fisher Ames's assertion that all the libraries in the United States were not adequate to provide sources for Gibbon's *Decline of the Roman Empire*, Kirkland also alluded to the possibility that the government might fund such an institution. He was not, however, particularly sanguine about the possibility: "When it is said to be desirable that steps should be taken to rival in literary advantages the establishments of Europe; to have at one or more of our most considerable universities or elsewhere in our nation a great repository of learning . . . and a wish intimated that this part of the literary interest of our country might be administered by the government, even at an expense equal to the cost of a single frigate . . . when these things are said or alluded to, the question is perhaps seriously moved . . . whether we have not now more books than we can read."[67]

Meanwhile, stigmas attached to the production of books that had marked classical republican political culture were falling away. George Watterston could claim that his literary attainments had secured him a post as Librarian of Congress. James K. Paulding, too, came to the attention of the Madison administration because of his writing and was appointed secretary of the Board of Navy Commissioners in 1815, a post that left him time to continue to pursue a literary career.[68] With a semiprofessional class of authors such as Watterston and Paulding being nurtured by means of government patronage positions, the government was, at least indirectly, fostering literary achievement. And Kirkland's claim that a dearth of library resources hampered U.S. writers provided Congress with a nationalistic rationale for devoting more attention to its Library. Ideas were circulating in the culture that the United States required a great national library, funded by the federal government and open to the public, to promote the literary accomplishment of which the country was generally believed capable given both the educational level of its citizens and its half century of development.

But after purchasing its new library from Jefferson, Congress generally refused to acknowledge any responsibility for advancing the cause of literature in America. Heedless of calls in the press for an expanded Library of Congress, in terms of either acquisitions or public access, Congress held to its utilitarian view of the institution as a legislative library with certain fringe benefits—it provided congressmen with light reading material and a place to socialize. Even when ideas about expanding the Library came from the body's own committee, Congress often resisted. The Joint Committee made a proposal in 1817 that its members be authorized to select "such books as they may deem proper to have deposited in the Congressional Library, out of the books which by the existing laws are to be deposited by the authors or publishers in the office of the Secretary of State, and are now lodged in the Patent Office." This modest request for a form of copyright deposit, which could perhaps have had a significant impact on Library collections, failed to become law. The request for a ten-thousand-dollar appropriation in the preceding year had also been opposed. Johnston reports that appropriations for books between 1817 and 1822 averaged a thousand dollars a year, the same sum that had been approved in 1806; there were increases in the annual appropriation to two thousand and five thousand dollars later in the period.[69] And in terms of access, for the most part Congress recognized only high-ranking government officials as authorized users of the Library, though people who did not have statutory privileges did sometimes use the books on the premises.

Legislative precedent clearly played a large role in shaping lethargic, unimaginative congressional action in regard to its library. In statute, by name, and by tradition, the Library was strictly legislative in nature. From the vantage point of the twentieth century it may seem inevitable that the Library of Congress should have become the national library of the United States, but virtually no one connected with the institution articulated such a role through the 1820s, with the significant exception of George Watterston. Edward Everett advocated collection of American books so that the Library could serve as a gauge of the progress of American literary history but beyond that seems to have lost, through hard experience with congressional frugality, any faith that the Library could transcend the limitations of narrow utilitarianism. These limitations might have reflected the residual influence of the association of literature and the fine arts with luxury and dissipation, considering that the kinds of books capable of turning the Library into something of greater scholarly import would had to have been procured from Europe.

Debate over the purchase of Thomas Jefferson's library to replace the destroyed Library of Congress in 1815 reveals much about competing American attitudes toward books and literature. The ideology of classical republicanism continued to exert an influence on Library of Congress development, as those opposed to purchasing Jefferson's library characterized the prospect as a dangerous encroachment of luxury infiltrating the federal government. In this view, the only justification for Congress to collect books was a narrow utility. On the other hand, the debate also allowed a burgeoning cultural nationalism to surface. For proponents of the purchase, a comprehensively collected Library of Congress would promote the progress of American letters and serve as a symbol of American devotion to cultural achievement. Much of Library of Congress history in the years before the Civil War can be understood in terms of these two poles of opinion.

The purchase was narrowly approved in 1815, giving Congress a library of greater size and intellectual range than it had ever before possessed. Certain ambitious members of the Joint Library Committee and other government officials, particularly Eligius Fromentin, John Quincy Adams, and Edward Everett, tried to build Library of Congress collections on the catholic model of the Jefferson library. For the most part, though, they were disappointed by a frugal Congress that continued to hold a utilitarian view of the institution. Collection development in the years following purchase of Jefferson's library often languished. When appropriations were approved, they were used to shore up the Library's traditionally strong subject areas: history, geography, law, politics, and economics. Congress altered its utilitarian conception of the Library to some extent during this period, however, as it became the site of recreation and social interactions for Congressmen and other members of Washington society.

President Madison made a significant move toward linking the Library of Congress with the literary culture of the nation through his appointment of George Watterston as the Librarian of Congress in 1815. This paved the way toward other patronage appointments, which would become a significant source of income to major American writers for the next several decades (and looked forward to the appointment of poet and writer Archibald MacLeish to the position in 1939). Watterston's appointment imbued the Librarian of Congress, formerly a position of no special authority in the world of letters, with a new cultural significance. Taking their cue from these developments, journalists and literary critics in the period from 1815 to 1829 called on the government to promote the cause of letters in America by more aggressively cultivating Library of Congress collections and making them more widely available.

For the most part, Congress ignored these calls. The appearance in print of arguments that the Library of Congress should take on a more comprehensive and democratic character represented the opening of a gap that would widen in succeeding decades between what influential literary and political figures believed the Library of Congress could represent and the policies that were enforced in regard to it by the Joint Committee, the Librarian of Congress, and Congress itself. The election of Andrew Jackson to the presidency in 1828 signaled a victory for populist, anti-intellectual sentiments that would continue to hamper Library of Congress growth.

CHAPTER FOUR

Jacksonian Democracy
and the Library,
1829–1843

The election of Andrew Jackson to the presidency in 1828 marked a shift in American political culture that is evident in the history of the Library of Congress, most visibly in the dismissal of George Watterston and the appointment of John Silva Meehan to the post of Librarian. The change in stewardship from a novelist with culturally nationalistic impulses to a self-effacing bureaucrat meant that the cultural authority of the position of Librarian of Congress declined precipitously. But Meehan was part of a larger trend in American politics that devalued high culture, championed the unlettered common person, and looked skeptically at federal agencies, an atmosphere that contributed to lost opportunities at the Library as Congress continued to develop collections on a narrow acquisitions model. While the press lobbied for a national library, Congress refused to acknowledge responsibility for providing one or for doing much else to promote the cause of American literature—such as legislating on behalf of international copyright.

The expanding print culture of the era came to include women, who participated in the literary culture of the nation both as readers and as writers. The national political culture, on the other hand, officially remained off-limits to them. When women in the 1830s mounted controversial challenges to this ideology, resistance was registered in subtle ways at the Library of Congress. Accounts of women at the Library and decisions made by the Joint Committee on the Library suggest that administrators responded to the incursion of women into the public space of the Library of Congress by creating a "women's corner" of light reading and illustrated books. Directing women's attention toward a class of books that had nothing to do with the political purposes for which the Library had been founded diminished the threat these patrons represented to the separate-spheres ideology of the day.

Librarian John Silva Meehan and the Politics of Cultural Authority

On 28 May 1829 newly elected President Andrew Jackson dismissed George Watterston and appointed one of his political backers, John Silva Meehan, as Librarian of Congress. A printer by trade, Meehan had no special qualifications for the post. He had been the publisher of a weekly Baptist newspaper in Washington before inaugurating the publication of the *United States' Telegraph*, a boisterously pro-Jackson newspaper, in 1826; Duff Green took over the journal within a few months. Meehan accepted the new job at the Library as a reward for establishing the newspaper and supporting Jackson's 1828 presidential campaign.[1] Rewarding supporters with political patronage positions was consistent with Jackson's stated intent to reform the federal bureaucracy. Believing that an entrenched bureaucracy was inimical to democracy and that any man of average intelligence was competent to administer government affairs, Jackson instituted the so-called spoils system of officeholding on the federal level. Ironically, though Jackson intended for the spoils system to encourage a healthy rotation in office, Meehan would hold the position of Librarian for over three decades, through the administrations of nine presidents.

Watterston's dismissal is comprehensible in light of the broader context of 1820s national politics. The removal was an attack on Watterston's political affiliations. During his tenure as Librarian, Watterston had formed a close relationship with one of Andrew Jackson's chief rivals, Henry Clay. Clay had been Speaker of the House in 1824 and helped to swing that year's presidential election to John Quincy Adams—though Jackson had won the most popular votes. When Clay was subsequently appointed secretary of state, traditionally a stepping-stone to the presidency, Jackson and his supporters famously decried a "corrupt bargain."

Clay acknowledged in a letter to Watterston his regret that "friendship for me may have been one of the causes which led to this exercise of vengeance upon you" and also compared the dismissal with "that act by which the famous Alexandrian librarian [*sic*] was reduced to ashes." On his own merits, Watterston supplemented his salary as Librarian by writing for the Whig *National Journal*, one of the most aggressive anti-Jackson newspapers and not incidentally the one that had led the attacks on the reputation of Jackson's wife, Rachel (who died just before Jackson took office).[2] Like many officeholders in Washington, Watterston found himself on the wrong side of the political fence with the ascendancy of Jackson.

But the replacement of Watterston with Meehan involved more than mere partisanship. Competing visions of the federal government's role in American culture were also at stake. In his belief that the Library of Congress was poised to become the national library, Watterston was aligned with politicians such as Clay and Adams who believed in a strong federal government with broad powers to initiate projects in the arts and letters. At his 1824 inauguration, for example, John Quincy Adams had called for such governmental projects as a national university, an astronomical observatory, and a federal role in promoting the advancement of literature. And in the 1830s, Henry Clay would advocate adoption of an international copyright law both to do justice by British authors and to support the development of American literature.

This patrician view of the relationship between the federal government and the world of letters was anathema to Jackson and his Democratic Republicans. Jackson rode to office on the strength of his military record and his reputation as the champion of states' rights and the common person. In the 1828 presidential campaign, Jackson's supporters succeeded in characterizing John Quincy Adams as an intellectual in the derogatory sense, a man of thought instead of action. Richard Hofstadter quotes a campaign slogan which held that the election was a contest between "John Quincy Adams who can write [a]nd Andrew Jackson who can fight." The Jackson camp argued that the learned Adams "was self-indulgent and aristocratic and lived a life of luxury."[3] Jackson's decisive victory proved that Americans responded to anti-intellectual demagoguery, and the Whig Party recognized that it would have to stoop to populist rhetoric if it wished to attract voters in the future. After this point, it became an even greater liability in American politics to be perceived as overeducated, aristocratic, or enamored of European culture. This boded ill for those who hoped the Library of Congress would transcend its legislative function.

After his dismissal, the indignant Watterston launched an editorial war in Washington newspapers that demonstrates the politics of cultural authority at work. In June 1829, the *United States Telegraph* and the *National Journal* devoted considerable space to coverage of the legality of Watterston's dismissal.[4] As had happened during discussion of the purchase of Jefferson's library, the debate carried over into newspapers in different parts of the country, and again the Library of Congress (or, by association, the Librarian) became a symbol open to competing interpretations.[5] Watterston charged that Meehan was "very ordinary," had "no fondness for reading," and was "never fitted for such a place." In other words, he implied that the democratic masses who took Jackson for their icon were unfit to wield the political power and cultural authority that Jackson's election conferred on them. Jackson's supporters countered that Watterston was "supercilious."[6] For them, he represented the pompous intellectual whose learning served no practical end, similar to their characterization of John Quincy Adams.

Debate over the appointment of Meehan shows how the Library of Congress offered politicians a site onto which opposing parties projected their ideas about the government's role in promoting culture. For Clay, in his letter to Watterston, the Library symbolized preservation of knowledge and devotion to high culture, and in sacking Watterston, Jackson had shown himself a representative of the forces of ignorance and barbarism. For Jackson, conversely, the kind of national library envisioned by Watterston would have symbolized a pernicious expansion of federal government power, akin to the National Bank whose charter Jackson revoked in his second term. By appointing the unassuming and obedient Meehan, Jackson (perhaps unwittingly—he might have had little knowledge of Watterston's ambitions for the Library) helped to ensure that the Library would continue along its foundational, utilitarian path of development.

The cultural authority of the Librarian of Congress suffered considerably under Meehan, who was content to step back into the shadows, deferring to the Joint Library Committee on all important decisions regarding the Library. A biographer describes Meehan as a "spectator" in the major acquisitions debates of the 1830s and 1840s.[7] The press took its cue from the retiring Meehan and correctly attributed guidance of the Library to members of the Joint Committee. In letters to the *National Intelligencer* in 1834 and 1835, correspondents argued over which members of the Joint Library Committee deserved credit for the quality of holdings, with one correspondent favoring Levi Woodbury and another championing the claims of Edward Everett, Guilian Verplanck, and Mahlon Dickerson. The Librarian was mentioned only in regard to the "civility and attention" he bestowed on visitors.[8] And in a spate of articles about libraries in America, which often touched on the Library of Congress, writers in the periodicals of the 1830s failed to name or even mention Meehan in connection with the institution.[9] Whereas Watterson had relished the platform that his position had given him to comment on literary affairs and the potential of the Library of Congress to become a national library, Meehan neglected to recognize or exert any cultural authority. It would not be until the era of Ainsworth Rand Spofford that the Librarian of Congress would again rise to national prominence. Refraining from voicing strong opinions about the place of the Library in American culture allowed Meehan to keep his job for decades and made it easier for Congress to persist in its narrow conception of the Library's importance. Now only individual members of the Joint Committee on the Library—and the ever vocal but largely irrelevant press— were left to lobby for its expansion.

Acquisitions in the 1830s and 1840s

The Journal of the Joint Committee on the Library, which contains annotations of the decisions of a series of Joint Committees during the period 1829–61, offers intriguing evidence of the way the Library was administered, shedding light in particular on Congress's unimaginative acquisitions policy—though some Joint Committees were more activist than others. The presence of Edward Everett increased the chances for an assertive committee, such as that of the Twenty-first Congress consisting of Senators Asher Robbins (chair: Whig, Rhode Island); Levi Woodbury (Jacksonian Democrat, New Hampshire); and Theodore Frelinghuysen (Whig, New Jersey), as well as Representatives Guilian Verplanck (Democrat, New York; a lawyer, writer, periodical editor, and, later in his life, Shakespeare scholar); James M. Wayne (Democrat, Georgia); and Everett (Whig, Massachusetts). This committee made an effort in March 1831 to rationalize its purchasing decisions when it resolved to "procure to be made out a complete catalogue of the remains of literature and science, and didactic works on the arts, contained in the ancient Greek and Latin languages," as well as the works of literature and science available in modern languages. The resolution, which was apparently disregarded by future committees, delegated to Edward Everett the task of cataloging the Greek and Latin works.[10] As Johnston points out, the committee had no one qualified to select the works in the modern languages, and no one learned enough to replace Everett in selecting Greek and Latin books when he left Congress.[11] Instead of following a methodical approach to purchases, therefore, committee members continued to purchase books for the Library according to their individual (and perhaps idiosyncratic) conceptions of the Library's needs. The committee routinely voted that three of its members be severally authorized to purchase fifty dollars' worth of books during each congressional recess.[12]

Purchases were generally carried out in large orders through book dealers Pishey Thompson in Washington and Obadiah Rich in London. But in the early 1830s members of the Joint Committee sometimes voted to acquire individual titles. Their wish lists generally included books in the subject areas of history, geography, economics, politics, and law, in conformity with the pattern set down since the Library had been founded. For example, on 9 January 1830 the committee of the Twenty-first Congress, first session (Robbins, Woodbury, Felix Grundy [a Tennessee Democrat], Everett, Wayne; and Verplanck) ordered, among others, the following titles: *The Jurist*, a periodical published in Boston; John Stuart Mill's *Political Economy*; Theodore Lyman's *Diplomacy of the United States*; Jefferson's *Memoirs and Correspondence*; and Basil Hall's *Travels in North America in the Years 1827 and 1828*. On the same day the Joint Committee directed that the laws of every state of the Union not yet in the Library be purchased "or otherwise obtained" (perhaps through exchange of public documents). Then, on 20 March 1830, this committee ordered that the Library acquire two copies of Jeremy Belknap's *History of New Hampshire*, David H. Burr's *Atlas of the State of New York: Containing a Map of the State and of the Several Counties*, "the best maps of the several states which are not already in the Library," and "all the books of reports, containing the decisions of the Supreme Court of each state." In March and April 1832, a new committee ordered the revised codes of the several states and a book on the state constitutions, while the committee of the following year ordered two additional copies of John Howard Hinton's *History and Topography of the United States*. In January 1835 another committee made sure to acquire recently published maps of Louisiana and North Carolina, and in July 1838 a map of Indiana was ordered.[13] All these books and maps covered the handful of subjects that had long been cultivated at the Library.

Occasionally, the Joint Committee ordered titles that applied directly to the legislative and political issues of the day. Andrew Jackson's support of Indian removal policies may have been the occasion for the Joint Committee ordering in 1830 James Haines McCulloh's recently published *Researches, Philosophical and Antiquarian, concerning the Aboriginal History of America*. The tariff was another major issue Congress wrestled with in the early 1830s, perhaps accounting for the Joint Committee's vote to order Robert Ellis's *British Tariff for 1829 and 1830* in January 1830 and six copies of the *Revenue Laws of the United States* on 17 January 1832. The most controversial political issue of the 1830s was whether to revoke or extend the charter of the Bank of the United States. Though such influential politicians as Henry Clay and Daniel Webster favored the bank, Andrew Jackson and his supporters opposed it, and Jackson removed federal deposits and set up new state banks once his second term began in 1833. Congressional need for information on this issue is reflected in an 1832 vote of the Joint Committee to purchase sixty copies of Matthew St. Clair Clarke and David A. Hall's *Legislative and Documentary History of the Bank of the United States, Including the Original Bank of North America*, "one for each member of the Senate, one for the Vice President, and one for the Secretary of the Senate—the balance for the Senate Library."[14]

Purchases were not always justifiable on utilitarian grounds, however. The list of desiderata from 9 January 1830 also included Coleridge's *Aid to Reflection* and Cooper's *Wept of Wish-ton-Wish*. On 7 March 1830 the same committee authorized the purchase of two German-to-English reference books, one dictionary and one grammar, an order almost certainly initiated by the German-educated Everett. With no explanation, the Joint Committee voted on 3 January 1834 to purchase twenty Bibles for use in the Library. And illustrated volumes of no discernible utility were also purchased with some frequency. In February 1830 the Joint Committee of the first session of the Twenty-first Congress ordered two illustrated volumes, Jacques Gerard Milbert's *Picturesque Itinerary of the*

Hudson River and Surrounding Parts of North America, 1828–1829, which included fifty-three lithographs, and John Martin's *Illustrations for Milton's "Paradise Lost"* (twelve plates), while the next incarnation of the committee, in February 1831, may have raised eyebrows when it resolved to pay Rogers & Co. the sum of eight hundred dollars for a work that had been commissioned by Napoléon, *Description de l'Egypt* (Paris, 1809–22), a massive, twenty-volume work with three volumes of illustrations. In January 1838 the Joint Committee ordered that a copy of Harrison Hall's new edition of Alexander Wilson's *American Ornithology* (with twenty-seven colored plates) be purchased for the Library, along with some more-staid Treasury Department reports.[15] Books by popular writers such as Cooper and Irving were probably the titles most requested by congressmen looking for light reading, while social visitors to the Library indulged the opportunity to handle and view expensive books with the latest innovations in engraving and illustration, books that without the collective purchasing power of the United States Treasury might have been difficult to come by.

Records indicate that the Library may at times have been neglected by its stewards in Congress. Very often the minutes of the committee indicate that it failed to meet or had to adjourn for want of a quorum. Some configurations of the committee appear to have made few if any significant purchasing decisions.[16] Such inactivity frustrated Edward Everett, who tended to argue for an aggressive purchasing policy. This impulse found expression in a diary entry of 26 February 1834, where he stated curtly that the "Library Committee met & did nothing."[17] Even when the Joint Library Committee was stirred into action, Congress might balk at its initiatives. Everett recorded in January 1835 that the committee resolved to request an appropriation of ten thousand dollars for the Library, which would have doubled the annual appropriation at the time. Congress chose not to approve the increase.[18] Writing in the *National Intelligencer* on 5 December 1834, a correspondent dubbing him or herself "A Friend to Literature" praised Everett and Verplanck for their "indefatigable" exertions to make the Library more useful, but contended nonetheless that the Library had admitted "a good deal of what may be called trash."

Congress was given an opportunity to acquire collections of a broader intellectual scope when a substantial private library came on the market in Europe in 1835. Richard Henry Wilde, a former congressman from

Georgia with a reputation as a poet and scholar, wrote from Florence in November 1835 to notify Congress of the availability of the library of the late Count Buturlin, in Wilde's phrase "a learned and curious bibliophile." He described the library as "fullest in those departments in which the Library of Congress is deficient, particularly the ancient authors, belles lettres, literary history, the fine arts, and the standard productions of France and Italy."[19] Washington's *National Gazette*, in advocating the purchase, appealed to the national pride and the aspersions cast on American literature by European critics: "We trust that Congress will . . . not allow so fine an opportunity to be lost of proving to the world that we are not a mere lucre-loving nation, devoid of all nobler aspirations than those of making and keeping money." The *Gazette* noted the increase of "the race of bookworms" in America and asserted that it was entitled to "some manifestations of kindness from our National Legislature."[20]

George W. Greene lobbied for congressional purchase of the Buturlin library in the *North American Review*, where he described the collection as "the nucleus of a great library, around which it would be easy to form a collection, that should leave us little to ask from the noblest libraries of Europe." Mindful of the republican bias against cultural products tainted with the stigma of aristocratic luxury, Greene defended the purchase against the charge that the Buturlin editions were unduly elegant for an American library, stating that "no public library . . . can be the work of a bibliomaniac. . . . Good, or in other words, correct editions answer every purpose of rare ones; the latter are rather the ornaments, than the appropriate furniture of a library."[21] "Public library" was a phrase that was applied quite vaguely in the nineteenth century to numerous library forms, most commonly to social libraries such as the Library Company of Philadelphia and Boston Athenaeum and to circulating libraries that rented books to the public. But Greene appears to have been using it instead as a synonym for "national library," a federally supported library that would follow a systematic acquisitions policy, starting with the purchase of the Buturlin collection, and would be accessible on liberal terms to scholars and the public.[22] Although arguments (tracing their lineage to the Revolutionary era) were still made that large European book collections embodied the danger of luxury, cultural nationalists in the 1830s suggested instead that American librarians look to the institutions of their European counterparts as worthy models of cultural achievement. As Neil Harris describes debate over the Buturlin collection, "the rhetorical strategy chosen to counter preachers of simplicity, equality, frugality, and their version of common sense was to align the cause of rare book collecting with the most potent and powerful American values: nationalism, mobility, and democratic access."[23] Critics, including Greene, pointed out that American writers needed access to books of the quality found in the Buturlin collection to elevate American literature to a level worthy of international acclaim.

Joint Library Committee member Senator William Campbell Preston of South Carolina touched on these themes in his report favoring purchase of the Buturlin library of twenty-five thousand volumes at a price of between fifty and sixty thousand dollars. Preston, who had studied in Europe, was well qualified to serve on the Library Committee given his interest in arts and letters. He was a classical scholar who would later become president of South Carolina College, and in the late 1830s he would support international copyright legislation in the Senate.[24] Preston's awareness of Library of Congress history (he spent several paragraphs describing that history in the report) was evident in the caution and prudence with which he defended his arguments for purchase. He invoked the always persuasive appeal of fiscal responsibility by pointing out that Congress had appropriated almost one hundred thousand dollars for the twenty-five-thousand volumes, many of little value, already in the Library. He compared the Library of Congress with the buildings that had been erected at the national expense, conceding that "it is not a substantive power of Congress to furnish means of knowledge or models of taste" but nonetheless averring that "a library is necessary; that it should have a certain degree of completeness and elegance is as proper as that the shafts of the columns around the halls should be polished or surmounted by a capital." Having tried to assuage the utilitarian impulses of the legislature, he appealed to its patriotism with statistics comparing America's libraries with those of European countries: "In all the public libraries of the United States, including those of schools and colleges throughout our wide territory and counting all the duplicates, there are not as many books as are contained in the Bibliothèque du Roi in Paris." Finally, he defended the large number of foreign-language books in the Buturlin collection by recommending its purchase as part of a larger plan to make the Library of Congress into a comprehensive national library: "The number of works in foreign languages would form an insuperable objection to the purchase if it was intended that the Library should be completed by it; but this the committee by no means believe to be the intention of Congress, and when the collection shall consist of 100,000 or 150,000 volumes, 30,000 or 40,000 in foreign languages may not be an undue proportion . . . If it be the purpose of Congress to extend the Library to 100,000 or 150,000 volumes, the committee think that the proposed purchase is very desirable."[25]

Unfortunately, the records of congressional debate from the period furnish no clue as to why the purchase was rejected. On motion of Henry Clay, the resolution to empower the committee to contract for purchase was tabled. Johnston conjectures that it was a partisan issue; after the removal of Watterston from office, "the Whigs could hardly entrust such a library to a Democratic Librarian."[26] While Johnston's explanation is plausible, it probably does not tell the whole story. After all, the party more likely to have been ideologically in favor of forming a national library would have been the Whigs, not the Jacksonian Democrats. The "if" clause quoted above is the most telling phrase in understanding congressional intent. Refusal to purchase the Buturlin library clearly implies that Congress did not intend to expand the Library's collections to 100,000 or 150,000 volumes. Rather, in a political atmosphere dominated by Jacksonian distrust of federal agencies, Congress continued to see its Library primarily as a tool for legislative activities.

To understand congressional frugality, it also helps to imagine the legislators looking over the catalog of the Library as they contemplated purchase. Given Wilde's description of the Buturlin library, its twenty-five thousand volumes would have been deposited primarily in these chapters of the catalog: chapters 30–32 on the fine arts; chapters 33–38 on various genres of poetry, romance, tragedy, and comedy; and perhaps chapters 42 and 43 on bibliography and languages, respectively. Thus a dozen or so chapters on which the Joint Committee on the Library had spent little attention in the years since purchase of Jefferson's library in 1815 would suddenly represent fully one-half of the Library's collections and dwarf other chapters on more immediately useful subjects such as politics, history, and geography. Purchase would have rendered the Library of Congress virtually unrecognizable to its chief patrons and largely unreadable to those who were not adept in foreign languages. Despite the nationalist arguments of the Joint Committee, this kind of acquisitions plan must have seemed almost inconceivable to many of the legislators. Thus Congress continued to ignore the precedent that had presumably been set by the purchase of Jefferson's books and confined the Library to a relatively narrow range of acquisitions.

Although Congress was reluctant to expand acquisitions into new areas, it did continue to support collections in areas in which members could clearly perceive the utility of the purchases; for many of them, given their training, law was such a subject. Recognizing this, in 1832 Congress moved to expand the law collections and created the first separate division of the Library. Law had always been one of the most valued subject classifications of the Library; law books represented over 18 percent of the collection in 1812 and over 14 percent in the 1839 and 1849 catalogs. Legislators with a background in the law often subjected this part of the library to particular scrutiny. Senator Robert Goodloe Harper introduced a bill in 1816 that would have appropriated two thousand dollars for a law library, and in 1817 the Joint Library Committee had requested a three-thousand-dollar appropriation for law books. The 1821 appropriation for the Library was targeted specifically for (along with maps) "the statutes and the reports of the decisions of the courts of law and chancery of the different states," and in 1824 Louis McLane of the House Ways and Means Committee identified law as one of the areas of the Library most useful to Congress.[27] On 9 January 1830 the committee resolved "that the laws of every state of the Union, not now in the Library, be purchased, or otherwise obtained." It made a similar resolution regarding the "digests, or revised codes, of the several states" on 17 March 1832. Apparently, successive committees were unsuccessful in accomplishing these goals: in 1840 the Joint Library Committee voted "that the Librarian prepare a letter to be addressed to the executives of the several states, requesting them to supply the Library of Congress with copies of the laws, journals, and documents of the states."[28]

In July 1832 Congress passed a law that provided for the expansion of the law collections and their physical separation from the rest of the Library. The books were to be moved to a location where members of Congress and the justices of the Supreme Court would have access to them; the justices were also empowered to make rules and regulations governing what the bill referred to as the "law department."[29] The legislation provided for a one-time $5,000 appropriation and an additional annual appropriation of $1,000 over five years. Another $5,000 was appropriated in 1837, and the $1,000 annual appropriation was then continued (and doubled in 1850). Separation of the law books represented not a movement to the periphery of the Library but a recognition and expansion of their utility. The unprecedented appropriations make it clear that law books remained central to Congress's vision of the purpose of its Library. And being made more readily available to the judicial branch of government represented an important step in the slowly evolving definition of the Library's functions.

Another important development arising from the 1832 legislation was the decision made by the Joint Library Committee in 1836 for Alexander Porter and William C. Preston to consult the Supreme Court on the subject of law books. After 1837, books for the law library were to be selected from a catalog provided by the chief justice. One of the primary sources of weakness in Library of Congress collections in the antebellum era had always been the unsystematic way that books were purchased according to the interests of individual members of the Joint Library Committee, membership of which shifted every year with the beginning of a new session of Congress. A catalog of desiderata compiled by experts in the field could only increase the value of this already highly regarded section of the Library.

Alexandre Vattemare and International Exchange

Congress in 1840 voted to support a novel method of acquiring cultural artifacts from Europe: the international exchange system proposed by the Frenchman Alexandre Vattemare. Although he first came to the attention of Europe as an entertainer (a ventriloquist), by the late 1830s Vattemare had also earned a reputation as the promoter of an exchange system whereby cultural institutions would exchange duplicates of their collections—including coins, medals, natural history specimens, and particularly books—with those of similar institutions of different nations for the purposes of expanding individual collections as well as promoting international amity. During his two trips to the United States (1839–41 and 1847–50), Vattemare achieved notable success, encouraging "the U.S. Congress, seventeen state legislatures, seven federal government departments, ten city corporations, thirteen colleges and universities, nine historical societies, and nine natural history or other societies" to participate in one form or another of cultural exchange.[30] When he arrived in Washington in 1840 with the hope of introducing Congress into the system of exchange, Vattemare bore letters of introduction from Washington Irving, Samuel F. B. Morse, and the French minister of public instruction François Guizot, as well as a testimonial from Library Committee member Guilian Verplanck.[31] Editors of American literary periodicals also championed Vattemare's exchange program. The *Southern Literary Messenger* declared that it would do "all we can to promote every such undertaking," including sending copies of the periodical to Vattemare, and articles in support of Vattemare appeared in the *Literary World, Holden's Dollar Magazine,* and *Norton's Literary Gazette.*[32]

In his 6 June 1840 report to the Senate on Vattemare's proposal, Library Committee member William C. Preston described the exchange system not principally in terms of the documents that the United States would receive but as an opportunity for the nation to display to curious Europeans the inner workings of the American political experiment: "The past and passing history of this Government, as imbodied [*sic*] in its published documents, necessarily produces the annual publication of many volumes, containing the most authentic and exact account of the progress of national events, and the working of our political machine. . . . To the intense and enlightened curiosity of the world is thus exhibited, at each step of the process, the new and great experiments we are making." Stressing Europe's interest in American political affairs, Preston appealed to national pride; by participating in exchanges, the United States would export its political know-how and spread democratic principles to Europe. Preston nonetheless also pointed out that America stood to gain more than simply a collection of government documents: "The rich accumulations of Europe in departments of learning as yet uncultivated by us, offer a most profitable exchange." The committee did not endorse the international exchange program to the extent that Vattemare would have wished, stating that "the full reciprocation . . . and enjoyment of such advantages, is alone within the power of the States. . . . But the committee believes that this Government may also, to a limited extent, advantageously enter into the proposed arrangement." Preston pragmatically justified the proposal with the assertion that "we should have the means, within the reach of Congress, of as minute a knowledge as authentic records can furnish in regard to foreign Governments."[33] Vattemare's program received congressional support because it met every requirement Congress had established in previous acquisitions debates: it was inexpensive (no appropriation was required) and had clear political benefits, without exceeding the limited responsibility that Congress felt it held in regard to literary affairs. Here was a way for the Library of Congress to receive valuable documents of a political as well as a literary character from Europe without the distasteful implication that the only way the United States could acquire culture was by buying the cast-off libraries of declining European aristocracies.

Ultimately, however, enthusiasm for Vattemare's proposal waned. In 1848 Vattemare returned to Washington, disappointed in the results of the exchange and asking Congress to appropriate money to establish an agency in Paris to effect exchanges. Congress appropriated two thousand dollars, appointed Vattemare its exchange agent, and gratefully acknowledged the books that Vattemare brought with him from Paris, but again in its report stressed its limited constitutional authority to participate in the exchanges, stating that "the great fields of literature, science, and art, belong almost exclusively to private individuals and associations, and the governments of the States."[34] By 1852, disillusioned with the results of the exchanges, Congress repealed the act of 1848 authorizing the exchange agency, and Meehan wrote to Vattemare to tell him that his services were no longer required.[35] McDonough attributes the failure of the exchange program to Vattemare's inability to win the trust of Meehan and the various members of the Library Committee, while Robert Stevens attributes it to Vattemare's "lack of success in securing adequate cooperation from the departments and agencies of the French Government."[36] While they were in Washington, at least two French diplomatic personnel told Meehan that they preferred exchanges to be carried out through official channels rather than through Vattemare.[37] Another problem was the quality of the publications received from Vattemare, which often were unbound or incomplete.[38]

Had Congress fully heeded the recommendation of its Joint Library Committee in 1840, Vattemare's international exchange plan could have had a major impact on acquisitions at the Library. In his report on the plan, Preston proposed an amendment to federal copyright law, which had just been revisited in 1831. Preston pointed out that the Library of Congress occasionally found itself with duplicate books suitable for exchange through Vattemare's agency. But these duplicates "might be increased by an amendment of the copy-right laws, directing three copies of every publication, under a maximum value, in the Congressional library."[39] Preston offered this idea almost as an afterthought, choosing not to append a resolution to this effect at the end of the report, and

Congress did not act on the proposal. Copyright deposits instead continued to go to the Department of State and would not become a reality in the Library of Congress until 1846; even then they proved not to be the boon to the Library for which supporters had hoped. But the wasted chance to consider copyright deposit in 1840, before the Smithsonian Institution had appeared on the scene as a rival depository, must be considered a lost opportunity.

The guarded support offered to Vattemare and congressional rejection of the Buturlin library reflect American politicians' anxious and conflicted appraisals of the value of the Old World's cultural treasures to the American political experiment. Congress in this respect resembled most of the country's major literary authors of the nineteenth century, from Cooper and Irving, through Emerson and Hawthorne, to Twain and Henry James, all of whom wrestled with the implications of their cultural debt to Europe, alternately embracing and rejecting European models in their creation of a national literature. In determining that cultural exchange should be left primarily to other institutions and to individual states and by rejecting a role as a supplier of books to the nation's scholars, Congress demonstrated a consistently conservative attitude toward its responsibility for cultivating the literary affairs of the nation, an attitude that kept the Library of Congress from flourishing as many writers would have wished.

The 1839 Catalog

Despite some missed opportunities, acquisitions did accrete at the Library of Congress. The new printed catalog of the Library issued in 1839 (the first since 1830) listed some 30,000 volumes (or 10,746 titles).[40] The 1839 catalog retained with slight modifications the organization into forty-four chapters imposed by George Watterston in 1815. This arrangement had been slightly altered from the system that Jefferson had devised for his library before selling it to Congress, which had in turn been derived from the Baconian classification of the faculties of the mind. Table 2 in the appendix shows a breakdown of each major subject area as a percentage of the entire catalog.

Analysis of the 1839 catalog shows that since acquisition of the Jefferson library, the personnel of the Joint Library Committee had continued to build on traditional strengths and to let areas deemed of limited utility to Congress remain in relative, but not total, neglect. The largest single chapter in the 1839 catalog was chapter 29, "Geography," with 1,584 titles, which accounted for almost 15 percent of Library holdings. The next largest single chapter of the library was chapter 24, "Politics," which had 1,200 entries and represented over 11 percent of the collections. The next two strongest areas of the collection, made up of multiple chapters, were history, which included some 1,855 entries, or over 17 percent of the collection spread over five chapters, and law, 1,590 entries, or about 15 percent of the collection, divided across six and a half chapters. Thus the four areas of geography, politics, history, and law, traditionally the Library's strongest subject areas, continued to dominate the catalog, accounting for nearly 58 percent of the collection.

As for the rest of the Library, science remained an area of importance; acquisitions in science were spread across some fourteen different chapters. One way of breaking down the science chapters is to divide them into pure science (including such areas as natural philosophy, zoology, botany, and mathematics) and applied science (agriculture, surgery, medicine, technical arts, and physicomathematics). By this method, pure science accounted for about 6 percent of the collection and applied sciences closer to 9 percent; stated more simply, around 15 percent of the entire Library was devoted to math, science, and technology. An age of rapid technological advances explains a need for the latest technical knowledge, though Congress generally did not act directly to promote individual industries. The Joint Committee had worked to improve its holdings in technical subjects in the 1830s, making a point of subscribing to the *Mechanics' Magazine* of London and ordering one hundred copies of the *American Journal of Improvements in the Useful Arts, and Mirror of the Patent Office*, edited by Ichabod L. Skinner.[41] The technical arts chapter devoted separate headings to such topics of contemporary interest as canals (seventeen titles), railroads (twenty-one titles), and the steam engine (twelve titles).

In the rest of the 1839 catalog, the belles lettres comprised about 14 percent of the Library, with some eleven chapters devoted to literature, languages, and criticism. Literature more narrowly defined as poetry, drama, and fiction accounted for 7.8 percent of the catalog. By comparison, the 1815 catalog had been made up of closer to 17 percent belles lettres, with about 10 percent of titles in poetry, drama, and fiction. Religion accounted for 4.7 percent of holdings, slightly less than in 1815, while such fine arts as architecture, music, gardening, painting, and sculpture occupied three chapters, or 2.7 percent, of the 1839 catalog. Miscellaneous subjects, including moral philosophy and a chapter devoted to polygraphical works (works on multiple subjects), filled out the remaining 5.4 percent. In short, the character of the Library of Congress as an institution devoted to collecting useful knowledge to help legislators in their work is evident in the 73 percent of the collection devoted to history, law, politics, geography, and science and technology, as well as in the more limited attention devoted to the subjects of religion, philosophy, and the fine arts.

Given that members of various configurations of the Joint Library Committee sometimes lacked expertise in book collecting, it is understandable that they would add to the Library's already strong chapters without radically changing the distribution of titles. The continuing strength of certain classifications was due both to the consistent congressional interpretation of the Library's mission and to developments in American history. The growth of the geography section over time into the largest single chapter of the Library was due in part, perhaps, to the enduring popularity of books of voyages and travels, which constituted a significant proportion of the universe of titles from which legislators had to choose. But it is also clear that as Americans moved west into territories claimed by other nations, titles in this area took on increased importance. It was natural that the overseers of a legislative library would want to keep the collections current in the areas of law and politics. Once the justices of the Supreme Court gained jurisdiction over the law library in 1832, areas such as common law, equity, and commentaries on the law were consistently well stocked. History remained important, though by 1839 titles in modern history exceeded those in ancient history by a ratio of seven to one, whereas it had been three to one in 1815. Naturally, as years passed, the field of history became larger, but it also seems likely that studying the classics for information relevant to legislation in America was not as much a concern in the practical, egalitarian Jacksonian era as it had been earlier in the century, in a political climate dominated by classical republican ideology.

Although the percentage of titles devoted to literature decreased somewhat between 1815 and 1839, this area was by no means neglected. The total number of titles had increased from 337 to over 800, as the Joint Library Committee continued to provide for the amusement of congressmen and their families by keeping up with the latest novels and poetry.

The romance chapter in the 1839 catalog, which had 339 entries, included most, if not all, of the popular fiction writers of the day. For example, the novels that British author Edward Bulwer-Lytton published during the 1830s—*Alice; or the Mysteries* (1838); *Earnest Maltravers* (1837); *Eugene Aram* (1832); *The Last Days of Pompeii* (1834); *Leila: or, the Siege of Granada* (1838); *Rienzi, the Last of the Tribunes* (1836); and *The Pilgrims of the Rhine* (1834)—found their way into the Library, in American imprints. Other British novelists represented in the 1839 catalog included G. P. R. James (three novels), Charles Dickens (four titles), and Frederick Marryat (seven titles). Contemporary American writers were also well represented. The Library had a complete run of the works of James Fenimore Cooper in addition to books by Washington Irving, John P. Kennedy (himself a member of Congress and a minor figure in the international copyright debate in the 1840s), and Catharine Maria Sedgwick. And the Library held a seventy-one-volume collection of British publisher Richard Bentley's standard novels series, which included both European and American authors published between 1834 and 1838. By 1840, purchase of popular novels would become automatic; in March of that year, the Librarian was authorized to purchase "any new work that may be published, from the pen of Cooper, Paulding, Irving, Marryat, Bulwer, Moore, etc. without waiting for specific orders in each case."[42] Since these titles had little utilitarian value, it is clear that providing light reading material to congressmen and their families was an important function of the Library.

If the Library of Congress somewhat resembled a social library of the era in providing its select clientele with the latest novels, in terms of holdings there were important differences. These are illustrated by comparing the 1839 Library of Congress catalog with the 1850 catalog of the New York Society Library (NYSL), which had served as the de facto congressional library in the 1790s (see table 2 in the appendix). In size, the two libraries were very similar: the NYSL had 35,000 volumes (around 12,000 titles) in comparison with 30,000 volumes (10,746 titles) at the Library of Congress. There were similarities within the collections too. At the NYSL, science, history, and geography were major collection areas. The library also included some 20 percent of the collection under the classification of science, though that consisted as well of metaphysics, ethics, logic, education, politics, and economics, all subjects that were classified differently at the Library of Congress. Taking away these subjects leaves about 13 percent, in comparison with 15 percent of the collection devoted to science at the Library of Congress. The geography section of the NYSL constituted about 12 percent of the collection, in comparison with around 15 percent in the congressional library. The NYSL classified about 15 percent of its collection as history, whereas the same figure was 17 percent in Washington. However, the New York library devoted a separate classification to biography, titles that would have been counted as history at the Library of Congress. Counting both the history and biography classifications, about 23 percent of the NYSL included books that would have been classed under history in the Library of Congress catalog. The stress on history and geography can be attributed to the popularity of these subjects among nineteenth-century readers.

Collections at the two libraries differed, however, in significant ways. Law and politics, subjects much less likely than history and geography to attract casual readers, were not stressed at the NYSL. The catalog of the NYSL listed only 330 titles, or 2.8 percent of the collection, in the sections on law, whereas the figure was 14.8 percent (1,590 titles) at the Library of Congress in 1839. With some 783 titles, or 6.7 percent, of the collection devoted to politics, the NYSL fell well behind the 1,200 titles (11.2 percent of collection) at the 1839 Library of Congress. In other areas that the Library of Congress had traditionally found of limited value, the NYSL was much better stocked. The NYSL catalog opened with theology, which included almost 1,200 titles, or some 10.1 percent of the collection, nearly double the proportion at the Library of Congress. And literature and the belles lettres were emphasized at the NYSL, which devoted separate classifications to poetry and drama, romances, and novels; together these sections added up to some 11 percent of the catalog, in comparison with about 8 percent at the Library of Congress. The total collections in the belles lettres—including subjects such as rhetoric, literary essays, dictionaries, and grammars—at the NYSL comprised 21.4 percent of holdings, in comparison with 14.1 percent at the Library of Congress. Comparison of the collections at the two libraries indicates how Library of Congress collections were peculiarly suited to the demands of a legislative library.

Copyright Law in the 1830s and 1840s

Cultivation of their Library was not the only way that members of Congress were enlisted in the cause of American letters by prominent writers of this era. The other issue on which the business of Congress intersected with American literature was copyright law. For the most part, the nation's literati were no more satisfied with congressional attitudes here than they were in regard to the Library. Writers did score a minor success in 1831, with the revision of the federal copyright act. The new copyright law extended the period of copyright protection from fourteen to twenty-eight years, allowed for the protection of musical compositions, and made it possible for widows (not widowers) and children of the author to apply for the fourteen-year renewal.[43] This victory, though, had not come easily. Instrumental in its passage was Library Committee member Gulian Verplanck of New York, but an even more dedicated proponent was lexicographer Noah Webster. Webster moved to Washington for ten weeks to personally lobby members of Congress for the bill, which increased the value of his own schoolbooks and dictionaries. He wrote of the experience that "few members of Congress feel much interest in such a law." These words were prophetic in describing the much more controversial proposals for international copyright that made it to Congress within a decade.[44]

The lack of an international copyright law meant that American publishers could reprint the latest English novels (or any books, in any language) without compensating the author or his or her publisher. Though the practice had been common for decades, international copyright became an issue in the 1830s with the rapid expansion of the American and international book trade. British publishers had the same opportunity for piracy, of which they increasingly took advantage, but in the 1830s American publishers were the worse offenders because of the wide popularity in America of cheap reprints of British books. Popular British novelists such as Bulwer and Dickens had the most to gain from international copyright, but many American authors, a handful of politicians, and certain members of the book trade—notably George Palmer Putnam in the 1840s—also began to perceive that justice required enactment of legislation to protect authors' interests on both sides of the Atlantic.[45]

The difficulty was getting Congress to recognize the justice of such a measure. Most congressmen, as Noah Webster had found out, expressed little interest in literary affairs. A significant exception was Henry Clay, who became the foremost proponent of international copyright in the Senate, introducing bills in February 1836, December 1837, December 1838, January 1840, and January 1842.[46] The only positive congressional report to emerge in this era came from the select committee that Clay chaired in the second session of the Twenty-fourth Congress, in February 1837. Committee members argued that British authors had a right to profit from their labor. But this principled argument could hardly be expected to prevail, thus the committee also noted that American writers and publishers were losing business owing to piracy on the other side of the Atlantic, which the proposed bill would remedy. And Clay tried to refute the protectionist argument of international copyright opponents by inserting into his Senate bill a manufacturing clause that would protect copyright only on the condition that the works were printed and published in the United States.[47]

None of Clay's bills ever reached the point of being brought to a vote, in part because of strong opposition from certain interest groups. Opponents of international copyright included large publishing houses such as Harper and Brothers which profited from the reprint trade; printers, bookbinders, and other members of the book trade who feared that their livelihoods would be at stake if American publishers lost their reprint business; and the large American reading public, who for the most part were quite satisfied with the present state of affairs in which British books sold in the United States at a fifth (or less) of their price in Great Britain. One of the most significant setbacks in the unfolding debate was a negative report by the Patent Committee issued in June 1838, in response to Clay's second effort to push a bill through Congress. This committee, chaired by Senator John Ruggles of Maine (a Jacksonian Democrat), leaned heavily on protectionist economic arguments, claiming dramatically that British authors "only want the aid of an act of Congress to enable them to monopolize the publication here as well as in England, of all English works for the supply of the American market!" Another argument calculated to appeal to republican sentiments was the committee's contention that the current legal situation served "to promote that general diffusion of knowledge and intelligence, on which depends so essentially the preservation and support of our free institutions."[48] The Patent Committee may have oversimplified the implications of international copyright, but its negative report nonetheless rendered subsequent proposals unlikely to pass.

The debate over international copyright is pertinent to Library of Congress history in two interrelated ways. First, it represents another area where Congress was pressed to do something on behalf of American authors. As long as American publishers could ensure risk-free profits from reprinting British bestsellers, supporters of international copyright pointed out, they had no incentive to publish the works of new American writers, and the cause of American literature was suppressed. The proposed law would encourage American writers and benefit "the cause of learning, of science, and of literature."[49] This argument, which was explained in a petition of American authors that Clay presented to the Senate in 1837, probably swayed such author-politicians as Preston and Verplanck, both members of the Library Committee who were sympathetic to international copyright. But to most members of Congress, with little abstract interest in the literary welfare of the country, economic arguments were more tangible. Ruggles had conceded in his report that lack of a law might be dampening the prospects for American literature but felt that the interests of authors were overshadowed by "other important interests, which no just or wise Government will overlook."[50] If international copyright would increase the cost of books and might put Americans out of work, these possibilities outweighed any appeal to cultural nationalism for a majority of legislators.

One more factor in the debate is the extent to which congressmen, through their Library, benefited from the status quo. The Library was well stocked with offending American editions of English works. A look at the Romance chapter of the 1839 Library of Congress catalog, for example, reveals that six of Bulwer's novels were collected in American editions, as were Lady Bulwer's *Chevely*, Charles Dickens's *Posthumous Papers of the Pickwick Club*, seven works by British writer Frederick Marryat, and eighteen titles by Walter Scott.[51] Congressmen could see simply by looking at the catalog of their Library how an international copyright law might affect their access to the latest popular English literature. This irony could not have been lost on legislators considering the petitions for international copyright signed by some of these same British authors, though no one found it decorous to allude to the situation in the course of debate. Congressional action and inaction on copyright law in the 1830s and 1840s further demonstrates what is clear from the history of the Library itself and from explicit statements by legislators: Congress recognized only the most limited responsibility (through domestic copyright law) to foster the growth of American literature.

The Library, the Press, and the Public

Throughout the Library's early history, newspaper correspondents and literary critics continued to press a recalcitrant Congress to expand the scope of the Library's collections and make them more available to the public. In the 1830s, these calls for a more extensive Library of Congress partook of nationalistic appeals for a distinctive literary tradition that would make the United States the cultural equal of Europe. To shame Congress into action, critics made comparisons between the Library of Congress, with thirty thousand volumes in 1839, and the national and university libraries of Europe, which often numbered collections in the hundreds of thousands. An anonymous correspondent to the *Intelligencer* (whom Library historian David Mearns conjectures might have been the European-born and-educated Francis Lieber) in 1834 voiced surprise at learning that only five thousand dollars was appropriated annually to the Library of Congress. Pointing out that even Harvard spent that much annually on its library, he wrote: "Surely we ought to expect a powerful and wealthy nation to make a more liberal appropriation than a mere College. . . . It seems particularly desirable that we should have . . . at least one grand and extensive Library, which shall contain all . . . the works that may be wanted for reference or consultation, in every department of human knowledge. . . . If we are ever to have such a Library, it must be that established by Congress, for the very obvious reason that there is not a single literary institution in our country that has funds sufficient for such an undertaking." This author concisely expressed the function of a national library and arrived at the surprising conclusion, given the Library's history, that the government was responsible for creating such an institution at the Library of Congress. He went on to contrast the Library with the major libraries of Germany, asking, "When will the United States, the boasted land of civilization and knowledge, afford to its students such facilities for the advancement of science and learning as these?"[52]

Secretary of War Lewis Cass, who would later become a member of the Joint Library Committee, made a similarly patriotic appeal for the Library of Congress to assume a national role in promoting American scholarship in a speech given to the American Historical Society in 1836. He believed the Library should be the one place in the United States "where every work may be found which has any relation, however remote, to the discovery, settlement, and history of America. . . . And why should not such additions be made to this collection, in all the departments of human learning, as will render it worthy of the age and country, and elevate it to an equality with those great repositories of knowledge, which are among the proudest ornaments of modern Europe?"[53] Two more examples should suffice to convey the tone of these appeals. Writing in the *North American Review* in 1837, in an extensive article on libraries in Europe and America, George W. Greene argued that the United States needed a library sufficiently well stocked to free American students from their dependence on European libraries, suggesting "that the enlargement of the library of Congress upon those broad principles . . . would reflect an honor upon the country, equal to the permanent advantages which it would secure to every member of the community." This sentiment was seconded by Charles Bowen in an article titled "Public Libraries" in the 1837 edition of *The American Almanac and Repository of Useful Knowledge*: "We do not see why Congress should restrict their views to anything short of having [the Library of Congress] rival the greatest establishments of this kind in Europe. . . . As many as half a dozen public libraries, of 200,000 or 300,000 volumes each, might, within the space of twenty or thirty years, be formed under the patronage and direction of the government."[54] Calls for government cultivation of library resources in America reached a rhetorical peak in the 1830s with the onus placed squarely on Congress to provide American scholars and authors with the books they needed to produce works of international renown. That these appeals to cultural nationalism were ignored by most members of Congress is amply demonstrated by the rejection of the Buturlin collection and the generally conservative acquisitions policies of the Joint Committee on the Library.

Expanded access was another issue taken up by the press in its campaign to revamp the Library. Greene acknowledged class barriers restricting library use in the country's major depositories and made a forceful argument for the admission of all classes to public libraries. He again praised Europe in this respect: "There is a republican liberality in the management of the great libraries on the continent of Europe, which is well worthy of our imitation. In these alone is the great invention of printing carried out to its full extent, by the free communication of all its productions to every class of society. No introduction, no recommendation, no securities are required." Greene apparently considered the custom of admitting users to the Library only on the introduction of a member of Congress antirepublican. Scholars in particular were interested in using the Library's collections both to carry on their individual work and to promote the greater good of creating a distinctive American literature. Greene noted how rapidly the wants of American authors were "extending beyond the bounds, which individual wealth can meet," and asked provocatively, "How far is our community prepared to supply these wants?"[55]

Residents of Washington asked similar questions. A correspondent labeling him- or herself "A Friend to Literature" in the *National Intelligencer* also criticized the rule that required an introduction by a member of Congress for a citizen to receive access to the books, arguing that "the Library" should be made free to the man of letters and science, who would thus have the opportunity to avail himself of its treasures, and diffuse its benefits among his countrymen." The writer further complained about the practice of closing the Library for a month when Congress was out of session, pointing out that this was a violation of the existing regulations. Registering a similar concern in 1844, a correspondent initialing himself "S. S. I." quizzed the editors of the *Intelligencer*: "Would it not be liberal, and better comport with the spirit of the times, if Congress would appoint one or two assistant librarians, and otherwise make provision which would render the *National Library* accessible at all hours of the day, and until eight o'clock at night, to all persons employed in the Departments?"[56] The designation of the Library of Congress as the "national library," of course, was more hopeful than descriptive in this period.

Complaints about access in the 1830s and 1840s seem at odds with George Watterston's observation regarding the state of the Library in the 1820s, when "the free ingress of strangers of all classes" struck him as a threat to the safety of the collections.[57] It appears that the Joint Committee on the Library tightened constraints on public use in this period and generally was disinclined to extend greater access to the collections. A minor concession was granted in 1830, when President Jackson approved a joint resolution extending Library of Congress privileges to the cabinet, the secretary of the Senate, the clerk of the House of Representatives, the chaplains of Congress, and former presidents when in the District of Columbia.[58] But most of the committee's decisions in regard to access during the period were restrictive. Everett noted in his diary, for example, that "Audubon's splendid work on ornithology is almost destroyed by being continually shewn to visitors." Two years later, the Joint Committee on the Library voted to purchase another copy of the work, with the explicit notation, "the same not to be exhibited to visitors." The Joint Committee generally appears to have been displeased with the number of people using the Library, voting on 31 March 1832 "that the rule relative to the admission of visitors be strictly enforced, and that the Librarian be directed to give public notice of the same." This was apparently the rule requiring visitors to be introduced by members of Congress. And in January 1834 the committee resolved "that the gratings put up for the security of the books, ought to be kept locked, and only opened by the Librarian on request."[59]

Although aware of the scholarly community's desire to use the Library at will, the committee preferred to grant access to such users on an individual basis. In February 1832 the Joint Committee voted to "permit Mr. Shackford, an officer of the Senate, to use the books in the Library," and in 1833 John Agg was specifically permitted "use of the Congress Library, during the recess of Congress, for the purposes mentioned in his letter to the Chairman of the Committee." The committee extended similar permission to William Clarke and Peter Force "to aid them in their proposed publication of the Documentary History of the United States." In contrast, a more liberal attitude toward visitors was expressed by the committee of the first session of the Twenty-eighth Congress, chaired by Rufus Choate, which in 1844 authorized the Librarian "to purchase cheap paper, to be supplied to persons who desire to make extracts from the books in the Library."[60] This evidence suggests that the Library went through periods of relative liberality and other periods when rules of admission were strictly enforced. Changes in the rules and customs governing access were dependent on such variables as the personnel of the Library Committee, the condition of the collections, and the number of visitors pressing for access. As collections became more valuable and would-be visitors more numerous, protecting the books may have taken precedent over making them accessible to members of the public. No amount of pressure exerted by members of the scholarly community in periodicals of the day appears to have had any effect on the way the Joint Committee conducted its business.

Women at the Library

It is not clear exactly when congressmen first began to allow members of their families to use the Library, but the practice dates from at least the early 1820s. In his 1822 novel about life in Washington, Librarian George Watterston had described "honourable members and their ladies . . . gazing at pictures" in the library rooms. In his next novel, Watterston placed a minor female character in the Library, where she could be found "absorbed in the perusal of a volume she held in her hand." This character, Amelia, turns out to be exceptionally well read, as becomes clear through her conversation, which "sparkled with wit, and epigrammatic brilliancy, and flowed with sentiment."[61] With the admission of casual visitors into its quarters, the Library became more than a place for official government work: it gradually developed into a space that served social purposes as well. But the mingling of women and books that this social space made possible eventually drew criticism.

Concerns over women's presence in the Library and in the Capitol began to be voiced in the 1830s. And not one of the women complained about was described as Amelia's intellectual equal. An *Intelligencer* correspondent wryly described the way users handled Audubon's *Birds of North America*: "Audubon's work . . . is handled—truly and literally, as well as roughly—by all sexes and ages. . . . It is gazed at by individuals of one sex more gaudy than the bird of Paradise, and by their attendants of the other, whose zoological studies . . . are governed by capillary attraction. . . . I beg that you will induce [the Librarian] to put Audubon, Wilson, and Bonaparte, aside, and suffer no one to examine them who is not acquainted with the proper manner of using books. These works were not purchased . . . for the amusement of loungers." Two years later, "A Friend to Literature" complained in the same newspaper that the Library was "but a literary lounge for visitors and members, to which all flock, to look at the specimens of the graphic art with which it abounds, or to pass away an hour in glancing over the pages of a fashionable novel."[62] While this second complaint is not necessarily aimed at women, it was taken up in a Washington pamphlet titled *The Champagne Club*, which dealt more explicitly with the gender of the loungers: "Crowds of pretty, fair ones with their pretty beaux filled the area and chatted and flirted and carolled their merry lays of laughter as they thumbed irreverently the hallowed and illumined pages of 'Paradise Lost' to look at the pictures." And in a later issue (also in 1835) *The Champagne Club* parodied "a group of laughing, chatting ladies" who "were *nonchalantly* turning over the elephant sheets of Audubon's ornithology."[63] Concerns over women's presence in the Capitol were not confined to the Library. Describing her visit to Washington in 1837, Harriet Martineau reported that the women sitting in the Senate gallery "came in with waving plumes, and glittering in all the colours of the rainbow, causing no little bustle in the place, no little annoyance to the gentlemen spectators, and rarely sat still for any length of time." She identified these women as "the wives, daughters, and sisters of legislators, women thronging to Washington for purposes of convenience or pleasure" and wished that they would "conduct themselves in a more dignified manner."[64]

The timing of these complaints about women in the Capitol is notable. While women socially connected to members of Congress had been able to use the Library for some time, grievances about this privilege were first lodged in print at the very cultural moment when women acting on behalf of various reform groups intruded on a number of public spaces that had previously been exclusive to men. Although women had tended to their communities from the eighteenth century through the 1820s in benevolent societies, new types of women's organizations arose in the 1830s to promote moral reform (to end or curb prostitution), temperance, and abolition. As Mary P. Ryan, Anne Firor Scott, and other scholars of women's history have noted, these movements frequently brought women into the public sphere to a degree virtually unprecedented in mainstream American experience.[65] The more activist wing of the Boston Female Anti-Slavery Society engaged in "new projects that increasingly brought them into the male preserve of law and politics," including appearances at "state legislative sessions, court hearings, and other political meetings to demonstrate their support for various antislavery measures."[66] Female members of the New York Female Moral Reform Society even ventured into the city's bordellos in 1835, where they prayed over prostitutes and their customers.[67] Such boldness outraged many citizens, who reacted violently in mob attacks on women's antislavery meetings in Boston in 1835 and Philadelphia in 1838. As Carroll Smith-Rosenberg describes the era, "Territorial conflicts between men and women resulted from these female offers to domesticate and sanctify men's newfound public space."[68]

On a federal level, women entered the political culture of the United States in the 1830s through abolitionist petition drives. This method of protest is of particular interest because it literally introduced women's names into congressional debate. One canvasser reported that she had encountered "various objections . . . to signing [a petition] . . . [because] some ladies seemed to consider it a departure from their proper place, and excused themselves by saying they did not wish their names to appear in Congress."[69] Although women defended the petition drives and abolitionist work in general as a moral rather than a political gesture, conservative critics "increasingly characterized women's petitioning as political meddling."[70] Southern lawmakers responded to the incursion of abolitionist discourse by persuading Congress to adopt the infamous "gag rule" of 1836, by which abolitionist petitions were automatically tabled without being read.

If women were overstepping the limits of the domestic sphere through the appearance of their names in the congressional record, how much more transgressive would be their physical proximity to books—the intellectual foundation for legislative authority—in the Library of Congress? Objections to the presence of women in the Library appear to serve a purpose similar to that of the gag rule that suppressed abolitionist petitions. Women who had access to and wished to read the books in the Library of Congress, with its holdings in law, political science, geography, and history, posed a threat to the ideology of separate spheres. This threat was neutralized by the insinuation that women were not interested or able to engage in serious reading. It is striking that not a single woman in the complaints is reading; all are carelessly skimming the volumes merely to look at the pictures. An image of gender-specific behavior in the Library of Congress that severely limits women's participation in the political realm is reflected and reinforced in these accounts, wherein the critics have rhetorically cordoned off the women from most of the knowledge in the Library and pushed them into a corner to look at picture books. These critics seem to have regarded women users of the Library as symbols of women's expanding participation in American political and literary culture, and their suggestions that women's access to books be curtailed should therefore be read as conservative opposition to the increased visibility and volubility of women in public spaces.

Arguing that women interfered with the utilitarian purposes for which the Library had been collected, they ignored the fact that congressmen themselves often resorted to the Library for purposes of light reading and socializing.

The distinction implicit in these complaints between serious books intended for the use of men and graphic works that tended to draw the attention of women puts in a new perspective some of the acquisitions decisions made by the Joint Committee in the 1830s. Recall that the committee ordered the purchase of several very expensive illustrated volumes in this period, including Milbert's *Picturesque Itinerary of the Hudson River*, Wilson's *American Ornithology*, Martin's *Illustrations for Paradise Lost*, and *Description de l'Egypte*. The committee also directed the Librarian to purchase in 1843 and 1844 the three-volume *Engravings of the Works of Sir Joshua Reynolds*, which included one hundred plates, and Henri-Louis Duhamel du Monceau's *Traits des Arbres Fruitiers*, a six-volume work published in Paris in parts from 1807 to 1835, with 153 colored plates. This was ordered from Little and Brown of Boston at the price of $325, a major expenditure at a time when the annual appropriation for the Library was $5,000.[71] The Joint Library Committee probably ordered these and other illustrated works, which clearly had no direct legislative value, largely as a means of amusing people, perhaps women in particular, who visited the Library for casual as opposed to professional purposes. The Library Committee thereby encouraged the development of the Library into a social as well as a reading space, purchasing works that, like the pictures, medals, and other artworks that adorned the walls of the Library rooms, helped to facilitate conversation among casual visitors.

Given that illustrated works appealed to and may have been purchased for the entertainment of women patrons of the Library, the catalog of literary holdings in the Library deserves a close look for evidence that the Library Committee sought to acquire books for a female constituency. A number of titles in the "Romance" section of the 1839 catalog, chapter 39, would have appealed especially to women readers. The Library held seven titles by novelist Catharine M. Sedgwick, a writer highly regarded by readers of both genders but whose work usually revolved around themes of feminine identity. The catalog listed at least two novels (*Flirtation* and *The Devoted*) by English romance writer Lady Charlotte Bury, another writer whose themes centered on "what it meant to be a woman in her time—emotionally, economically, physically."[72] English moralist writers of a previous generation, including Maria Edgeworth and Amelia Opie, were also very popular among American women readers and were well represented in the Library of Congress catalog, with two and eight titles, respectively. And by 1849, collections of women authors, including such domestic novelists as Fredrika Bremer and Caroline Norton, had increased markedly. One can imagine wives and daughters of congressmen being swayed by the force of custom, if nothing else, to direct their attention toward illustrated books and fictional works that treated women's themes. These works would have been considered safe and appropriate for women readers, who were known to be large consumers of novels and believed to be especially interested in works on domestic subjects. Essentially, it appears that the Joint Library Committee appropriated money for costly illustrated volumes and women's fiction in part to create a small space within the Library's reading room where casual visitors—women in particular—would be separated from the power and influence represented by the rest of the collection.

If the Library Committee did in any way distinguish between books appropriate for women's and men's uses in the Library, it was acting consistently with general trends in the literary culture of the period. Literary reviewers in the 1830s subscribed to a belief that women fiction writers were a special and inferior subcategory of novelists in general. Fiction by women was evaluated on the basis of the fidelity with which it upheld the status quo in regard to women's place in society; women authors were placed into a cultural niche whose purpose was "to neutralize the threat of the woman author by setting her to work on behalf of true womanhood."[73] The relegation of women to inferior authorial status was implicitly recognized by the Joint Committee on the Library in the list of literary authors mentioned earlier whose books were automatically collected—Cooper, Paulding, Irving, Marryat, Bulwer, and Moore. All were men, though women novelists were becoming equally popular among general readers. In the eyes of the Library Committee, only fiction by notable male authors was important enough to warrant collection on a standing order basis.

To put this analysis of women and the Library in a larger cultural context, note that the practices of physically separating men from women and providing different books to each group of readers were not uncommon in nineteenth-century libraries. Joseph Robinson's circulating library and reading room, established in 1809 in Baltimore, serves as one example. This library included a room "for the sole use of women; it contained in addition to reading tables and writing desks 'a Piano Forte for the purpose of trying music.' The two upstairs rooms were habituated apparently only by men."[74] The piano in the women's reading room not only would have made reading difficult, but its very presence sent women a message that they were not necessarily expected to use a library for reading.[75] Nor was Robinson's library alone in segregating readers by sex. Mechanics' and mercantile libraries were often not available at all for women. When they were, female readers might have been directed to certain segments of the collection considered appropriate for them. This happened in 1842 at the Apprentices' Library Company of Philadelphia, where a committee "offered resolutions providing for establishment of a separate library for girls," which was eventually opened with "about eighteen hundred volumes 'peculiarly adapted for the reading of females.'"[76] In 1856 the library had 11,450 volumes in the boys' library and 5,050 in the girls' library. And in the late 1850s, both the Mercantile Library Association of New York and the Town Library of New Hampshire found it necessary or desirable to separate readers by gender.[77] This practice continued into at least the 1880s, when librarian William Poole published an article in the *Library Journal* advocating gender segregation in small library buildings, a suggestion that was put into practice at the Carnegie library opened in 1893 in Allegheny City, Pennsylvania.[78] In the words of architectural historian Abigail A. Van Slyck, gender-specific reading rooms in the nineteenth century endorsed the assumption "that serious readers and female readers were distinct groups" and served "to reinforce—even to naturalize—a socially constructed hierarchy of library readers based on class and gender."[79]

The evolution of the Library rooms into a space where men and women conversed and socialized brought women into close proximity to books that would normally have been considered outside their sphere of interest. The women who, through family or social connections, were in a position to pursue both serious and light reading at the Library of Congress posed a challenge to the idea that women occupied the bottom level of a hierarchy of readers and therefore required only a limited range of books to satisfy their reading needs. This challenge was noted and addressed in different ways in the 1830s, primarily through complaints about women in the Library. Those objections fit into a historical pattern of anxiety about increased access to books by new classes of readers. The offending women in these anecdotes should be regarded as, in effect, the sisters of George Watterston's fictional "Richard L...." from Connecticut. Watterston had described "vulgar intruders" such as Richard as a danger to the Library's collections in order to challenge the propriety of their presence in the Library rooms. Similarly, the concerns expressed in the 1830s for the safety of the collections mask an uneasy recognition of the implications of women having access to a world of knowledge that had previously been off-limits. Thus the Library rooms in the Capitol became a site where dramas of class conflict and gender exclusion played out, a development that seems only natural given that the books amassed there were collected with the specific intent that they serve as instruments for exercising political power.

Libraries and Cultural Trends in the 1830s and 1840s

The cultural climate in which the Library of Congress was situated in the 1830s and early 1840s encompassed contradictory trends, some favorable and others less friendly to Library development. New institutions appeared on the scene that in different ways facilitated the spread of books and libraries throughout American society. Sunday schools achieved widespread acceptance and popularity in the 1830s. According to the *Eighth Annual Report* of the American Sunday School Union (ASSU), published in 1832, some 3,360 ASSU-affiliated schools reported having a library.[80] Meanwhile, the years 1829–31 saw the American Tract Society (ATS) and the American Bible Society (ABS) set goals—not ultimately achieved—of putting religious tracts and Bibles in the hands of every American. These efforts, according to David P. Nord, constituted the "realization that the creation of mass media was possible in America."[81] Sunday schools and tract societies saturated the country with books, albeit of a narrow range of content, making them an increasingly familiar presence in the American home.

The growth of the American lyceum during this period reveals a newfound interest among Americans in means of self-education. Founded in 1826, the lyceum movement spread rapidly in the late 1820s and early 1830s, particularly in New England, but throughout other areas of the country as well. Originally intended to provide a scientific education for workmen, "the main methods were the use of lecture-demonstration courses organized by public-spirited citizens and the assembling of local libraries of technical books." An early pamphlet promoting the idea included the argument that lyceums call "into use neglected libraries and giv[e] occasion for establishing new ones."[82] Thus the lyceum nurtured a habit of adult education that continued to shape the American character until the Civil War, while contributing modestly to the growth of the nation's library resources.

Another important trend of the era was the availability of books to a widening sphere of readers through a variety of new library forms. The genteel proprietary library, essentially an eighteenth-century institutional form, experienced a general decline in the nineteenth century.[83] A number of new institutions developed, which promoted increased access to books. Mechanics' or apprentices' libraries were formed by employers to give their mechanics access to technical information and general education, as well as to keep them from engaging in the unsavory distractions of the nineteenth-century city.[84] The mercantile libraries, occupying a higher socioeconomic plane, ensured that clerks entering the merchant class would be sufficiently educated in its values to sustain its respectability.[85] Referring to these and other library forms, Joseph Yeatman describes an unprecedented proliferation of libraries between 1815 and 1840 which "began to serve the needs of an increasingly diverse middle-class audience." The institutional form known at the time as the free public library, which would achieve national prominence with the foundation of the Boston Public Library at midcentury, made an early appearance in this period. The town of Peterborough, New Hampshire, established a library in 1833, "open without charge to all residents of the town and maintained by public funds."[86]

Amid these developments, some Americans were thinking about libraries in new ways. In 1829, the twenty-two-year-old Henry Wadsworth Longfellow, studying in Göttingen, wrote to his father proposing some changes at his hometown's society library, the Portland Athenaeum: "Perhaps the *Town* would do something towards enriching the Library . . . let the Library be made public. . . . Let a librarian be appointed by the *town*, with a moderate salary. . . . then throw open its doors—and let it be as public as the town pump."[87] Longfellow was inspired by what he had seen of the availability of books at the Sorbonne and the public libraries of Paris. Individual Americans who had been educated in Europe, including Longfellow and Edward Everett, warmed to the idea of universal access to large, publicly funded libraries.

Americans' ambivalence toward government funding of cultural and educational institutions, however, is evident in reactions to the common-school movement of this period. Developments such as the migration from farms toward towns and cities, an industrializing economy, and the expansion of suffrage made primary education an increasingly pressing need throughout the country. Reformers in Massachusetts, New York, and other areas of the country pushed for statewide systems of tax-supported public schools at the elementary level. The late 1830s saw such developments as the appointment of educational reformer Horace Mann as secretary of the Massachusetts Board of Education in 1837 and the establishment of a common-school system in Philadelphia by 1840. Even these apparently benign institutions met with resistance, however. Rural farmers were reluctant to be taxed for schools that they believed would prove useless to their children, and conservative clergy regarded with suspicion the premise of a nonsectarian education.[88]

In a few states, including New York, Massachusetts, and Michigan, the foundation of common schools also involved the establishment of school district libraries, which, had they been successful, would have signaled a shift in attitudes toward public expenditures for books.[89] Ultimately, though, the school district library movement failed. Public apathy weighed heavily on these libraries. Many citizens, especially in poor rural districts, did not take kindly to the idea of being taxed for the purpose of creating a library, so that "the appropriations which were gathered from a reluctant, impecunious population were not large enough to yield satisfactory libraries."[90] While educational reformers recognized a need for governmental funding of library resources, the public did not embrace the idea. If this modest scheme, which was in keeping with the long-standing national tradition of diffusing useful knowledge through cheap printed media, met with public disapproval, then it is not surprising that calls were not heeded for the federal government to expend tens of thousands of dollars to create a central depository of specialized books for the use of the nation's professional authors and scholarly community.

Finally, an abiding characteristic of literary discourse in America during the 1830s was the call for a distinctive national literature. Emerson's optimistic declaration in 1837 that "our day of dependence, our long apprenticeship to the learning of other lands, draws to a close," belied the anxiety that American literati generally felt about the state of American letters.[91] Timothy Flint opined bluntly that "we are a people too young to have a literature," and John L. O'Sullivan agreed that "we have no national literature." Critics wrung their hands over the low quality of American literature, with Flint, among others, arguing that the government should do more for the cause of American letters.[92] But calls for a national literature may have had an equivocal relationship with the cause of a national library. Cultural chauvinists such as O'Sullivan demeaned European influence over an emerging national literature, and readers who shared his prejudices might have been little disposed to see a national library on a European model as the best way to stimulate American letters.[93] Ray Frantz contends that if the cultural chauvinists had prevailed, "the concern for a national literature would have had little influence on the promotion of libraries." He credits more cosmopolitan literary nationalists with actively encouraging the development of libraries as an essential precondition for American literary growth.[94]

The fortunes of the Library of Congress declined following the inauguration of Andrew Jackson. Jackson's election represented the victory of Democratic populism and distrust of government over the ambitions of such Whigs as John Quincy Adams and Henry Clay, who envisioned Congress assuming an active role in promoting the arts and culture in America. At the Library of Congress, these political positions were personified by Librarian George Watterston and his successor, John Silva Meehan. In place of Watterston, a novelist and literary critic who promoted the Library as a symbol of American cultural development, Meehan was a quiet, meticulous civil servant with no inclination to regard the Library of Congress as anything more than a useful tool for government officials.

   Collection development continued at a steady but slow pace, with the most resources devoted to the areas of history, geography, law, and politics and new attention given to science and technology. In this period, two important opportunities for expanding collections were squandered by Congress. Purchase of the Buturlin library was rejected, despite the recommendation of the Joint Library Committee, a development that clearly signaled the wishes of Congress that the Library continue to serve a limited, utilitarian function. And William C. Preston's advocacy of a copyright deposit law, which could have had enormous implications for the Library, was overlooked during consideration of Vattemare's proposals for international exchange. Yet international exchange of duplicates and public documents and a separate appropriation for the new law division were advances in collection development that passed congressional scrutiny because of their utility and the relatively small amount of funding they required.

Women with family or social ties to members of Congress used the Library of Congress in the 1830s, as they had in the previous decade. But during a period of increased visibility of women in both the literary and political cultures of the United States, their presence in the Library began to be challenged. The collections in the Library were both tools and symbols of political power and social authority, and women's access to these books challenged the ideology of separate spheres. A backlash of complaints arose, to which the Joint Committee on the Library apparently responded. Collections of expensive illustrated volumes and light fiction, much of it devoted to women's concerns, were designed to appeal to casual users of the Library and, it seems likely, to divert their attention from the more serious and useful books, thus diminishing the threat posed by women in the Library.

An ideological faith in diffusion of knowledge continued to be a powerful concept encouraging the spread of information in America. But a diffusion of knowledge was not necessarily consistent with the centralization of resources in a large library in the nation's capital. The trend in the 1830s and 1840s toward increased access to books encompassed mostly private rather than public ventures. The lyceum, the Sunday school, and the new library forms of the era were either profit-making ventures or the result of the philanthropic impulses of private citizens. When state governments ventured into the arena of supporting educational and cultural institutions, as in the case of common schools and school district libraries, they usually met with significant resistance. The idea that the country required a large central library to help American writers achieve international prominence was supported by only a handful of intellectuals. Though American writers and scholars with progressive ideas often repeated their demand for a Library of Congress that more closely resembled the national libraries of Europe, Congress fell squarely in line with public sentiment as it refused to acknowledge federal government responsibility for creating such an institution. This continued to be the case during the period beginning in 1845 when Maryland senator James Alfred Pearce joined the Library Committee and, as chair from 1846 to 1862, exercised unprecedented authority over its development.

CHAPTER FIVE

James Alfred Pearce,
the Smithsonian Institution,
and the Question
of a National Library,
1844–1859

In the 1840s and 1850s American scholars, librarians, and journalists continued to bemoan the country's lack of library resources and pressed Congress to establish a national library with comprehensive collections and liberal access policies. But their attention was no longer focused exclusively on the Library of Congress. The story of the Library in these years is inextricably linked with that of the Smithsonian Institution, to which national library proponents shifted their attention in the 1840s and early 1850s. The debate over the mission of the Smithsonian Institution illustrates the competing claims for federal government patronage of humanist scholarship and research science. It also reveals the enormous influence over library history in America wielded by Maryland senator James Alfred Pearce, who was simultaneously chairman of the Joint Library Committee and a powerful member of the Board of Regents of the Smithsonian Institution.

But Pearce's key role in the Smithsonian debate involves something of a puzzle. In 1845, Pearce had enthusiastically championed the "library plan" for the Smithsonian. But in 1854, as a member of the Smithsonian Board of Regents, Pearce authored the acerbic special committee report that scuttled this plan permanently. Trying to account for Pearce's change of heart leads one into a tangled thicket of personal loyalties and broader political issues, including areas as seemingly diverse as copyright law and sectional hostility. Two purposes of this chapter will be to document Pearce's volte-face and to propose several factors that might have contributed to both the content and the tone of the 1854 special committee report.

With the failure of the library plan at the Smithsonian, the way was open for the Library of Congress to step into the role of national library that had so often been forced on it by eager editors and scholars. That it did not was due largely to the conservative view of the institution held by Pearce. Like most of his colleagues in Congress, Pearce viewed the Library primarily as a legislative library for the use of Congress, secondarily as a source of popular literature and a social space for legislators, and only incidentally as a resource for scholars or the public. Pearce's autocratic reign over the Joint Committee on the Library meant that a true national library would not come into being in Washington until after the Civil War.

Joint Committee Chairman James Alfred Pearce

Born in 1805 in Virginia but raised in Maryland, James Alfred Pearce graduated from Princeton, studied law, and then moved into public life as a member of the Maryland legislature. He was elected to the United States House of Representatives as a candidate of the Whig Party in 1834, 1836, and 1840. He joined the Senate in 1843 and was elected to four successive terms, dying in office in 1862. With the dissolution of the Whig Party in 1852, Pearce, like many of his colleagues, switched allegiance to the Democratic Party, the only home left for southern politicians as the nation's politics became increasingly sectional. In some ways, Pearce fitted the ideal of the southern planter-aristocrat. His colleague in the Senate, William Pitt Fessenden, described him posthumously as "a southern man and a slaveholder" and "a participator in the consequent struggle for permanent southern ascendancy." This encomium obscures Pearce's support of the Union after the outbreak of the Civil War, though he continued to defend the interests of slaveholders in the Senate.[1]

According to Fessenden, Pearce was suited by talent and inclination to serve on the Library Committee. Commenting on Pearce's intellectual attainments, Fessenden characterized him as "distinguished as a scholar in early life, thoroughly imbued with a love of letters and of science, delighting in books."[2] Undoubtedly his nineteen years of membership on the Joint Committee on the Library allowed Pearce to cultivate and indulge his scholarly interests, but they did not make him sympathetic to suggestions that the Library of Congress should take on a more significant role in the nation's literary culture. Ainsworth Rand Spofford, the Librarian of Congress who would guide the institution toward becoming the country's de facto national library later in the century, must have been referring to Pearce—and perhaps to sometime Library Committee member Jefferson Davis as well—when he complained to Ralph Waldo Emerson, visiting the Library of Congress in 1862, that the Library "has been under Southern domination, and as under dead men."[3]

Pearce joined the Library Committee in December 1844 during the second session of the Twenty-eighth Congress and became its chairman in January 1846 with the opening of the Twenty-ninth Congress. From that time until his death, he retained an impressive command over every aspect of its operations, becoming the most influential figure controlling the Library's development between the eras of Jefferson and Spofford. Librarian John Silva Meehan's letterbooks show that he never made decisions without first consulting Pearce and rarely felt impelled to make any substantive suggestions about book acquisitions, Library privileges, or any other area of Library policy, aside from occasional recommendations regarding the book agent who could offer the Library the most advantageous prices. After Pearce's death, Meehan's successor as Librarian of Congress, John G. Stephenson, affirmed in the 1863 annual report that Pearce "has had more than any other man the control and direction of the Library. . . . He has left his mark on the Library ineffaceably."[4]

Pearce's conservative vision of the Library's role is evident in the reports he authored while a member of the Library Committee as well as in the comments he made during the early years of the Smithsonian debate. He addressed the Senate on the subject of the Smithsonian Institution on 13 January 1845 and supported Rufus Choate's proposal that it become a comprehensive national library. Pearce argued that "the libraries of the government . . . cannot, with due regard to the interests of national legislation, be transferred for public use as a national library. By carrying out the suggestion of the senator from Massachusetts, a great national library worthy of the country and of the donor of this fund, may be established."[5] When Pearce later retreated from the library plan and opposed Charles Coffin Jewett's attempts to turn the Smithsonian into a national research library with comprehensive acquisitions, he maintained the view that the Library of Congress should not become such a library. Indeed, he guarded against extending the privileges of the Library to anyone beyond the users approved by statute. When the judges and solicitor of the Court of Claims petitioned for the right to use the Library in 1858, Pearce reported on behalf of the Library Committee that "it is inexpedient to extend the privilege of taking books from the Library of Congress further than is now allowed by law. . . . The number of books taken out of the library by parties entitled to do so is quite large, and, indeed, often so large as not unfrequently to impede very seriously the researches of those making extended inquiries. This inconvenience increases with every addition to the number of privileged persons, and it has been so obvious to the Library committee that they have long opposed all applications made for the extension of the privilege." The degree of control he expected to exercise over Library policy is evident in his peevish complaint in the same report that the last addition made to the list of borrowers had been enacted "without reference to the Committee on the Library, and without due consideration."[6]

Of course, there was a difference between taking the books from the Library and using them for reference purposes on the premises, a practice that had often been granted to scholars. Pearce did not oppose this use of the Library, stating in the report that "although [the] rules are silent as to the use of books by visitors, they are, in fact, allowed the use of books by reading them while there." He asserted that "this is greater liberality than is usually practiced in great libraries," a statement that was simply inaccurate in regard to many of the great European national libraries of the nineteenth century, as well as to the Boston Public Library, which had opened its doors to the public four years earlier, in 1854.[7] Pearce probably had in mind the great proprietary libraries of the United States, whose more elitist institutional structure and clientele would have suited his patrician sensibilities. Pearce thought of the Library of Congress largely in terms of the proprietary library form, which, though it was the model on which the Library had originally been based, was soon to become dated in comparison with the new free public libraries of the mid- to late nineteenth century in America.

James Smithson's Bequest and Acquisitions at the Library

Attitudes about libraries, literature, humanist scholarship, scientific research, and the responsibilities of the government toward them all in mid-nineteenth-century America are revealed nowhere more clearly than in the debates that took place regarding the disposition of the money that English chemist James Smithson bequeathed to the United States upon his death in 1829. Over the objections of a few congressmen such as John C. Calhoun, who considered acceptance of the bequest both unconstitutional and "beneath the dignity of the United States," a sum of over five hundred thousand dollars was accepted by Congress in 1836. For the next decade successive Congresses debated the nature of an institution that would bear Smithson's name and would accomplish "increase and diffusion of knowledge among men," the only two instructions Smithson had left to the frustrated legislators.[8]

Among the most prominent suggestions made in the 1830s and 1840s for using Smithson's money were the establishment of a national university, an idea that traced its roots to George Washington, and erection of an astronomical observatory, the latter of which was championed by John Quincy Adams. In the popular press other ideas were promoted, such as a college of natural sciences and a university specifically for graduate studies that would supply teachers and professors to the country's educational institutions.[9] That the bequest might somehow affect the state of American literature was first suggested in Congress by Library Committee chairman Asher Robbins of Rhode Island. Intoning in 1839 that "we have not a national literature of [a high and immortal] character," Senator Robbins proposed the creation of a new model of educational institution devoted both to science and literature.[10] Once the link between the Smithsonian and the cause of American literature was established, it was a small step to the idea that the money be used to found a national library, an idea that resonated with certain members of the Joint Committee on the Library.

Many of the same congressmen who served on the Joint Committee were also influential voices in the debate over the disposition of James Smithson's bequest. As a result, acquisitions decisions at the Library in the 1840s should be seen in light of concurrent developments in regard to the Smithsonian Institution. And a major decision faced by the Library Committee in 1844 involved whether to purchase a large library that had come on the market and had been offered to Congress: the library of the Durazzo family of Genoa. C. Edwards Lester, United States consul at Genoa, communicated the offer in January 1844, characterizing the collection as "one of the choicest private libraries in Europe," containing over ten thousand volumes in history, law, jurisprudence, and the classics, available at a price of thirty thousand dollars.[11] On the basis of a negative report by the Library Committee, submitted on 7 June 1844 by George Perkins Marsh of Vermont, Congress elected not to purchase the collection.

In its report, the Joint Library Committee adhered to the utilitarian standards of acquisition that Congress had traditionally followed. Marsh reported that the committee had conducted an examination of half of the library's catalog and found only eleven works in English of over eighteen hundred titles counted; some six hundred of these works were in Greek and Latin. Since Congress had always purchased most of its books in English, this alone might have been reason enough to reject purchase. The committee also found "few works which have not been superseded by later authors or editions." Thus the books might have been valuable for other reasons, but they could not have provided useful information to Congress. Marsh concluded that the Durazzo library was "principally interesting as furnishing abundant material for literary history, and in this respect it is of great value; and, though it would be a highly desirable acquisition to a well-endowed literary institution, it is not, in the judgment of the committee, suited to the purposes of Congress."[12]

Previous library historians have justifiably interpreted rejection of the Durazzo library as simply another instance of congressional frugality and shortsightedness. The decision certainly fits the pattern of limited appropriations observed by Congress since the hotly contested purchase of the Jefferson library. But a negative report by the Joint Library Committee is notable, especially given the personnel on *this* committee. The author of the report, George Perkins Marsh, was one of the most learned members of Congress in the 1840s and was ideally suited to guide the Library Committee toward a wider acquisitions policy. Marsh was a linguist who had mastered French, Spanish, Portuguese, Italian, German, and Scandinavian languages and had authored *A Compendious Grammar of the Old-Northern or Icelandic Language* (1838). He was also a Whig and therefore ideologically disposed toward federal support of the arts and sciences. His authorship of the negative report on the Durazzo library seems highly inconsistent with later statements he made regarding libraries. In April 1846, for example, speaking in the House of Representatives on the subject of the Smithsonian, Marsh said of the Library of Congress that "there is no one branch of liberal study, even among those of greatest interest to ourselves, in which it is not miserably deficient."[13] Moreover, in 1848 Marsh would write to a friend that "nothing is more imperiously demanded by all great American interests than enlarged, multiplied, & diversified collections of books."[14] Entertaining these sentiments about libraries generally and the Library of Congress in particular, why would Marsh have authored a report against acquisition of the Durazzo collection?

It could be that the committee had learned its lesson from debate over the Buturlin collection and had given up on the idea of a national library. But a close look at the timing of the report suggests that members of the Library Committee hoped as strongly as ever to establish a national library in Washington; they simply had turned their ambitions to a different institution. Both Marsh and Rufus Choate, chairman of the Joint Committee on the Library, were already anticipating the creation of a Smithsonian Library. On 6 June 1844, just one day before Marsh filed the report on the Durazzo library, Senator Benjamin Tappan of Ohio, another member of the Joint Library Committee, introduced a bill proposing to establish the Smithsonian Institution. And Choate's counterproposal, that the Smithson bequest be used to finance a great national library, would follow in a matter of months. In June 1844, then, it seems quite likely that New England Whigs Choate and Marsh already had their eyes on the Smithson bequest as the most probable route to acquiring a national library. They therefore saw no reason to append the Durazzo collection to the Library of Congress, which appeared unlikely ever to transcend its primarily legislative function. The "well-endowed literary institution" Marsh mentioned in his report probably referred to his hopeful vision of a library to be established using Smithson's half-million-dollar bequest to the United States.

The Rise of the Library Plan for the Smithsonian

The debate over the ultimate form of the Smithsonian Institution picked up speed after Democrat Benjamin Tappan of Ohio introduced bills into the Twenty-eighth Congress in June and December 1844. Senator Tappan's proposed institution was to include professors of natural history, chemistry, and astronomy and other lecturers in the arts and sciences.[15] Neither bill passed, but they did serve as the stimulus for Rufus Choate's competing proposal for a national library in 1845.[16] On 8 January 1845, in one of his most memorable speeches to the Senate, Choate proposed that a large portion of the income, possibly "twenty thousand dollars a year for twenty-five years," be devoted to book purchases for a national library.[17] Because Choate's speech was evidently quite persuasive—the Senate accepted Choate's amendments to the Smithsonian bill and agreed to appropriate most of the income to a library—the terms in which he couched his argument are worth considering in detail.

Choate must have been acutely aware of the arguments that could be raised against a large national library, because he cannily attempted to circumvent them in his speech. For example, Choate made the case that "a various and ample library is one of the surest . . . instrumentalities to increase and diffuse knowledge." He made this claim by arguing that putting adequate library resources for serious scholarship within reach of American scholars would "raise the standard of our scholarship . . . and communicate an impulse to our educated and to the general mind. . . . Let [the scholars] . . . go back and make distribution among their pupils; aye, through the thousand channels and by the thousand voices of the press, let them make distribution among the people!"[18] Besides establishing that a library would satisfy the terms of the bequest and achieve the republican goal of diffusing knowledge, Choate also made a shrewd fiscal argument that "when you have laid it out, you have the money's worth, the value received, the property purchased, on hand to show for itself and to speak for itself." Moreover, the minimum staffing requirements of a library meant the creation of "so few jobs and sinecures; so little salaried laziness." In this way Choate anticipated and countered the assertions that a large library would include many books that contained the refined and useless musings of antiquarians and philosophers by focusing on the physicality of the books, their tangible financial value as pieces of property. Next, Choate turned to the political advantage of purchasing a library. Taking account of the precarious relations between the North and the South, intensified in the 1840s by the question of whether slavery would be permitted in the new territories, Choate claimed that the scholars who came to the library from disparate parts of the country would "go away not only better scholars but better Unionists. Some one has said that a great library molds all minds into one republic. It might, in a sense of which he little dreamed, help to keep ours together."[19]

Given the history of resistance to great libraries in America, Choate's most important line of argument was probably his claim that "a rich and public library is no antirepublican monopoly." Aware of the charge that extensive libraries transferred to America the wretched excesses of European aristocracy, Choate contended that "I do not . . . desire any more than you . . . to introduce here those vast inequalities of fortune, that elaborate luxury, that fantastic and extreme refinement. But I acknowledge a pang of envy and grief that there should be one drop or one morsel more of the bread and water of intellectual life tasted by the European than by the American mind." Choate deflected the association of books with luxury by figuring them, in an adroitly republican gesture, as the most basic necessities of the intellectual life—its bread and water. Senator Tappan spoke after Choate in opposition to a national library and invoked the example of the Library of Congress, for which an annual appropriation of five thousand dollars "enabled the committee to procure everything coming out in print worth procuring" and which still contained "more than half the books that he would not take a gift of for the cost of transportation to Ohio."[20] But Choate's arguments prevailed in the Senate, which passed a bill to the House that appropriated the bulk of the income to book purchases for a national library.

The debate continued for a year and a half in the House, where Indiana Democrat Robert Dale Owen was the most eloquent opponent of the national library plan. The son of English socialist reformer Robert Owen and a critic of American institutions during his early life, Owen became "an eloquent exponent of Manifest Destiny" after ten years of life in the West. Instead of a library, Owen advocated a normal school that would instruct teachers in the science of education. Having previous experience with adult education through popular lectures and cheap tracts, and having experienced the "backward state of agricultural and common school instruction in the West," Owen made a proposal that squared well with the populist ideology of his party and long-held American ideas about the diffusion of knowledge.[21]

The most interesting parts of Owen's 22 April 1846 speech to the House defending his bill are his attempts to discredit the library proposal by characterizing it as an elitist venture of little practical value. Owen held that he prized libraries in their proper dimensions as much as any other person but that more effective ways existed to distribute the benefits of knowledge than accumulating a library of one hundred thousand volumes to match Göttingen or Paris. Owen asked: "Are there 100,000 [volumes] in the world worth reading? I doubt it much. . . . Books are like wealth. An income we must have to live. . . . Beyond a certain income the power of wealth to purchase comfort, or even whole-some luxury, ceases altogether." In addition to associating books with wealth and luxury, much as the Federalists who opposed the purchase of Jefferson's library had done, Owen undertook to subvert Choate's equa-tion of books with intellectual bread and water. After quoting that pas-sage from Choate's speech, Owen argued: "It grieves me not that the fantastic taste of some epicure in learning may chance to find on the book shelves of Paris some literary morsel of choice and ancient flavor, such as our own metropolis supplies not. I feel no envy if we republicans are outdone by luxurious Europe in some high-seasoned delicacy of the pampered soul."[22] These clever permutations of the metaphor linking books and food suggestively express the opposing sides of the conflict, which had been debated since the earliest days of the nation, about the value of books to the republican experiment. If a national library were established, for whose consumption would its books be intended? Would its acquisitions appeal to the popular taste, or would the library perpetu-ally cater only to the appetites of a small scholarly elite? At the most basic level, would the books represent nourishment or poison to the republican constitution?

The question was next taken up by Marsh, who argued in the House on 23 April, 1846 that he considered the library "the most valuable feature" of the plan for the Smithsonian. Marsh revisited the food metaphors and slyly transmuted them into an argument for inclusiveness in acquisitions, accompanied by universal access to a national library: "[A] national library . . . must embrace all science—all history—all languages. It must be extensive enough, and diversified enough, to furnish aliment for the cravings of every appetite. We need some great establishment that shall not hoard its treasures with the jealous niggardliness which locks up the libraries of Britain, but shall emulate the generous munificence which throws open to the world the boundless stores of literary wealth of Germany and France." Reconciling in some measure the positions of Choate and Owen, Marsh argued for an institution that would be able to satisfy "epicurean" intellectual tastes with its unlimited collections but would also be accessible on the most democratic basis to American citizens. Marsh impressed on his colleagues the need for such a library by pointing to the Library of Congress, contending that although the Li-brary held forty thousand well-chosen volumes, its collections were still, as has been quoted, "miserably deficient."[23]

The debate over the Smithsonian suggests how ill-suited the Library of Congress was to become a national library in the 1840s. The primary advocates of such a library, Choate and Marsh, both active members of the Library Committee, expressed little confidence in the Library as a resource for American scholars. Library Committee member Tappan disparaged the abstruse quality of the Library's collections. If even a member of the Library Committee had this dismissive attitude toward books, then persuading Congress as a whole to expand the scope of acquisitions at its Library was clearly a doubtful proposition. And as we have seen, soon-to-be Library Committee chairman James Alfred Pearce was convinced that a government library could never double in function as a national library. The Smithsonian therefore seemed the most likely institution to step into a void that the Library of Congress could not fill.

In August 1846 President James Polk signed into law a bill establishing the Smithsonian Institution, with the specification that no more than twenty-five thousand dollars annually should be devoted to the gradual formation of a library.[24] Congress had decided to invest the principal of Smithson's bequest and to use the annual income from the interest to fund the institution perpetually. Thus the large sum of twenty-five thousand dollars out of an annual income of thirty thousand dollars represented a stunning (but temporary) victory for the national library proponents. Although the bill provided for a building that would house a geological and mineralogical cabinet, a chemical laboratory, a library, a gallery of art, and lecture rooms, only the library's appropriation was specified.

The Demise of the Library Plan

The Smithsonian Board of Regents, which inherited the debate over the exact amount of income its library should receive, was not unanimously sympathetic to the national library plan. The Board of Regents was a body appointed by Congress whose membership continually shifted. It included "the Vice-President of the United States, the Chief Justice, and the Mayor of Washington, three members of the Senate, three members of the House of Representatives, and six other persons, not members of Congress, two of whom must be members of the National Institute and resident in Washington, and the other four, inhabitants of States, no two of the same State."[25] The board in 1846 included both Choate and Owen, as well as other members on both sides of the library debate. The prospects for a national library at the Smithsonian suffered a setback when the board settled on Princeton physicist Joseph Henry as secretary of the institution in December 1846. Henry arrived at the Smithsonian "with a completely worked out program for the 'increase and diffusion of knowledge' that had very little to do with a library."[26] Henry favored a program that he considered more strictly in accordance with the terms of Smithson's will, consisting primarily of original research in the physical sciences (to increase knowledge) and publication of its results (to diffuse knowledge). Rather than settle on either a library or Henry's plan exclusively, in January 1847 a committee on organization reported the so-called compromise resolutions that allocated one-half of the income for the library, museum, and gallery and the other half for original research and publication of scientific transactions. It was also in January 1847 that the Board of Regents decided to appoint an assistant secretary to take charge of the library; the proponents of the library plan eventually succeeded in persuading Charles Coffin Jewett to accept the position. Although the board had decided to delay purchase of books for several years until a building had been erected to keep them, the library faction maneuvered to bring Jewett to Washington by 1849 to begin overseeing library operations, lest their aims for a national library be left solely at Henry's discretion.

At the time of his appointment, Jewett was the most eminent librarian in America. His catalog of the Brown University library had attracted national attention.[27] And although he knew before he began his duties at the Smithsonian that Henry was not interested in acquiring a national library, he nonetheless went to Washington with plans for the library that would involve implementation on a national scale. A letter from Jewett to Henry was appended to the 1848 annual report of the Board of Regents, in which Jewett concurred with the suggestion of Alexander Dallas Bache, another member of the board, that the library should be "a supplemental one, and a centre of bibliographical reference."[28] He proposed to collect the catalogs of all the principal libraries of the United States and from them to form a national union catalog so that scholars could write to the Smithsonian to find out where in America to locate individual titles necessary to their work. To this extent, Henry concurred with Jewett's plans.

But Jewett's plans for the Smithsonian library went further. The boldest and most complicated scheme that Jewett conceived and began to implement was one for stereotyping the union catalog. Cataloging libraries in the nineteenth century involved immense logistical problems; the time required to prepare and print a catalog ensured that it would be out of date as soon as it was published. Under Jewett's plan to surmount these difficulties, the Smithsonian would publish guidelines that individual libraries could use in compiling catalog entries in a uniform fashion. The libraries would then send the catalogs to the Smithsonian, where stereotype plates would be created for each title. Having at the Smithsonian separate plates representing the titles of all the works in American libraries would allow the institution to print and periodically update a national union catalog and to print catalogs every few years for individual libraries that joined the system. Had it worked, the system would have made the Smithsonian the center of the American library world, but mechanical problems arose, and then Jewett was dismissed.[29] The large scale of this project is emblematic of Jewett's ambitious plans for the Smithsonian library.

Despite Jewett's early report indicating acquiescence with creating a "supplemental" library at the Smithsonian, neither he nor certain members of the Board of Regents had ever given up on the idea of the Smithsonian library becoming the national library of America. Jewett's reports to the Board of Regents eventually came to reflect a sharp divergence between his views and Henry's. In the third annual report of the Board of Regents, Jewett (in his assistant secretary's report on the library, dated 13 December, 1848) noted that "the large libraries of Europe, containing from 200,000 to 800,000 volumes, some of them selected with great care, have not been found large enough to meet the wants of her scholars." After registering "the complaints of our scholars" as to the deficiency of library resources in America, Jewett brashly asserted that "to supply these wants, or, in other words, to place American students on a footing with those of the most favored country of Europe, is the design of the Smithsonian Library." Responding to Jewett's designs for the library in the fifth annual report, Henry stated, with reference to the library, that "the idea ought never to be entertained that the portion of the limited income of the Smithsonian fund which can be devoted to the purchase of books will ever be sufficient to meet the wants of the American scholar."[30] By contrast with his assistant secretary, Henry envisioned a library that would be complete in the transactions of learned societies and current books of scientific interest sufficient to support the work of the scientists whose research was published in the *Smithsonian Contributions to Knowledge*. Not surprisingly, relations between Henry and Jewett became increasingly acrimonious as a result of their contrasting visions of the library's function. The two engaged in a number of heated exchanges between December 1852 and September 1853.[31]

In his annual reports to the Board of Regents in the early 1850s, Jewett continued to press the case for a national library by citing evidence of growing national interest in libraries and scholarship. In his capacity as Smithsonian librarian, he had compiled statistics on libraries in America, which he appended to his annual report and also published in 1851 as *Notices of Public Libraries in the United States of America*. The widely admired *Notices*, published in an edition of six hundred copies, was almost exhausted by 1853, and the Smithsonian issued a second edition in 1859.[32] Jewett appealed to public interest in the library (not just interest among librarians or scholars) in the fifth annual report. He contended that "a record of visitors . . . showed an average of sixteen thousand a year" to the library, which then contained about nine thousand volumes collected through exchange, copyright deposits, and a minimal number of purchases (the library would not be entitled to devote its share of the annual income to book purchases until the building was completed). He admitted that some of the visitors were merely curious but maintained that "many are led by a love of study."[33]

Perhaps the strongest statement of a national interest in the Smithsonian library was made at the conference of American librarians held in September 1853 in New York, which unanimously elected Jewett its president. Organized by New York bookseller Charles B. Norton, the conference attracted eighty-two participants from thirteen states, representing forty-seven libraries.[34] In his final annual report as Smithsonian librarian, Jewett tried to use the support he had garnered at the convention as political clout in his rift with Henry by reprinting the conference resolutions. The librarians had resolved "that the establishment of a great central library for reference and research, while it is demanded by the condition of the United States as to general civilization and intellectual advancement, is especially interesting to this convention from the bearing it would have upon libraries throughout the country." And further: "we deem such an establishment as being eminently worthy of support from the national treasury; and that in no way can the government better promote the progress of learning through the whole country, than by placing a central national library under the administration of the Smith-sonian Institution."[35]

Support from the librarian's convention and evidence of public interest in the Smithsonian library could not smooth over the bitter personal relationship that had developed between Henry and Jewett, however, nor was it able to persuade the majority of the Regents of the necessity or desirability of a national library. With the building nearing completion, Henry brought before the Regents in 1853 the question of how the annual income should be distributed in the coming years. The board appointed a special committee chaired by Regent (and Chairman of the Joint Committee on the Library of Congress) James Alfred Pearce to investi-gate the question, and in May 1854 the committee recommended that the board repeal the compromise resolution devoting half the annual income to the library. Aware of the dispute between the secretary and his assis-tant, in July the regents affirmed Henry's right to terminate an insubor-dinate assistant. Jewett was immediately dismissed from his post, effec-tively bringing to a close the prospects for a national library at the Smithsonian Institution.

Examination of the report of the special committee of the Board of Regents on the organization of the institution is central to a complete understanding of how and why the national library proponents were finally defeated. Not only does the report include the reasons that were urged for repealing the compromise resolution and thereby drastically reducing the Smithsonian library's budget, but it also records Pearce's remarkable reversal on the question of a national library—he had con-curred with Choate in 1845 that "this munificent bequest" would "accom-plish the injunction of the donor, by such an increase and diffusion of knowledge among men as a complete national library . . . would un-doubtedly insure."[36] In the 1854 report, Pearce took the position that Congress's original ceiling of twenty-five thousand dollars placed on expenditures for a library was merely a spending limit but in no way an injunction to spend all or nearly all that amount. He then launched into a more abstract discussion of whether a great library could accomplish the increase and diffusion of knowledge that Smithson's will had re-quired, and came to the following conclusion: "Neither of these purposes could be accomplished or materially advanced by the accumulation of a great library at the city of Washington. This would be to gather within the walls of a building here those fruits of learning which had been reaped elsewhere. It would be the *hiving* of knowledge, not its increase and diffusion." Pearce went on to contend that given the provisions of Smithson's will, the collection of a great library would have been "palpably absurd" and "a preposterous abuse of terms." And on the nature of the library that the Smithsonian should ultimately possess, Pearce wrote: "It is not believed to be advisable to accumulate in the Smithsonian Institution great masses of books, without reference to their peculiar character and value. What we want, and what the act of Congress contemplates, is not a collection of everything which learned dullness and literary folly as well as real wisdom and sound science have put into print—a vast and unwieldy repertory, in which the trash as well as the precious may be found—but a library of *valuable* books pertaining to all departments of human knowledge."[37]

One member of Pearce's special committee dissented from the May 1854 report. James Meacham authored a minority report, which was in effect the last defense of the library plan. A Whig from Vermont, Meacham believed that the compromise resolutions themselves had been contrary to the will of Congress, which had expressly intended for the Smithsonian to become a national library. In his spirited report, Meacham pointed out that aspects of the "active operations" of conducting research and publishing results that was the current mission of the Smithsonian had been proposed and rejected in Congress before the library plan had met with its approval. Meacham derided Pearce's claim that a library represented the hiving of knowledge and persuasively demonstrated how a library contributes to both the increase and diffusion of knowledge (he dryly pointed out that the *Smithsonian Contributions to Knowledge* would accomplish exactly these ends by being consulted in libraries). Without making any overt statements about Pearce's unusual reversal on the library plan, Meacham quoted from Pearce's original comments in support of Choate's proposal. But Meacham's charges that the Board of Regents had circumvented the will of Congress through wheelings and dealings behind closed doors—he called it "an affair of the closet"—had no bearing on subsequent events.[38]

Explanation of Pearce's Reversal

While it is perhaps no more surprising for a nineteenth-century politician than a modern one to reverse positions on an issue, Pearce's radical about-face on the question of a national library nonetheless demands inquiry.

Commenting on the change of heart, C. Hale wrote in the *North American Review* that he was "almost inclined . . . to explain the inconsistency . . . by attributing the authorship of the [special committee's report] to some other pen than his own."[39] This possibility, however, is difficult to admit. The report was signed by Pearce, who chaired the committee. Moreover, a number of Pearce's acquaintances wrote him soon after publication of the report to congratulate him on its clarity of expression or otherwise comment on its content.[40] One correspondent, Harvard botanist Asa Gray, seemed to bend over backward not to impute to Pearce an awkward reversal of opinion. Gray wrote apologetically of a published comment on the affair, "I see however that the expression I have inadvertently used that you had 'changed your mind' may be deemed objectionable, and may not be true." Gray explained that when Pearce made the 1845 speech, he could not have known that Congress would be able to secure the services of "so truly a scientific, high-minded and incorruptibly honest and disinterested a person as Prof. Henry" to run the Smithsonian.[41] As Gray saw it, Pearce had not exactly changed his mind but had reevaluated the options after Joseph Henry, one of America's foremost scientists at the time of his appointment, entered the picture.

Gray's explanation has much to recommend it. Henry and Pearce developed a warm personal friendship after Henry arrived in Washington. As early as 1851, Pearce wrote to Henry, "I am very obliged to you and Dr. L. for the mineralogical specimens & the matting in which they were arranged. My children will find them a source of amusement & instruction & will prize them highly."[42] Henry also provided detailed instructions to Pearce on installing lightning rods on his estate, even studying architectural plans of the house and having the lightning rods custom-made.[43] That Pearce and Henry shared a personal animosity toward Jewett is revealed in a letter Henry wrote to Pearce in 1855. Discussing the congressional investigation into management of the Smithsonian that followed Rufus Choate's angry resignation from the Board of Regents after the demise of the library plan, Henry wrote to Pearce with evident glee that "Jewett has ordered 1000 copies of the whole investigation before the committee of the House. He did not know at the time he did this that Mr. Witte's report was to form a part. It will cost him about 2000 doll."[44] The conspiratorial tone suggests that Henry knew Pearce would share in his delight at this unexpected expense incurred by the librarian. It would not have been difficult to dislike Jewett.

The debate over the Smithsonian library had been both public and acrimonious, and Henry felt that Jewett had treated him unfairly. In a letter he asked Pearce, "Shall I come out in the Intelligencer with the facts of the case as exhibited in a correspondence between Mr. Witte and myself? Can I induce the next Congress to allow me to put on record an answer to Mr. Jewett's papers? As the matter now stands on the records of Congress I am not fully exonerated from the charges which were made against me."[45] And both Henry and Pearce might have found Jewett's personality noxious; Jewett's biographer concedes that "egotism, resentfulness of affronts . . . and a certain quickness of temper" were among his less appealing personality traits.[46]

Through his friendship with Henry, Pearce also became persuaded by 1854 of the superior utility of scientific research over the more humanistic benefits of a library. Pearce's special committee report included two paragraphs in which he defended the value of pure scientific research on utilitarian grounds, arguing that "the most valuable and productive of the arts of life, the most important and wonder-working inventions of modern times, owe their being and value to scientific investigations." Meacham took note of this line of reasoning, which he considered fallacious, complaining in his minority report that "we are prone to draw our analogies too much from the physical sciences, when we think of the increase of knowledge," and asserting that "all knowledge is worthy of support."[47] Pearce's close friendship with the country's leading proponent of pure scientific research might have helped to convince him that money expended on scientific investigation promoted national interests more visibly and effectively than a library could. His responsibility as Joint Library Committee chairman for the publication of the multivolume account of Charles Wilkes's exploring expedition might also have contributed to Pearce's privileging the utilitarian benefits of research in the hard sciences.

The new copyright deposit law of 1846 also appears to have played a role in Pearce's decision. In the act establishing the Smithsonian, Congress had included "the first Federal provision for the use of copyright deposits to enrich American libraries."[48] The law directed that copyrighted articles be sent to both the Library of Congress and the Smithsonian but provided no penalty for noncompliance. Some publishers were unaware of the law, while others ignored it, so the materials received were not highly valuable. David Mearns characterizes the deposits received during this era as "Sunday school texts, juveniles, indifferent prints, engravings, and other classes of current material least likely to serve the immediate purposes of research."[49] Pearce's statement in the special committee report about amassing "a vast and unwieldy repertory, in which the trash as well as the precious may be found," probably had reference to these deposits. Next to the transactions of learned societies that were quickly filling up the shelves through exchanges, the schoolbooks, musical scores, and patent medicine labels must have seemed odd shelf mates. Though he saw little value in certain ephemera brought in by the copyright deposit law, Jewett was cognizant of the great utility of copyright deposit in building up the collections of European national libraries. He often lobbied in his reports to the Board of Regents for a stronger deposit law which would ensure that "all the products of the American press may be gathered, year by year, and preserved for reference."[50] Henry, on the other hand, saw the accumulation of ephemeral literature on the shelves of the Smithsonian as a burden to the institution, for the postage required to receive the material and the shelf space to store it.

Quite possibly, his experience at the Library of Congress led Pearce to share Henry's opinion. Having had virtually sole responsibility over book purchases for the Library for several years, Pearce might have wondered whether twenty to twenty-five thousand dollars could be advantageously expended for books. The Library of Congress book budget had been five thousand dollars annually, yet Tappan had argued that most of its books were not worth the cost of transportation. Meanwhile, the copyright deposit items were accumulating rapidly at the Library of Congress, and an increasing amount of Librarian Meehan's time (later, that of his assistant E. B. Stelle) was taken up with the labor-intensive tasks of cataloging these deposits and acknowledging their receipt. Space was also a problem. In 1849 Meehan had written to Obadiah Rich, the Library's book agent, that "the rooms for the accommodation of our Library are now so thoroughly filled, that we find it very difficult to take in any more books."[51] It is conceivable that Pearce watched with skepticism as both the Library of Congress and the Smithsonian Institution received large numbers of relatively valueless accessions that drained the time and energy of library personnel and took up increasingly scarce shelf space. The copyright deposit law of 1846 probably led Pearce to reevaluate his support of a national library that would have collected all the productions of the American press.

A comprehensive copyright deposit law also violated a strongly held principle of Pearce's in regard to management of a government library: his belief that its holdings should remain nonpartisan. This attitude is evident in an 1847 letter from Librarian Meehan. Trying to convince Pearce to subscribe to a new periodical, Meehan wrote of its editor: "He intends that his work shall not be *political*, in a party sense, & has already received for it the promise of contributions . . . from the most . . . eminent gentlemen known as writers of all parties."[52] Confirmation of this attitude comes from Benjamin Perley Poore, who observed in his memoirs that "Mr. Pearce was a devoted friend of the Congressional Library, and during his long service on the Committee having it in charge he selected the books purchased. In doing this he excluded all works calculated in his opinion to engender sectional differences, and when the *Atlantic Monthly* was established he refused to order it for the Library." *Atlantic Monthly* editors James Russell Lowell and Francis Underwood were well known for antislavery views that made their periodical, launched in 1857, "soundly hated in the South."[53]

While Pearce could try to exclude antislavery materials from the shelves of the Library of Congress on the somewhat artificial grounds that they were partisan (it was clearly just as partisan a decision *not* to shelve the *Atlantic Monthly* as it would have been to collect it), he did not possess a similar authority over accessions at the Smithsonian Library. Jewett espoused in one of his annual reports the value of collecting all the productions of the U.S. press, with the rationale that "the interest with which those who in 1950 may consult this library would view a complete collection of all the works printed in America in 1850, can only be fully and rightly estimated by the historian and bibliographer, who has sought in vain for the productions of the past."[54] If in 1845 Pearce had envisioned a national library as presumably existing above the realm of politics or sectionalism, he must by 1854 have realized that Jewett's acquisitions policies would result in the Smithsonian Library becoming something quite different and inescapably political. The chapter on "ethics" in the 1861 catalog lists nineteen books on the subject of slavery that had been received in the Library of Congress through copyright deposit.[55]

Pearce confronted a world of print in the 1850s in which the boundaries between literature and politics were dissolving. Frank Luther Mott quotes the superintendent of the eighth census, who discovered a 100 percent increase in the number of political papers and periodicals published between 1850 and 1860. Mott also notes an abundance of political discussion even in the nonpolitical periodicals of the day, writing that "it seemed impossible for the individual or the periodical to keep away from politics altogether for long."[56] The impact of slave narratives of the 1840s and 1850s such as Frederick Douglass's *Narrative of the Life of Frederick Douglass, an American Slave* (1845), as well as a new willingness on the part of literati such as Emerson and Henry David Thoreau to speak and write on the issue of slavery after the Compromise of 1850 (and its attendant Fugitive Slave Law), would have impressed on a southern senator how literature could exert an influence over political realities.

No literary event signifies the inextricable link between literature and politics in the print culture of the 1850s better than the publication of *Uncle Tom's Cabin* in book form in 1852. Harriet Beecher Stowe's best-selling novel foregrounded the nation's most contentious political issue, galvanizing the abolitionist movement in the North and inspiring denunciations in the South. No doubt to Pearce's chagrin, *Uncle Tom's Cabin* found its way into the Library of Congress catalog of 1861, where a typographical mark indicates that it was a copyright deposit, not a purchase. A surprising and suggestive link exists between the publication of *Uncle Tom's Cabin* and Pearce's derisive comments in the 1854 special committee report attacking the library plan. Simply put, Smithsonian librarian Charles Coffin Jewett was the brother of John P. Jewett, publisher (in book form) of *Uncle Tom's Cabin*. It seems inevitable that a slaveholding senator from Maryland would have resented John P. Jewett for his role in publishing the most influential antislavery polemic of the period, a feeling that would perhaps have affected Pearce's relationship with Charles Jewett. Though it does not wholly account for Pearce's turnabout on the library plan, the opportunity to cast ignominy on a member of the Jewett family, added to what we know of Pearce's personal friendship with Joseph Henry, might help to explain Pearce's unusually vitriolic dismissal in 1854 of a library plan that he had supported nine years earlier.

Finally, one might speculate that changes in the availability of information in the rapidly transforming print culture of mid-nineteenth-century America also influenced Pearce's decision. Diffusion of knowledge had been for early republicans an indirect process of civic education. Books could be collected in a central location like the Library of Congress, consulted by the social elite, and knowledge of them diffused through hierarchical channels to the masses. This was the mode of diffusion that a southern gentleman such as Pearce, born early in the century and believing in the ordered and deferential society that southerners touted in defense of their way of life, would have subscribed to. But by the middle of the nineteenth century, the expansion of American print culture made new sources of information available to a widening sphere of readers through a much more direct, egalitarian process. In the words of Richard D. Brown, "the generous access to information was exhilarating . . . men could acquire information on their own in the marketplace, more or less on an equal basis."[57] The trend in American culture toward a direct model of diffusion was best symbolized in 1854 by the opening of the Boston Public Library, which was expressly designed to bring books to the city's less privileged residents in the form of a "free public library," a type of institution hitherto virtually unknown in the United States.

National library proponents welcomed the prospect of information diffusion on the broadest scale, and the institution they envisioned would have represented a federal commitment to encouraging diffusion of knowledge through immediate, direct public access to the books on the shelves. Marsh had argued that the country needed an institution where "the poorest and humblest aspirant may slake his thirst for knowledge, without money and without price."[58] And Jewett had supported his case for the library plan by citing a yearly average of sixteen thousand visitors to the Smithsonian collections.[59] Moreover, what would have made the information disseminated from a national library different from that found in the expanding marketplace of periodicals and cheap books was its prospective social and political utility. While noting dramatically increased access to information among ordinary Americans in the 1840s and 1850s, Brown also points out that "the new communications environment in which all were encouraged to participate created a kind of information competition in which people of education, wealth, and social rank enjoyed distinct advantages."[60] The kinds of information available in periodicals, bookstores, and circulating libraries did not represent the scholarly depth, intellectual richness, or social cachet that were present in the volumes on law, politics, and history shelved in the Library of Congress, where Pearce kept a close watch over both access and acquisitions. In other words, the proposed national library would have represented a distinct (if limited) leveling of the playing field in the competitive information environment of midcentury Washington.

Would the southern aristocrat Pearce have looked favorably at the notion of tens of thousands of citizens, including the "poorest and humblest" whom Marsh had sketched, gaining access to books that had in his lifetime been the more exclusive possessions of their social betters? The jealous guardianship he exercised over borrowing privileges at the Library of Congress indicates otherwise. As a member of the southern gentry, Pearce held a vested interest in preserving the advantages that social rank gave him. Perhaps Pearce argued so inconsistently and vehemently against a national library in 1854 because he recognized and deplored, on some level, what had not yet become entirely clear to him in 1845: the egalitarian tendencies of a rapidly expanding culture of information. The goal of bringing a wide range of popular and scholarly books to all classes of readers as voiced by national library proponents would have struck Pearce as symbolizing a very different relationship between knowledge and power than was generally endorsed by the southern slaveholding aristocracy. His 1854 special committee report, therefore, might reflect an uneasiness with the blurring of social distinctions implicit in the expanding midcentury culture of letters, a sentiment which he obviously would have found it impolitic to express but which nonetheless could have played a role in his decision.

Consequences and Significance of the Smithsonian Debate

After the dismissal of Jewett, Choate sent a letter to the Senate in January 1855 tendering his resignation from the Board of Regents and suggesting that it had violated the law by repealing the compromise resolutions. The letter, which aroused the ire of fellow regent Senator Pearce, prompted both houses of Congress to appoint committees to look into the affair and contributed to the air of controversy surrounding Jewett's dismissal. Major literary periodicals, including the *North American Review*, the *Christian Examiner, Putnam's Monthly*, and the *Southern Literary Messenger*, weighed in with their respective opinions on the Board of Regent's performance in managing the Smithsonian.[61] Not surprisingly, the *North American Review* was strongly critical of the actions of the Board of Regents and especially of Pearce's report. Had the Regents been faithful to the law and expended twenty-five thousand dollars annually on books, C. Hale argued, "there would be at Washington a magnificent library containing two hundred thousand volumes." He charged the board with mismanagement of the funds in allowing only a "niggardly appropriation" for books during the preceding eight years. He considered the question of whether a library accomplishes the tasks of increase and diffusion of knowledge a point "sufficiently clear" as not even to warrant argument.[62] In the *Christian Examiner*, W. H. Hurlbut was less charitable on this point, mocking Pearce's statement about the hiving of knowledge in a national library. He wrote: "And if it be true of libraries, that their magnetic influence can only cover the spot where they are located, we shall have to adopt a system of literary *ambulances*. The Boston Athenaeum and Gore Hall must be set on wheels, and conducted by nomadic scribes through the length and breadth of the land." In a less playful vein, he accused the Board of Regents of both "gross dereliction of duty" and "violations of law."[63]

Other periodicals defended Pearce. In *Putnam's Monthly*, T. M. Brewer exonerated the Board of Regents, taking the position that because Smithson had been a chemist, he probably would have favored the original scientific research that Henry promoted rather than a library. Brewer quickly articulated, however, his desire that the federal government should establish with funds from its "overflowing treasury . . . a great national library at Washington, worthy an educated and enlightened nation."[64] The writer in the *Southern Literary Messenger* voiced the strongest opinion in favor of Pearce, agreeing with him that a library "provides no direct instrumentality for increasing knowledge in the sense of the will, or for diffusing it in any sense at all." He also quoted an article on libraries from the *Edinburgh Review* of November 1820, in which it was argued that the great value of libraries had been somewhat mitigated by the invention of the printing press, which ensured both the diffusion and the preservation (through multiplied copies) of knowledge. But as in *Putnam's*, this writer expressed a hope that one day Congress would "find it within the scope of its constitutional powers and obligations to provide, as Mr. Choate says, that 'the soul of this country may eat as good food and as much of it as the soul of Europe.'"[65] Even the writer most strongly in favor of Pearce's position (who was perhaps prompted in some degree by sectional rivalry to defend the honor of a southerner against attacks by New England intellectuals) agreed with Choate that a national library funded at government expense was a desirable goal for the Republic. Interestingly, none of these authors mentioned the Library of Congress as a fit institution to assume this role. But the Library was in the process of recovering from a disastrous fire, and with Pearce at the helm these authors must have entertained little hope that it would realize their ambitions for a national library in the foreseeable future.

Previous scholars have offered varying assessments of the significance of the entire Smithsonian affair, from the debates in the 1840s through the dismissal of Jewett. Jean Matthews astutely points out that the controversy encapsulated a growing rift between traditional humanist scholars and researchers in the hard sciences. Scientists thought of knowledge in terms of scientific method and proving or disproving hypotheses to produce new truths and therefore valued books that could serve as "a compact working library of current works." In contrast, the traditional scholars, many of them historians, were "hoarders, to whom anything and everything might be valuable, however slight its intrinsic worth."[66] The disagreement over the efficacy of copyright deposit illustrates this conflict perfectly. Henry looked with disdain on the "light" literature pushing the volumes of scientific transactions off the shelves, whereas Jewett wanted to collect everything printed in America for the benefit of future bibliographers and historians. Matthews concludes that this was a debate the humanists were bound to lose, not only because the image of the research scientist was more vigorous, active, and masculine than that of the timid, passive scholar "encumbered by musty books," but also because the scientists somewhat cynically resorted to utilitarian arguments about the mechanical applications of pure research to bolster their case, a mode of argument that clearly had an impact on Pearce.[67]

Agreeing with Matthews in regard to the national interest in science that the debate uncovered, Nancy Gwinn adds that the Smithsonian conflict "showed clearly the depth of cultural nationalism in the new democracy."[68] Choate had skillfully capitalized on national feelings of cultural inferiority in the speech that won the Senate over to the idea of a national library in 1845. Supporters of a national library based their arguments on the idea that the nation's pride in its cultural achievement was at stake in the debate. On the other hand, the fate of the Smithsonian library plan also shows that the effects of cultural nationalism ran up against limits imposed by political realities. Given repeated calls for a renewed commitment to a national literature and a link between library resources and literary nationalism made explicit in the national press, it would seem that the intellectual currents of the day strongly supported the establishment of a national library. But the course of events re-created here suggests that other influences, such as the unforeseen effects of a

copyright law, a rift between the period's humanist and scientific communities, an intensifying politicization of literary discourse, and the pull
of personal friendship might have weighed more heavily than nationalist
sentiments on decisions affecting the growth of cultural institutions in
the country. All the librarians and journalists who lobbied for expanded
library resources as a necessary precursor to the development of a viable
national literature, despite their sincerity and zeal, simply could not
overcome the political will of a single powerful, conservative senator who
occupied key positions at both the Library of Congress and the Smithsonian Institution. In his measures checking the growth of the Library
of Congress and in his authorship of the report that signaled the defeat
of the library plan at the Smithsonian, Pearce arguably had as much
influence over U.S. library history as many better-known figures who, in
a spirit of cultural nationalism, acted for rather than against the expansion
of public library resources.

Developments at the Library in the 1850s

Certainly one of the most important events to occur at the Library of
Congress during the period under discussion was the catastrophic fire of
24 December 1851. Upon investigation, the architect of the Capitol,
Thomas U. Walter, determined that a chimney had caught on fire. From
there the fire was communicated to the timbers of the library wall. In
other words, the design of the building was at fault, and Walter believed
that "no human forethought or vigilance could, under the circumstances,
have prevented the catastrophe," which destroyed 35,000 of the Library's
55,000 volumes.[69] Within just over a year, and apparently with little
debate, Congress had appropriated $93,000 for a new library room and
$85,000 for books.[70] In light of the ongoing debate over the future of the
Smithsonian Library, the destruction of the Library of Congress offered
legislators an opportunity to clarify its function and reconsider the character of its holdings. A correspondent to the *National Intelligencer*, whom
Johnston conjectures must have been Jewett, tried to initiate such a
reevaluation. On 8 April 1852 he wrote that "the new library should be a
systematic collection of books, chosen with competent bibliographical
learning for a specific and well-defined purpose." The correspondent
clarified that purpose in an article that appeared on 14 April: "It is
intended for use; principally for the use of Congress during their sessions
. . . and incidentally for the use of the public." A national library, on the

other hand, would be "accessible to all students" and would "*aim* at possessing every book." The author proposed the Smithsonian Institution as the suitable site for the much-needed national library.

Ultimately, however, Congress neglected this opportunity to clarify the purpose of the Library of Congress and essentially returned to business as usual. When it was suggested that the Library appoint a book agent to help make purchasing decisions after the fire, Meehan wrote to Pearce, "I am sorry to see that the project of an agent to select and purchase books for us is again revived. It will not meet with favor in Congress, I think. . . . [Members of Congress] have no idea of placing Congress in a position which admits that they cannot select the books they need." Pearce's Joint Committee on the Library flirted briefly with a suggestion that it systematize the collections when it resolved on 18 August 1852 "that it is expedient to procure complete lists of books in the various chapters included in the catalogue of the Library; and that the chairman be instructed to address scientific and literary gentlemen on the subject." For some reason Pearce failed to undertake this duty, however, and on 3 March 1853 the committee resolved instead "that for the purpose of collecting a Library for the Congress of the United States, on the most complete and systematic plan, the Librarian be requested to prepare as soon as may be, catalogues of books according to chapters . . . under their respective heads and according to the language in which they are written." Johnston sums up the wisdom of this resolution, remarking that "it was unfortunate that the selection should be made by one man, and that one a person of very limited bibliographical experience." Meehan was not up to the task and simply relied on the old catalog in compiling the Library's want list. A correspondent of the *New York Daily Tribune* signing himself "F. S." criticized the Joint Committee in May 1852, arguing that "what has already been done toward replenishing the empty shelves of the Congressional Library, has been directed rather by booksellers, eager for lucre, than by a bibliograph, or bibliophile, or any systematic intellect whatever."[71]

The chance to revisit the question of booksellers for the Library was also passed over in the years immediately following the fire. Johnston writes that "no one seems to have suggested that it would be well to advertise for bids for supplying the losses of the Library, and that the catalogues of the old Library be placed in the hands of American and European booksellers." A single resolution along these lines was offered in March 1853, apparently by Library Committee member and educational reformer Horace Mann. Of the catalogs that Meehan was supposed to compile, the resolution stated, "that when said catalogues shall be prepared, all persons who wish to supply the books so designated, may take a copy thereof and propose terms for furnishing the same; and those persons who, all things equal, shall propose to furnish the books on terms most economical to the government, shall have the contracts awarded to them."[72]

An interesting pair of letters reveals just how far Pearce and Meehan would go to avoid any change in their accustomed mode of doing business. Meehan wrote to Pearce in May 1853 to reassure him that, despite Mann's resolution, he believed that full authority for purchases still rested in Pearce's hands: "Mr. Mann's resolution creates some difficulties, and I believe that it offers not a single advantage over the mode we were pursuing to restore the Library to the elevation it had attained at the time of the fire. . . . I think, however, that it was not Mr. Mann's intention to transfer the direction of the purchases of books from the Chairman of the Committee, and invest the power in the Librarian." Pearce evidently directed Meehan to attempt to circumvent the resolution by writing to Lewis Cass of Michigan, who would join the Joint Library Committee at the start of the Thirty-third Congress in January 1854, when Mann would no longer be a member. Meehan told Cass that "we had to regret that a resolution, passed by the committee, at the last day of its existence, was preventing necessary and indispensable additions of books. He [Pearce] wrote to you, yesterday, and gave you the information more particularly. I hope you will concur with him in the opinions he advanced in his letter, and enable him to order books from our very competent, trustworthy, and obliging agents, who have stood the tests of fidelity for many years, without any failure."[73] In this way, Pearce and Meehan contrived to transact most of their business with *Rich Brothers* of London, ignoring Mann's resolution rather than institute any more complicated (but potentially more economical) scheme. Meehan's letter to Pearce is also interesting for its clear statement that all Pearce wished to accomplish in the way of book purchases after the fire was to restore the Library of Congress to its earlier level of holdings. Meehan informed Rich Brothers on 28 February 1856 that "the orders for the Library will be more limited in future, for some time, than they have been hitherto since the fire. But they will be as liberal as they ever were before our unfortunate accident. Our new Library already outnumbers the old one more than one thousand volumes, and our shelves are now once more overflowing." Meehan congratulated Pearce in 1856 for having purchased thirty-six thousand books in a few years, replacing thirty-five thousand that were lost. He wrote that "we have not replaced every book that was lost . . . but we have been very successful in all our efforts to regain valuable works hitherto ordered to be purchased."[74] Pearce succeeded admirably in re-stocking the Library of Congress in a period of four years after the disastrous fire, but his ambitions for the Library stopped there. Appropriations for books returned to the level of five thousand dollars per year and stayed there through the end of the Civil War.

After the debate over the Smithsonian and recovery from the fire of 1851, Pearce presided over a Library whose functions continued to be curtailed. Two developments of the late 1850s that occurred during his chairmanship of the Joint Committee are further evidence of his conservative vision of the Library's sphere. The first involved distribution and exchange of public documents. For decades, the Library had retained responsibility for collecting the publications of Congress and distributing them not only to members but also to institutions within the states. A statute of 1828 directed that various official publications be sent "to the public library of the legislature of each state in the Union, and one copy each to such universities and colleges as may not already have received them, and one copy to one incorporated Atheneum in each state." And the Library had been integral to Alexandre Vattemare's ambitious international exchange program. But a law of 1857 took both these duties away from the Library. Distribution of congressional publications was transferred to the Department of the Interior, and exchange of documents with foreign countries was now to be handled by the Department of State.[75] This law meant that the Library would no longer receive the materials it sometimes acquired in exchange for its public documents and further reduced the extent to which the Library reached beyond Washington to interact with other American institutions.

The second development came in 1859 with the repeal of the copyright deposit provision of the 1846 act that had established the Smithsonian. At Secretary Henry's behest, and undoubtedly with Pearce's consent, copyright activities were consolidated at the Patent Office, which also received the twelve-thousand-volume copyright library from the Department of State, which had received deposits from 1790 to 1846. John Cole describes the new arrangement as a "severe setback" to the idea of deposit for use, a concept not to be resurrected until 1865, when Pearce and Meehan had both left the scene and Ainsworth Rand Spofford had taken over as Librarian of Congress.[76] Copyright deposits had never been the boon to collection development that Charles Coffin Jewett had envisioned, but their withdrawal from the Library of Congress nonetheless meant that it would have to rely entirely on its annual appropriation for book purchases and therefore give up any pretensions toward comprehensiveness in its collections.

Pearce, then, was chairman of the Joint Library Committee at a time when the Library's functions were pared down so that in 1859, at least in terms of functions, the Library much more closely resembled that which George Watterston had presided over in 1815 than the one that Spofford began to create after the Civil War. Jewett's vision of a national library in Washington that boasted massive collections given over to scholarly inquiry, thousands of visitors annually, and a leadership role in the American library community was moribund, as the Smithsonian devoted itself to scientific research and Pearce streamlined the Library of Congress to its statutory function as a legislative library and little else. Most striking is the way these final two developments of the antebellum era removed the Library of Congress from the public eye. Copyright deposit had ensured that authors and publishers were aware of the Library as a repository for the nation's literary output—at least those who complied with the weak copyright law. Exchange of public documents had given the Library domestic and international visibility, encouraging librarians throughout the nation to see it as a resource and possibly a symbol of the nation's cultural life. Removal of these functions meant that these constituencies no longer had any reason for the Library of Congress to enter their consciousness at all.

Expansion of Libraries and Publishing in the Antebellum Era
That the Boston Public Library opened with an intention of reaching the city's poor residents in the same year that Pearce's special committee report denied that a large public library could accomplish diffusion of knowledge illustrates how the federal government largely ignored the democratization of American print culture that characterized the middle decades of the nineteenth century. In January 1848 the state of Massachusetts passed legislation authorizing the city of Boston to establish and

maintain a public library, a statute that Jesse Shera notes was "the first official recognition by a state governing body of the principle of municipal library support."[77] The prime movers of the Boston Public Library, most notably Boston Brahmin George Ticknor, intended it to serve simultaneously the light reading demands of the common citizens of Boston as well as the researches of more serious scholars, in particular those who had been impeded in their inquiries by financial inability to purchase the books they required. In other words, it was to function similarly to the national public library that Marsh and Jewett had envisioned, combining the qualities of democratic access with a collection of books worthy of scholarly research (with the important added benefit that the Boston Public Library circulated its books). In the arguments urged in favor of the Boston library, books were no longer the enemies of republicanism but rather upheld its principles through their ability to diffuse knowledge and inculcate public morality. Ticknor saw a free public library as "the crowning glory of our public schools" and wrote in the report of the trustees of the library that "it is of paramount importance that the means of general information should be so diffused that the largest possible number of persons should be induced to read and understand questions going down to the very foundations of the social order."[78] Ticknor took it for granted in 1852 that a public library was consistent with the goal of diffusion, making Pearce's opinion that a Smithsonian library would necessarily have constituted the hiving of knowledge seem strangely anachronistic.

The proponents of a free public library in Boston also believed that books ameliorated civic virtue by diverting the lower orders from more destructive or subversive pursuits, an argument that had also been raised in support of mechanics' libraries earlier in the century. A report submitted in 1852 by the Joint Standing Committee of the Public Library reminded Massachusetts legislators that "we educate, to restrain from vice, as much as to inculcate sentiments of virtue; we educate, to enable men to resist the temptations of evil, as well as to encourage and strengthen the incentives to good."[79] This view of libraries was advanced in reference to the Library of Congress in a plea voiced in the *National Intelligencer* for an extension of the Library's hours. Writing of the Library of Congress and the Smithsonian, a government clerk with a taste for scholarly pursuits said that "for all purposes of practical benefit to me and those similarly circumstanced, these libraries might as well be at the antipodes of the city. . . . The libraries are open during our hours of business, and closed at all other hours." He went on to mention that "books and the society of cultivated men would go far to preserve [young government clerks] from the follies and vices of city life."[80]

These sentiments mark a transformation in the American perception of large, publicly funded book collections. In the early Republic, extravagant government libraries were seen as a potential threat to republican simplicity. Though this argument was raised by some in the Smithsonian library debate, libraries by the 1840s and 1850s were just as likely to be seen as propagators of middle-class values and defenders of the social order. This remarkable change was no doubt related to the development of the American publishing industry during the same period. The extraordinary growth of periodical publishing at midcentury, for example, contributed to the atmosphere of rapidly expanding access to information documented by Brown. From the penny press era of the 1830s there emerged in subsequent decades a "new generation of penny papers," including the *New York Tribune* (first published in 1841) and the *New York Times* (1851), with circulation figures in the tens of thousands. The number of magazines published in the United States rose from an estimated 100 in 1825 to 600 in 1850, with the start-up of such notable general-interest magazines as *Harper's* in 1850 and the *Atlantic Monthly* in 1857. Frank Leslie's *Illustrated Newspaper* (considered a magazine, title notwithstanding) started publication in 1855 and within a few years boasted a circulation of 164,000, a figure that would have been simply astounding merely a generation before. In short, the American public was confronted with a proliferation of printed information that changed the relationship between the common citizen and the printed word.[81]

Book publishing experienced a similar expansion, probably contributing even more directly to the changing view of libraries in the country. When expensive books had been mostly imported from Europe and possessed by the affluent classes in the eighteenth and early nineteenth centuries, they were more easily associated with wealth and aristocratic vice. By the middle of the nineteenth century, the connection was much more difficult to make. According to an often quoted estimate, the American publishing industry had grown from a 2.5-million- to a 12.5-million-dollar industry between 1820 and 1850. Moreover, literary publishers of the 1840s had begun to elide the distinction between the culture of books and the presumably more diffusive and more republican culture of periodicals by issuing the first American paperback books. Among the most notable of these were the "supplements" or "extras" (produced on steam presses, sometimes in editions of tens of thousands), reprints of entire novels sent through the mail masquerading as newspapers to evade high postal rates. Of this first paperback revolution in American publishing, John Tebbel notes that "cheap books appeared in profusion from many publishers, some in cloth, others softbound, most selling for less than a dollar" between 1845 and 1857.[82]

This expansion of publishing was linked with rising literacy rates, changes in the technology of printing, and improvements in book distribution via canals and railroads, all of which lowered the prices of books and consequently expanded the size of the purchasing public. Ronald Zboray cautions against a naïve understanding of the impact of technology on reading in America, contending that "innovations in printing technology by no means caused such a drop in the price of books as to make them widely available."[83] Keeping in mind Zboray's corrective, it nonetheless seems a plausible argument that in comparison with the early decades of the nineteenth century, books became inexpensive and plentiful enough at least to members of the middle class to make arguments about luxury largely invalid, thereby eroding some of the resistance to libraries in the public consciousness. This change in the relationship between Americans and their books explains in part why the library plan got as far as it did.

The dominant figure in Library of Congress history in the years leading up to the Civil War was Maryland senator James Alfred Pearce. Pearce held to a narrow view of the Library's mission, believing that the Library could not adequately fulfill its responsibility to Congress if it were also pressed into service as a national library. Pearce presided over a quick reconstruction of the Library rooms and restocking of the shelves after the fire of 1851. But he opposed any broadening of the Library's collections or services. Given his views about the limited public function of government libraries, Pearce's simultaneous chairmanship of the Joint Committee on the Library and membership on the Board of Regents of the Smithsonian Institution ensured that a national library collected under the auspices of the federal government would not become a reality until after he left the Senate—Pearce died in office in 1862.

Indeed, Library of Congress history in this period cannot be fully understood without close attention to the early history of the Smithsonian Institution. Collection development decisions were influenced by ongoing debate over the disposition of James Smithson's bequest. Discussion of the mission of the Smithsonian reprised long-standing American debates about the role of the federal government in supporting cultural institutions, while introducing new elements such as the conflict between scientific research and humanist scholarship, personified at the Smithsonian by the figures of physicist Joseph Henry and librarian Charles Coffin Jewett. These factors surfaced in Pearce's 1854 special committee report of the Board of Regents, which killed the library plan and authorized Henry's dismissal of Jewett. The report also reflected Pearce's conservative response to the increasingly democratized and politicized nature of American literary culture at midcentury.

It might have seemed to some observers that developments in the print culture of the time ushered in a new and more favorable climate for the creation of a national library. Books became more familiar and plentiful objects in American homes, making their connection with an unwholesome luxury much harder to defend. The successful campaign for the Boston Public Library showed that new ideas were emerging about the propriety of the government providing resources for scholars and general readers, and the temporary success of the library plan for the Smithsonian Institution bore witness to these changes. But changes in the relationship between Americans and books encroached slowly on the political culture of Washington, where ideological resistance to federal support of cultural institutions was a venerable tradition. Since the founding of the Library, the federal government had consistently maintained that it bore little or no responsibility for the promotion of American letters. Immediate utility was the justification that Congress most readily recognized when it came to collecting books, though it also provided for the recreational reading needs of members and their families. These were the purposes that the Library served throughout the 1840s and 1850s.

CHAPTER SIX

Congressmen Use Their Library, 1840–1859

Because James Alfred Pearce and his colleagues in Congress elected not to turn the Library of Congress into a national library in the 1840s and 1850s, the institution's main users continued to be not scholars or the public but the congressmen and government officials for whom it had been founded, as well as their family members and friends. Politically, congressional concerns in the 1840s and 1850s centered largely around the issue of territorial expansion as the United States pursued an imperialist vision embodied in the phrase "manifest destiny." Not surprisingly, their Library came to reflect this and other political issues of the era as congressmen assembled books that could help them in their day-to-day business. Recreationally, the Library of Congress continued to serve, as it had for decades, as an art gallery, social space, and a source of the day's popular literature. These facets of the Library are revealed in the acquisitions decisions of the Joint Committee on the Library as well as in the architecture of the Library, particularly the rooms constructed after the fire of 1851. The uses made of the Library by its primary constituents in the 1840s and 1850s is the subject of this final chapter on antebellum Library of Congress history.

Acquisition of Useful Knowledge in the 1840s and 1850s

The year 1849 marked the publication of a new catalog of the Library of Congress, which shows that a handful of core subjects useful to Congress continued to occupy the attention of the Joint Committee on the Library. In the decade since publication of the last full catalog, the Library had grown considerably, from thirty thousand to forty-five thousand volumes.[1] Despite this growth, the distribution of titles in various subject areas remained relatively constant. The leading subject areas in 1839—geography, politics (a chapter that included economics as well), history, and law—continued to dominate holdings a decade later, representing 58 percent of the collection. Geography (14.9 percent of collections) and politics (11.2 percent) were still the largest and second largest single chapters in the catalog; the important areas of history (17.9 percent) and law (14.4 percent) were each spread over multiple catalog chapters. Science and technology (a categorization that embraces some fourteen catalog chapters) accounted for 17.5 percent of the collection in 1849, whereas it had been around 15 percent in 1839. Collections in imaginative literature made up close to 7 percent of the 1849 catalog (a slight decline from 1839); religion, 4.5 percent (slightly less than in 1839); and fine arts, 2.7 percent (same as 1839); other areas, including philosophy, criticism, belles lettres aside from imaginative literature, and books with multiple subjects, rounded out the remaining 10 percent of the catalog. Table 2 in the appendix provides a breakdown of major subject classes in the 1849 Library of Congress catalog as a percentage of the entire catalog.

Examples of some individual purchasing decisions made by the Joint Committee on the Library will serve to give an idea of the kinds of books on law, politics, history, and economics that the Library acquired in the 1840s and 1850s.[2] Books on international law had been in demand at the Library since it was founded. In 1845 the Library Committee ordered five copies of Henry Wheaton's *History of the Law of Nations in Europe and America* (1845). In 1858 the committee ordered three copies of Joseph Chitty's recent edition of Vattel's *Law of Nations* (1855) and three copies of the sixth edition of Wheaton's *Elements of International Law* (1855). On American law, Jonathan Elliot's *Debates on the Adoption of the Federal Constitution* (1845) was ordered in 1845. The committee ordered Jonathan French's 1857 compilation *Constitutions of the States and United States* (three copies) and Luther Stearns Cushing's *Lex Parliamentaria Americana* (1856) in 1858.[3]

Some of the accessions in catalog chapter 24, "Politics," were simply records of Congress's own debates, which the Joint Committee was continually working to complete. In 1840 the committee ordered the Librarian to complete four sets of Gales and Seaton's *Debates in Congress* and the *Congressional Globe*, and in 1846 it authorized purchase of the thirty-one-volume edition of Gales and Seaton's *Debates*.[4] In an era when the question of tariffs was an ongoing point of ideological contention, books on economics were frequently consulted. These books were also included in chapter 24, which accounts in part for the size of this chapter. Early in the 1840s the Library Committee voted to purchase Samuel Hazard's *United States Commercial and Statistical Register*, a periodical that the committee kept current in subsequent years. In a single purchase order of 1842, the committee listed Charles Pope's *Yearly Journal of Trade, Comprising Law of Nations, Laws of Customs and Excise*, a new edition of Adam Smith's *Wealth of Nations*, and Georg Thomas Flügel and Francis J. Grund's *Merchant's Assistant, or, Mercantile Instructer* [sic]. In 1846 the committee ordered George Tucker's *Progress of the United States in Population and Wealth* (1843). Many of these works were no doubt consulted by congressmen as they took their positions on the Walker tariff reduction that passed in 1846.[5]

Political memoirs and campaign biographies also fell under the purview of the Joint Committee. Shortly after William Henry Harrison was nominated as the Whig presidential candidate in 1840, the committee ordered S. J. Burr's *Life of William Henry Harrison* (1840) and a history of the War of 1812 (Harrison was a war hero from his victory in the Battle of Tippecanoe). In 1846 the committee ordered Calvin Colton's campaign biography *The Life and Times of Henry Clay* (1843). Retired for the time from the Senate but still a widely admired figure on the national political scene, Clay was preparing in 1846 to run for the presidency in 1848. And shortly after it was published, the Library purchased three copies of the first volume of Thomas Hart Benton's political autobiography, *Thirty Years View* (two volumes, 1854, 1856), which detailed his long career in the Senate.[6] Though these were books with obvious political implications, they were classed under history in the 1861 catalog.

American history had always been a subject cultivated by successive

Joint Committees on the Library. Standard works of history such as Jared Sparks's twenty-five volume *Library of American Biography* and works by George Bancroft and William Prescott were acquired in the 1840s, along with some older materials, such as volumes of pamphlets related to the War of 1812. In June 1846 the committee ordered John Warner Barber's editions of the state historical collections of New York, New Jersey, Massachusetts, Connecticut, and New Hampshire. Later that year the committee ordered a copy of the *Journal of the New York Colonial Legislature, from the Years 1691 to 1765.*[7] When Obadiah Rich, the Library's London bookseller for many years, offered to sell Congress his valuable collection of books relating to America, the committee showed marked interest. Meehan wrote to Rich in 1845 that the committee wanted the books but had been unable to pass a separate appropriation, which it felt was necessary to complete the purchase.[8] The offer appears to have been put on hold in the late 1840s, perhaps pending the outcome of the Smithsonian debate, and the fire of 1851 made other purchases more immediately necessary. For the most part, the committee chose not to acquire historical manuscripts, though they were frequently offered by booksellers. Congress in 1850 extensively debated purchase of the manuscript of George Washington's farewell address to the nation. Joint Library Committee chairman Pearce came out against the purchase, opining that "the Library Committee do not think that they are authorized to purchase manuscripts which are valuable as relics merely."[9] With a few significant exceptions, the principle of utility continued to guide the Joint Committee's decisions.

In an age of revolutionary technological advances, the Joint Committee on the Library purchased books and periodicals to help members of Congress keep abreast of the latest developments. In 1840 the committee ordered Henry Schenck Tanner's *Map of the Canals and Railroads of the United States* (1840), and in a single purchase order of 1846 it listed Alfred Vail's *Description of the American Electro Magnetic Telegraph Now in Operation between the Cities of Washington and Baltimore* (1845; the link had been established a year earlier), the *Telegraphic Dictionary and Seaman's Signal Book*, the *Railroad Journal*, and the *Mechanics' Journal.*[10] Despite these and other purchases, the quality of the science and technology collections at the Library can be inferred from a comment by James D. Dana, a scientist from the United States exploring expedition, when he was told in 1846 that he would have to live in Washington while preparing his report: "It is perfectly absurd that I should be able to prepare my reports in a city where there are no books!"[11]

Some of the most interesting accessions of the period are books that were clearly needed for information on unfolding historical events. For example, the United States was beginning to pursue more extensive trade relations with Asia in the late 1840s. Caleb Cushing completed a trade agreement in 1844, the Treaty of Wanghia, which secured important trade privileges for the United States with China. In 1849, in response to this developing relationship, the Joint Committee ordered that "a copy of the *Chinese Repository*, in fourteen volumes (1833 to 1846), be purchased from Dr. J. C. Hepburn, of New York, at the price of sixty dollars."[12] This was a periodical edited by missionaries Elijah Coleman Bridgman and Samuel Wells Williams and provided some of the most up-to-date information about the region that Congress could acquire. Similarly, the United States was attempting to open trade relations with Japan through the diplomacy of Commodore Perry in the early 1850s. Meehan wrote to Pearce in 1852 that "we have now, in the Library several of the most recent works on Japan—and others, of old date, have been placed on our orders."[13] Meehan probably had in mind titles such as *Japan and the Japanese in the Nineteenth Century* (1852) and Charles MacFarlane's *Japan: An Account, Geographical and Historical* (1852), which were cataloged by 1861.

The most exciting developments in foreign affairs in this era were the European revolutions of 1848, which inspired a number of purchases by the Library Committee. In 1850 the committee ordered Meehan to "purchase, immediately, or order from abroad, or at home, all the works of any reputation touching the modern history, present condition, and prospects of Hungary and Germany." In response, Meehan sent Rich Brothers of London a list of some fifteen titles wanted for the Library, including Frederic Shoberl's *Scenes of the Civil War in Hungary, in 1848 and 1849* (1850); *Review of the French Revolution of 1848* by Frederick Chamier of the United States Navy (1849); John Paget's *Hungary and Transylvania* (1850); and *Austria in 1848 and 1849* (1850) by Franz Xaver Pillersdorf. Meehan asked the booksellers to send the volumes "by the first opportunity, in a mail steamer."[14]

Obviously, one of the most controversial domestic political issues of the 1840s and 1850s was slavery. The Library was stocked with books arguing both sides of the question, some purchased and some obtained by other means. On 11 March 1842 the Joint Committee ordered the *Proceedings of the Anti-Slavery Convention* held in London in June 1840. Interestingly, this order was made with William C. Preston of South Carolina chairing the committee. Other works on slavery received by the Library in this period came from a lobbying effort on the part of the Quakers of England. In 1846, Isaiah Forster, George Stacey, and William Foster of the Society of Friends presented the Library with copies of John Candler's *Brief Notices of Hayti* (1842); *A Brief View of Slavery and the Slave Trade in British India* (1842); *Testimony of the Society of Friends against Slavery and the Slave Trade*; several annual reports of the British and Foreign Anti-Slavery Society; and the *Proceedings of the General Anti-Slavery Convention* held in London in 1843.[15]

By 1861, according to the new catalog of that year, chapter 16, "Ethics," included fifty-seven books and several volumes of pamphlets on slavery.[16] A minority of the books were actually purchased by decisions of the Joint Committee: four were donated, nineteen arrived through copyright deposits, four came from international exchanges, and six had been inherited from Jefferson's library. Many of the books were arguments against slavery, including the proceedings of various antislavery societies and Hinton Helper's *Impending Crisis of the South* (1857), a controversial work written by a southerner opposed to slavery which was a copyright deposit. The Library also held the works of southern apologists, including George Fitzhugh's *Sociology for the South* (1854), Frederick A. Ross's *Slavery Ordained by God* (1857), and George S. Sawyer's *Southern Institutes* (1858); these three works also were copyright deposits. Considering that Pearce reportedly tried to exclude from the Library material that would inflame sectional prejudice, it is not surprising that only six of the fifty-seven books on slavery in the 1861 catalog were actually purchased while Pearce chaired the committee: Wilson Armstead, *Tribute for the Negro* (1848); *Brief Notice of American Slavery, and the Abolition Movement* (1846); William Chambers, *American Slavery and Colour* (1857); Marshall Hall, *Two-Fold Slavery of the United States; With a Project of Self-Emancipation* (1854); Sir William Gore Ouseley, *Notes on the Slave-Trade* (1850); and *Pro-Slavery Argument; As Maintained by the Most Distinguished Writers of the Southern States* (1852).

The Library and Manifest Destiny

A look at the geography chapters of the 1839 and 1849 catalogs, along with other documents, shows how the Library of Congress became a site where the expansionist impulses of politicians and settlers were registered in the concrete forms of books and maps about the West. During the intervening decade, the United States acquired Texas, the Oregon Territory, and a large chunk of northern Mexico, including present-day California, Nevada, Utah, Arizona, and parts of Colorado and New Mexico, extending the boundaries of the Republic to the Pacific. Meanwhile the Library was making acquisitions as well. Sections 5, "America," and 6, "Maps," from catalog chapter 39, "Geography," grew significantly during this decade, from 616 titles and 51 maps in 1839 to 851 titles and 80 maps in 1849, with the most notable acquisitions related to places where the United States had territorial interests or ambitions.

In 1839, for instance, the United States had been eyeing the Mexican province turned independent republic of Texas for decades. But the geography chapter of the Library of Congress catalog of that year had only three titles: Mary A. Holley's *Texas: Observations, Historical, Geographical, and Descriptive* (1833); Chester Newell's *History of the Revolution in Texas* (1838); and *Visit to Texas* (1836). By 1849, the United States had annexed Texas (in 1845), and the Library had tripled its holdings on the geography of the area with six more-recent titles: Henry Stuart Foote, *Texas and the Texans; or, Advance of the Anglo-Americans to the South West* (1844); Mathilde Charlotte Houston, *Texas and the Gulf of Mexico; or, Yachting in the New World* (1844); George W. Kendall, *Narrative of the Texan Santa Fe Expedition* (1844); William Kennedy, *Texas: Its Geography, Natural History, and Topography* (1844); Francis Moore, *Description of Texas* (1844); and F. B. Page, *Prairiedom: Rambles and Scrambles in Texas* (1845). The Library by 1849 also held a State Department–sponsored map of Texas published in 1844 and recent maps of the United States integrating the annexed territory.[17]

An initial Texas annexation treaty had been submitted to the Senate by Secretary of State John Calhoun and defeated in April 1844, but Congress voted in favor of annexation in February 1845 and Texas was admitted as a state in December. There is little doubt that some of the titles listed above and others relevant to Texas were consulted by members of Congress during annexation debates. Extant in the Library of

Congress Archives is an invoice book covering the years 1841–62 which documents to the day when many books were shipped by booksellers or received by the Library. According to the invoice record, a copy of Kennedy's book on Texas geography and Moore's *Description of Texas* were received from Washington bookseller Franck Taylor in May 1844. Nicholas Doran Maillard's *History of the Republic of Texas* (1842) and David Urquhart's *Annexation of the Texas: A Case of War between England and the United States* (1844) were shipped by Obadiah Rich in September 1844. In ordering books, the Joint Library Committee anticipated the needs of Congress so that members would have access to pertinent material about Texas in time to respond to developing political events.[18]

A process of territorial acquisition reflected and encouraged by Library of Congress acquisitions emerges with greater clarity in the case of Oregon. In 1836, as American missionaries and settlers began to migrate in increasing numbers to this territory occupied jointly by the United States and Great Britain since 1818, President Jackson sent William A. Slacum to investigate. Slacum reported favorably to Congress in December 1837, and efforts began in earnest to acquire Oregon from Great Britain. The 1839 catalog indicates that Congress had seven books about the area, two derived from the Lewis and Clark expedition and five published in the 1830s: Ross Cox, *Adventures on the Columbia River* (1831); Timothy Flint, *The Far West; or a Tour beyond the Mountains* (1831); Washington Irving, *Astoria* (1836) and *The Rocky Mountains*, now popularly known as *The Adventures of Captain Bonneville, U.S.A.* (1837); and Samuel Parker, *Journal of an Exploring Tour beyond the Rocky Mountains* (1838).

Irving's works were probably the best-known books on Oregon and can be considered representative of expansionist sentiment in America. *Astoria* was the history of John Jacob Astor's attempt in the decade following 1810 to establish a fur-trading empire headquartered on the Columbia River. *The Rocky Mountains* detailed the adventures of Captain Bonneville, a member of the United States Army who took a leave of absence to pursue his own commercial interest and the territorial interests of the United States through an exploration of the area west of the Rockies in 1832–33. While these books were written with literary rather than political intent, they both argued more or less explicitly that acquisition of Oregon was in the national interest. Irving had written in *The Rocky Mountains* that American traders would not be able to establish themselves in the area "until the question of territorial right is adjusted between the two countries. The sooner that takes place, the better." He also pointed out that "the great valleys of the lower country . . . are calculated to give sustenance to countless flocks and herds, and to sustain a great population of graziers and agriculturists."[19] By their mere popularity, these books piqued the interest of Americans in Oregon. And the interesting choice to classify them in the chapter on geography might signify something about how the Joint Library Committee viewed them, as Irving's other works were classified under either history or romance.

The principal political issue in regard to Oregon in the 1840s was whether the dividing line with Great Britain's possessions in Canada would be drawn at 49° N or at 54°40' N. As sentiment moved in favor of an "All Oregon" position and negotiations were ongoing between the State Department and Great Britain, minutes of the Joint Library Committee show members seeking additional information about the area, often information with a decidedly expansionist spin. On 3 March, 1840 the committee ordered John K. Townsend's *Narrative of a Journey across the Rocky Mountains* (1839) and Jason Lee's "account of his travels in the same country." Townsend was an ornithologist who had accompanied an exploring expedition from Wyoming down the Columbia River to the Pacific Ocean; Jason Lee and his nephew Daniel were Methodist missionaries in the Oregon territory. Jason Lee had traveled through northern states drumming up settlers for Oregon and in 1838 had petitioned Congress to extend United States laws over the territory.[20]

The Library Committee continued to acquire books on Oregon in the 1840s. During the 1844 presidential campaign the Democratic Party, whose candidate was James Polk, resolved in its party platform both to acquire Texas and to refuse to cede to Great Britain any of the Oregon Territory. On 18 December 1844, in anticipation of Polk's incoming administration, the Library Committee voted that a bill be reported for the purchase of fifteen hundred copies of Robert Greenhow's *History of Oregon and California* (1844). Greenhow was the librarian of the State Department, and this book, based on his official report, included the argument that a dividing line at 49° N had no particular historical authority, and thus the United States could hold out for 54°40'.[21] The 1849 Library of Congress catalog listed twenty copies. A little over a year later, as Secretary of State James Buchanan was negotiating a treaty with Great Britain in January and February 1846, the committee reviewed titles by

Wyndham Robertson, including *Oregon: Our Right and Title*, which it decided to purchase.[22] It is difficult to say for certain to what extent partisan motives influenced these purchases. The committee that ordered the copies of Greenhow's book was chaired by Massachusetts Whig Rufus Choate and had an equal number of Whigs and Democrats. The committee that ordered the Robertson title, however, was dominated by Democrats and chaired by a southern Whig. In any case, Greenhow's work and other recent accessions on Oregon were available to Congress in the spring of 1846, when it debated the issue of serving notice to Great Britain that the United States would terminate its treaty of joint occupation of the Oregon Territory.[23] This position eventually gave way to a more conciliatory mood, especially in light of the beginning of the Mexican-American War. A treaty with Great Britain settling on the forty-ninth parallel was ratified in the Senate in June 1846, and a bill creating the Oregon Territory passed in 1848.

The full story of congressional interest in information about Oregon is found in the 1849 catalog itself. Between the 1839 and 1849 catalogs, the Library had acquired seven titles about Oregon, eight about Oregon and California together, and a number of relevant maps. Many of these books, of course, embodied the country's expansionist mood. Thomas J. Farnham's *Travels in the Great Western Prairies* (1843) was a work of propaganda in support of acquisition. And explorer John C. Frémont's *Report of the Exploring Expedition to the Rocky Mountains in the Year 1842 and to Oregon and North California in the Years 1843–44* (1845), which had been published under the auspices of Congress and became a bestseller, also extolled the virtues of the West for American settlement.[24] The expansionist ideology advanced by books in the Library did not trump other political realities, as the compromise position reached with Great Britain over Oregon suggests. But the collection of books with imperialist aims seems nonetheless to have had the potential to form a cycle wherein a developing political situation engendered a need for information, which itself embodied and fueled the expansionist mood. This cycle is perhaps best perceived in regard to U.S. interest in Mexico.

The most extensive accessions connected with U.S. territorial ambitions in the 1840s involved areas that the nation would eventually win from Mexico in the Mexican-American War. American expansionists had wanted to acquire the Mexican province of California since Andrew Jackson's administration, but interest increased significantly in the late

1830s and early 1840s as American settlers moved across new overland routes to California and published their glowing accounts in books, pamphlets, and newspapers. The 1839 catalog had little specific information about California, with four titles about the area, three of which dated from the eighteenth century. On Mexico itself, which had gained its independence from Spain in 1821, the Library was better stocked, with over twenty titles, twelve dating from the years since the revolution.

The Joint Library Committee's interest in information about California during the 1840s coincided with growing tensions between the United States and Mexico over such issues as Mexican debt to American creditors and, after 1845, the American annexation of Texas. This was an act that Mexicans resented, in part because it looked like a precursor to United States designs on California. The political situation became explosive in January 1846 when President Polk ordered General Zachary Taylor's belligerent move across the Nueces River into disputed territory. When a Mexican force surrounded a party of Americans in April, killing three U.S. soldiers, a pretext for war had been established. Once Congress declared war in May 1846, the need for useful information took on a new immediacy, and the Joint Library Committee and Librarian John Silva Meehan set to work. On 30 May 1846, for example, the committee ordered Waddy Thompson's *Recollections of Mexico* (1846). Thompson was a former minister to Mexico whose disparaging account of the Mexican army in this book suggested that American conquest of the region could be easily achieved.[25]

Congress also needed maps of Mexico as members followed the progress of the war and, later, debated the peace treaty. In May 1847, Librarian Meehan acknowledged receipt from J. G. Bruff of Washington of copies of two maps: *Map of the Valley of Mexico, and the Surrounding Mountains*, and *Map of the Seat of War in Mexico*. On 11 February 1848 the Library Committee resolved that the secretary of war be contacted to find out whether he had "a correct map of Mexico and Texas, showing the operations of the Army in the present war, and the boundaries of Texas as established and claimed at different times." The war was over by late 1847, and terms of peace negotiated but not yet ratified. Joint Library Committee activity in early 1848, therefore, indicates a need for information as Congress debated the controversial peace treaty, which was accepted by the Senate on 10 March 1848. On the day of ratification, the Joint Library Committee directed the Committee on Engraving to con-

tract for maps of the battles in the valley of Mexico and Cerro Gordo
and of operations at Vera Cruz, in enormous quantities: fourteen thousand for distribution and twelve hundred for the use of both houses of
Congress.[26]

The invoice book indicates that the Library of Congress received
a flurry of acquisitions about Mexico in response to the Mexican-
American War. On 17 December 1847 bookseller Franck Taylor delivered
to the Library several books on the area, including Geronimo Boscana,
Life in California (1846); Albert M. Gilliam, *Travels in Mexico, during the
Years 1843 and 44* (1847); Benjamin Moore Norman, *Rambles by Land and
Water; or, Notes of Travel in Cuba and Mexico* (1845); Michel Chevalier,
Mexico before and after the Conquest (1846); and Thomas J. Farnham, *Life
and Adventures in California* (1846), this last of which "outdid all compet-
itors in its fulsome praise of the province."[27] The largest single purchase
order of books related to Mexico arrived from bookseller Cooley, Reese
& Hill of New York in December 1848. This list included at least eleven
titles related to Mexico, a few dating from the sixteenth and seventeenth
centuries and others of more-recent vintage. Among the former would
be included Agustin Davila y Padillo, *Historia de la Fundacion y Discurso
de la Provincia de Santiago de Mexico* (1596). Among the latter were a
seven-volume collection of books on various aspects of Mexican culture
and Philip Young's *History of Mexico* (1847), which included an account
of the Mexican-American War, ongoing when the book was published.[28]
A very expensive purchase related to Mexico was approved by the Joint
Library Committee on 14 January 1848 when it ordered Edward King,
Lord Kingsborough's nine-volume *Antiquities of Mexico* (1831–48) at the
price of $350 (the work was obtained and almost immediately destroyed
by fire in 1851). Later in 1848, Meehan wrote to the United States consul
at Mexico City, John Black, requesting newspapers and public documents of the Mexican government for the use of the Library.[29] Evidently
the Librarian and the Joint Committee had put out the word to booksellers in the 1840s that the Library of Congress was interested in just
about any information on Mexico that could be acquired.

The geography chapter of the 1849 catalog further documents the
extent of congressional interest in California and Mexico. The Library
acquired fourteen books on California in the 1840s, more than tripling its
holdings of 1839, and eighteen books on Mexico—most of them of much
more recent vintage than the twenty-four titles listed in the 1839 catalog.

A representative example of the expansionist sentiment in many of these works is Richard Henry Dana's *Two Years before the Mast* (1840), which detailed the attractions of the land while denigrating the laziness of its Mexican settlers; the book has been described as "probably the most influential single bit of California propaganda" published in the era.[30] Even books that were not overt arguments for American conquest could be used by legislators to further an imperialist agenda. British diplomat Alexander Forbes argued in favor of British possession of California in *California: A History of Upper and Lower California* (1839), while French diplomat Duflot de Mofras voiced his country's interest in the territory in *Exploration du Territoire de l'Oregon, des Californies et de la Mer Vermeille* (1842). Both these works, which appear in the 1849 catalog, were pointed to by expansionists as evidence that if the United States did not acquire California, then a European power would acquire a foothold on the Pacific coast.

Very few books on the West seem to have escaped the notice of the Joint Committee on the Library. Though a few available titles were not purchased, reasons for their absence can usually be perceived. For example, Lansford Warren Hastings's *Emigrants' Guide to Oregon and California* (1845), Thomas James's *Three Years among the Indians and Mexicans* (1846), and Overton Johnson and William H. Winter's *Route across the Rocky Mountains* (1846) were published in Cincinnati, Waterloo, Illinois, and Lafayette, Indiana, respectively; the committee was probably not aware of their existence. Fictional works, such as Frederick Marryat's *Narrative of the Travels and Adventures of Monsieur Violet, in California, Sonora, and Western Texas* (1843) and Percy Bolingbroke St. John's *The Trapper's Bride: A Tale of the Rocky Mountains* (1845), were probably deemed of little political value, whereas Victor Tixier's *Voyage aux Prairies Osages, Louisiana, et Missouri, 1839–40* (Paris, 1844) was likely not purchased in keeping with the Joint Library Committee's general aversion to foreign-language books. In other cases, the books were merely a republication of information congressmen could have found in periodicals. This may have been the reason for not purchasing Charles Folsom, *Mexico in 1842*, published by the author in New York in the same year, and A. J. Allen's *Ten Years in Oregon* (1848). These instances bring up the important point that much of the most useful information on western lands probably came to congressmen and other government officials through periodical rather than book publication. Some oversights are ultimately difficult to explain, however, such as Rufus B. Sage's *Scenes in the Rocky Mountains, and in Oregon, California, New Mexico, Texas, and the Grand Prairies*, published in Philadelphia by Carey and Hart in 1846.

To assess the role that the Library of Congress played in regard to American imperialism in the antebellum era, recall that other territories, which were not eventually acquired by the United States, were nonetheless coveted by the most ardent expansionists of the age. This is particularly true of Central America, where the United States had two pressing interests. First, many southern politicians were worried that addition of new western states to the Union would upset the balance of political power in the Senate between free and slave states which had been maintained since the Missouri Compromise of 1820. Therefore, southerners looked to acquire Cuba or areas of Central America that they considered suitable for the expansion of American slavery, even though most of these countries had already abolished slavery. Second, with the United States after 1848 stretching along the Pacific coast from California to Oregon, Americans saw much to gain from building a canal across Central America to link territory on the Pacific Ocean with the rest of the country. The two most plausible places for a canal were in Nicaragua and the Isthmus of Panama, in New Granada.

In light of these interests, Congress sought books about Central America. In the 1840s the Joint Committee asked Obadiah Rich to send John Lloyd Stephens's *Incidents of Travel in Central America, Chiapas, and Yucatan* (1841) and Frederick Catherwood's *Ancient Monuments in Central America, Chiapas, and Yucatan* (1844). Though these books were destroyed with the rest of the Library's collections in geography in the fire of 1851, Pearce and the Joint Committee evidently worked hard to restock this key subject area as quickly as possible. In 1853, when former Arkansas senator and recently appointed minister plenipotentiary to Central America Solon Borland inquired about works in the Library of Congress relevant to the region, Librarian Meehan was able to provide a list with sixteen separate titles, including Henry Dunn's *Guatemala; or, The United Provinces of Central America in 1827–8* (1828); George Washington Montgomery's *Narrative of a Journey to Guatemala* (1839); American commissioner Ephraim George Squier's *Nicaragua: Its People, Scenery, Monuments, and the Proposed Interoceanic Canal* (1852); and other general books on American geography.[31] The Library's thorough holdings on this region might have had something to do with James Alfred Pearce's active role in defending the Clayton-Bulwer Treaty of 1850, which limited British claims to dominion over parts of Central America and allowed for both nations to join in promoting a waterway to join the Atlantic and Pacific Oceans.[32]

United States interest in Central America peaked in the mid-1850s. Filibuster William Walker appeared in Nicaragua in June 1855 with a band of American adventurers and established a government by October. Though President Pierce had taken a stand against filibustering, support for Walker in late 1855 and early 1856 was strong among American expansionists in the press and in the government, including Secretary of War Jefferson Davis. Meanwhile, the United States and Great Britain were at odds over the region. The British claimed possession of a colony on the Mosquito Coast, a possible eastern terminus of an interoceanic canal, while the United States believed that the Clayton-Bulwer Treaty affirmed the Monroe Doctrine and prohibited British colonization. Tensions were so high that a U.S. Navy captain bombarded a British port on the coast in 1854, and there was talk of war in both countries.[33]

To help Congress respond to these developments, Meehan and the committee set about purchasing additional books on Central America. In February 1856, Meehan wrote to Rich Brothers to request a long list of titles about the region spanning several centuries. The list included, among others: George Alexander Thompson, *Narrative of an Official Visit to Guatemala from Mexico* (1829); an additional copy of Dunn's *Guatemala*; George Henderson, *An Account of the British Settlement of Honduras* (1809); John Wright, *Memoir of the Mosquito Territory, as Respecting the Voluntary Cession of It to the Crown of Great Britain* (1808); Orlando W. Roberts, *Narrative of Voyages and Excursions on the East Coast and in the Interior of Central America* (1827); and Thomas Young, *Narrative of a Residence on the Mosquito Shore* (1842).[34] As had been true with land in the West, movement of Americans into new territory inspired purchases at the Library of Congress, though in the case of Central America, interest in the region cooled with the onset of the Civil War. On the whole, the catalogs of 1839 and 1849 and other records indicate that the Library in the 1840s performed precisely the role envisioned for it in the 1780s by James Madison: it collected materials that assisted Congress and the president in pressing and defending American territorial interests. The 1849 Library of Congress catalog is more than a list of titles; it can also be read as a document onto which the ideology of manifest destiny is prominently inscribed.

The Library and Antebellum Literary Culture

Chapter 34 of the 1849 Library of Congress catalog, "Romance," reflects congressmen's interest in the varied literary culture of the antebellum era. This chapter grew from 339 titles in 1839 to 469 titles in 1849, counting by number of entries. This method of counting is somewhat imperfect, however; sometimes a single entry would include all an author's works (as was the case with James Fenimore Cooper's twenty-eight separate titles), whereas in other cases each novel would be given a separate catalog entry (as was done for Herman Melville's four titles). In terms of the actual number of book titles, the Library in 1849 contained over seven hundred separate novels and romances. Most of these were acquired by purchase, though some of the books published after 1846 were deposits sent to the Library in compliance with the new copyright law of that year. The size and richness of this chapter of the Library amply demonstrate that in the 1840s and 1850s the Library continued to serve as a source of popular literature for government officials and their families.

The 1840s were a period of growth and diversity for literary publishing in the United States and Great Britain, and the purchasing decisions of the Joint Committee on the Library mirror some of the dominant strains of this print environment. For example, American publishers such as Wiley and Putnam, in their Library of American Books, sought to showcase the talent of American writers and in doing so began to establish a number of "standard" authors as the country's leading literary lights.[35] If one judges by the 1849 catalog, the Joint Committee partook of this cultural nationalism when selecting books. Most of the writers who had emerged by the 1840s as America's premier authors of fiction, many of them published by Wiley and Putnam, appear in chapter 34. The catalog lists numerous works by James Fenimore Cooper, Washington Irving, Catharine Maria Sedgwick, and James K. Paulding. The Library also owned Nathaniel Hawthorne's *Twice-Told Tales* (1842), the poet Henry Wadsworth Longfellow's prose romance *Hyperion* (1839), and three works by Herman Melville—for the moment considered merely a sea adventure novelist—*Typee* (1846), *Omoo* (1847), and *Mardi* (1849), the last of which was a copyright deposit.

With the interesting exception of Edgar Allan Poe, major southern fiction writers were also collected at the Library.[36] This might have had something to do with the number of southern legislators who often sat on the Library Committee but was just as likely simply the product of these authors' national popularity. Chapter 34 listed *Horse-Shoe Robinson, Rob of the Bowl,* and *Swallow Barn* by John Pendleton Kennedy; *Georgia Scenes* by Augustus Baldwin Longstreet; and ten novels by popular South Carolina novelist William Gilmore Simms. Interestingly, while Kennedy and Longstreet were listed in the 1839 catalog, Simms was not. All seven of Simms's books published in the 1830s and listed in the 1849 catalog were acquired sometime after their initial publication. Acquisition of ten Simms novels between 1839 and 1849 might have been initiated by Senator William C. Preston, a fellow South Carolinian and leading member of the Joint Library Committee in the late 1830s and early 1840s.

Though American writers were coming into their own in the 1840s, the print culture of the era was decidedly international. British authors enjoyed great popularity on this side of the Atlantic, and the 1849 Library of Congress catalog listed many works by the leading British authors of the day. Because these works could not have been copyright deposits, they were certainly purchased by the Library Committee. Moreover, most of these titles were pirated editions, as the Library of Congress continued to benefit from the lack of an international copyright law. Chapter 34 of the catalog listed numerous titles by such popular British writers as Edward Bulwer (seventeen titles, ten in American imprints); Charles Dickens (fifteen titles, seven American imprints); G. P. R. James (fifteen titles, seven American imprints); and Frederick Marryat (ten titles, only one of which was published in London). The works of Sir Walter Scott, too, had all been collected in earlier decades and remained a fixture of this chapter, with nineteen separate titles, all of them in American editions. The Library also held 112 volumes from English publisher Richard Bentley's Standard Novels series, which included popular writers from both sides of the Atlantic.

Women fiction writers figured prominently in the print culture of the 1840s, and their contributions were not ignored by the Joint Committee on the Library. American women novelists were represented by, among others, Catharine Maria Sedgwick, who appears in the catalog as author of seven novels and a book of tales and sketches. Domestic novelist Caroline Gilman's *Recollections of a Southern Matron* (1839), which has been described as the genesis of "the novel of Southern womanhood," and *Love's Progress* (1840) were also on the shelves.[37] Among international women authors, the Library held four novels by Swedish writer Fredrika Bremer and five by English noblewoman turned romance novelist Lady Charlotte Bury. Her works, including *The History of a Flirt, Related by Herself* (1841) and *The Willfulness of Woman* (1844), all appear in London editions. It seems likely that women writers who covered domestic subjects in their fiction were collected by the Joint Library Committee to cater to the women readers (mostly wives and daughters of government officials) who had access to the Library.

Though writers like Sedgwick, Gilman, and Bury generally subscribed in their works to the separate-spheres ideology of the era, the Joint Committee sometimes purchased the work of more controversial women writers. The catalog listed an 1847, three-volume, English-language edition of the *Works* of French feminist George Sand, notorious at the time for her outspoken views on women's rights as well as for her defiantly unconventional lifestyle. The Library also owned seven novels by Marguerite, Countess of Blessington (Margaret Power Farmer Gardiner), a writer whose adventurous, flamboyant lifestyle (it was rumored that her stepdaughter's estranged husband was her lover) became the subject of scandal.[38] Amid these inclusions, it is hard to explain the conspicuous absence of Charlotte Brontë's *Jane Eyre*, which was published to wide acclaim, if also some controversy, in England and America in 1847. The book was in the Library by 1851, when it was borrowed by Attorney General John J. Crittenden.[39]

Publishers of the era recognized that families and children constituted an important market for fiction. The Joint Committee on the Library understood this as well, making purchases with these readers in mind. That the Library was resorted to frequently by family members of all ages and both genders is abundantly clear from the committee's purchasing decisions. In 1841, for example, the committee ordered a copy of Jessie Olney's *Family Book of History* (1839), as well as La Fontaine's *Fables*, in French and English, translated by Elizur Wright (1842). Two titles ordered in 1843, both authored by Robert Sears, were also aimed at a family audience: *Bible Biography; or, The Lives and Characters of the Principal Personages Recorded in the Sacred Writings; Practically Adapted to the Instruction of Youth* (1842), and *The Wonders of the World, in Nature, Art, and Mind* (1843). Other titles in the catalog indicate a readership of children and young adults. The catalog lists four books by Eliza Leslie, whose fiction and conduct books instructed young American women in manners and domestic duties.[40] Two of Leslie's books of the 1830s, *Pencil Sketches* (1833) and *Pencil Sketches, 2d and 3d Series* (1835), were purchased by the committee, while her works from the late 1840s were acquired through deposit. All these books, which clearly served no utilitarian function, would have fit snugly into a reading niche at the Library aimed at entertaining and instructing the families of congressmen.

Given a limited purchasing budget and an expanding publishing industry, the Joint Library Committee could not collect all the popular fiction published in the 1840s. Works that clearly fit into the parameters of Library Committee selection criteria often did not make it into the Library, at least not on first publication. Historical romance was extremely popular with American readers and well represented in the 1849 Library of Congress catalog by authors such as Cooper, Simms, Sedgwick, and Robert Montgomery Bird. But the novels of William Alexander Caruthers and Joseph Holt Ingraham, though popular and published by well-established presses, did not make it into the Library.[41] Similarly, while the Library Committee purchased Victor Hugo's *The Hunchback of Notre Dame* (a translation published in Philadelphia in 1834), for some reason it did not acquire Alexandre Dumas père's *The Three Musketeers* and *The Count of Monte Cristo*, both of which were available in English translations in the 1840s. And although American women novelists were often collected, the novels of Maria McIntosh and Ann Sophia Stephens were overlooked.[42] These apparently arbitrary choices were probably dictated by financial constraints.

In some cases, though, by looking at what the Joint Library Committee elected not to purchase from the universe of titles available, certain exclusionary criteria can be cautiously inferred. One class of novels that the committee omitted entirely from the Library was the "radical democrat" fiction of the 1840s. As described by David S. Reynolds, this school of authors exposed the squalor of the living conditions of the urban poor and chastised the wealthy for their indulgence and immorality, relying on sensationalist imagery and black humor to hold readers' attention. Their cheaply produced books were popular among working-class readers and widely enough known that members of the Library Committee, and certainly the booksellers who supplied the Library, must have been aware of them. Most prominent was George Lippard, whose *Quaker City; or, the Monks of Monk Hall* (1844–45) sold 60,000 copies in its first year of publication and 150,000 in the subsequent five years.[43] With imagery that bordered on the sadistic and the pornographic as well as radically subversive political themes, it is not surprising that the Library Committee elected not to purchase this book or any others by Lippard or fellow radicals George Thompson and George Foster. The radical democrat perspective was inspired by two European urban exposés, Frenchman Eugène Sue's *Les Mystères de Paris* (published in translation in London in 1844) and Englishman G. W. M. Reynolds's *Mysteries of London* (four volumes, 1845–48). Interestingly, while Lippard and Reynolds were not collected, the Joint Committee did purchase a translation of Sue's *Les Mystères de Paris*. For some reason, radical French writers such as Sue and Sand were more likely to be collected than American works that broached similar themes.

A genre which would have been of particular interest to congressmen but which they seem to have scrupulously avoided collecting was the novel of political satire. Nathaniel Beverly Tucker's *Partisan Leader* (1836) was published anonymously in Washington by prominent editor Duff Green; the Library Committee could not have been unfamiliar with it. Tucker was a nationally known supporter of slavery and states' rights, and his futuristic novel, which was set in 1848 and featured a civil war brought on by the secession of several southern states, was intended as an attack on Martin Van Buren's presidential campaign. Another work along these lines that the Library Committee eschewed was Thomas Dunn English's novel *1844; or, The Power of the "S. F."* (1847), which is about "a secret society of underhanded Democrats trying to defeat the Whigs in the election of that year."[44] Works of overt political content were obviously bound to antagonize certain members of the Library Committee, which always consisted of members of both major parties. The decision not to purchase a novel like this would have been consistent with Library Committee chairman James Alfred Pearce's desire to keep collections above the fray of partisan discourse.

It could have been this spirit of nonpartisanship that explains the otherwise unaccountable absence of Johnson Jones Hooper's *Some Adventures of Captain Simon Suggs* (1846), which was based on the exploits of a character who was already well known through periodical publication when the book came out. Published in Philadelphia by Carey and Hart, the book went through six editions in five years. However, the principal character, Simon Suggs, an unethical backwoods politician, was a caricature of Andrew Jackson, and the book itself was structured as a parody of a campaign biography.[45] If there was an agreement to avoid works of overt political satire, this might have worked against Hooper. Other humorists whose work was less political in nature, including Thomas Bangs Thorpe and Thomas Chandler Haliburton, were both included among Library of Congress collections. After 1846, because of copyright deposit laws, the Library Committee was unable to make such distinctions, accepting works of whatever political or partisan stripe. Hence both Harriet Beecher Stowe's *Uncle Tom's Cabin* and Caroline Lee Hentz's *The Planter's Northern Bride*, an apologia for slavery written to counter Stowe's popular indictment of the institution, were included in the 1861 catalog as deposits.[46]

Illustrated works representative of the highest-quality products of American and European publishers continued to be purchased for the Library of Congress in the 1840s and 1850s. These books served no utilitarian function but would have been appropriate objects of attention for casual visitors to the Library. The purchasing power of the federal government allowed it to acquire engraved volumes that were out of reach for individual consumers and even for libraries. Superintendent Joseph Cogswell was probably referring to some of these expensive works when he told Meehan in 1855, after viewing the Library of Congress collections restored since the fire of 1851, that the Astor Library "cannot afford to purchase such books."[47] In this regard, John J. Audubon's works were continual favorites. Meehan informed a would-be bookseller in 1851 that the Library's copy of *Birds of America* had survived the fire, bragging that it was "one of the very best; it having been selected for us by Mr. Audubon, and bound in the most substantial manner for us, under his own care and supervision."[48]

Some of the other expensive purchases authorized by the Joint Committee on the Library in the 1840s and 1850s include George Catlin's *North American Indian Portfolio* (1844), with 25 leaves of plates; John Sibthorp's *Flora Graeca* (in ten volumes published from 1806 to 1840), with 966 colored plates on botany; and John Boydell's *Illustrations of Shakespeare*, the 1852 American edition of which boasted 100 copper plates.[49] Restoring losses after the fire, the Library acquired a copy of "the great work on Egypt, commenced under the auspices of the Emperor Napoleon and completed under the auspices of King Louis XVIII"

(*Description de l'Egypte*, Paris, 1809–22), along with catalogs of two French museums from Dr. J. S. Ludlow of Philadelphia, for $500.[50] The Library drew its share of casual visitors, including women and children with family or social connections to government officials. The popular novels and illustrated volumes appear to have been purchased with such visitors in mind, with the Joint Committee on the Library acting under the assumption that the more serious areas of the collection devoted to law and politics would have been inappropriate or of no particular interest to women patrons, in accordance with the separate-spheres ideology of the day.

Borrowing Practices at the Library

Charge records of congressmen offer a glimpse into the daily workings of the Library and testify both to the utility of the holdings and the popularity of the literary titles in the catalog. It should be kept in mind, of course, that the charge records are certainly not an accurate record of all the books members of Congress actually consulted, for much of their use of the Library for official purposes was probably conducted on the premises and therefore left no written record. What the charge records do preserve, though, are the titles of books that members wished to have available longer than necessary for simple fact checking. Occasionally, congressmen used the Library almost exclusively for the practical purposes envisioned when it was founded. During the Thirty-first Congress in 1850–51, Senator Henry Clay checked out only a handful of books, including acts of previous Congresses, the *Federalist* papers, and an eight-volume compilation of the laws of the United States. Arkansas senator Solon Borland, upon his appointment as minister plenipotentiary to Central America in April 1853, checked out three recently published works on Central America, the only books he requested in this period.[51]

More typically, congressman and government officials requested a range of books for both professional reasons and light reading, making for some curious juxtapositions. Explorer and California senator John Charles Frémont checked out four books in 1850. In addition to two books of a professional nature, a Spanish-language edition of the constitution of Mexico and an edition of Vattel's *Law of Nations*, Frémont requested George Sand's *Works* and Thomas de Quincey's *Confessions of an English Opium-Eater*. In skimming the charge records of Senator Daniel Webster in the same period, one finds a similar blending of books for professional and personal uses, including Jonathan Elliot's *Debates on the Adoption of the Federal Constitution*, an edition of Vattel, Anna Jameson's illustrated *Court Beauties of the Reign of Charles II*, and a couple of volumes from an anthology of British drama.[52]

Sometimes the books checked out by congressmen were almost exclusively intended for light reading. In 1850–51 Senator Jefferson Davis of Mississippi charged twenty-nine works, most of them literary, including the works of George Sand, romance novels and fables, a volume of sermons, and a couple of encyclopedias. Only three titles were of potential professional value: a volume of the acts of Congress, *Niles' Register* (a nonpartisan periodical that provided printed documents and speeches on current political questions), and Frederick Grimké's *Considerations upon the Nature and Tendency of Free Institutions*, a recent work of political science. The fifteen works on Davis's charge records covering 1853–55— his years as secretary of war in the Pierce administration—were all literary or historical, including de Quincey's *Confessions of an English Opium-Eater*, two editions of Shakespeare, and the Countess of Blessington's novel *Country Quarters*. During the Thirty-second Congress of 1851–53, twenty-five separate titles were charged to the account of Senator Sam Houston of Texas, including one Bible, Thomas Wright's *Narratives of Sorcery and Magic*, and twenty-three novels, nine of them from an English publisher's Library of Foreign Romance series. Houston's use of the Library was more circumspect during the Thirty-third Congress of 1853–55, when his charges included works of clear political utility such as *Niles' Register* and Alexander Jones's *Cuba in 1851*, which detailed the unsuccessful filibustering expeditions of General Narciso López, in addition to a novel and other light reading.[53]

The records of Houston and Davis, among others, show how Library privileges were extended to family members and friends of congressmen and other government officials. Librarian Meehan penciled a note into the records whenever a book was checked out by someone else on the user's account. The twenty-three romance novels charged to Sam Houston in 1852 and 1853 were actually loaned on his behalf to one Miss Barber. A note next to Jefferson Davis's charge records in 1854 indicates that Maria Edgeworth's works were returned to the Library by his wife, Varina. Attorney General John J. Crittenden's wife received three novels from the Library in 1850; Stephen Douglas's wife checked out the *Oeuvres* of French poet and satirist Nicolas Boileau Despreaux in the same year;

and a daughter of Senator Thomas Hart Benton, perhaps Jessie Benton Frémont (both wife and daughter of senators), borrowed Lady Morgan's *France* and Thomas Moore's *Life of Byron* in October 1853.[54] The lending of books to acquaintances, wives, and children of government officials sometimes made it difficult for Librarian Meehan to track down unreturned volumes.[55]

These records help to fill out the picture of the multiple functions the Library served in the 1840s and 50s. The Library was available to a certain class of women users, though the books they checked out were almost always novels and other light reading, suggesting a segregation of the collections by gender, though one that was created, it would seem, by custom and inclination rather than imposed by regulation. The presence of acquaintances and relatives of members of Congress indicates that the Library rooms were a place where members of Washington society might meet and socialize, perhaps using the books, as well as the artwork exhibited in the rooms, as a starting point for conversation. Finally, the charge records show that a library collected according to a rationale of utility was resorted to as frequently for entertainment purposes as for professional ones. The fear of luxury characteristic of attitudes toward books and literature in the early Republic gave way to a more comfortable relationship between government officials and their books in the mid–nineteenth century, as the publishing explosion of the period, among other cultural trends, made books a familiar and less threatening element of the cultural landscape.

The Library as Art Gallery and Social Space

The Library space in the Capitol served interrelated social and aesthetic functions that had little to do with the printed page. Since 1824, the Library had been located in an elegant room (ninety feet long, thirty feet wide, and thirty-five feet high) designed by Charles Bulfinch, on the west front of the Capitol. Here, the Library provided visitors in Washington with an art gallery where paintings, busts, and medals were attractively displayed. The presence of works of art in the Library encouraged visitors to use the space for purposes other than reading and research; the artworks invited comment and facilitated conversation. The Library in the 1840s displayed bronze medals, presented to Congress by George W. Erving in 1822 for the explicit use of the Library, which depicted historical events of Napoléon's reign. Upon visiting the Library in 1837, Harriet

Martineau called them the "most beautifully composed piece of history" that she had seen.[56] Also on view in the Library were plaster busts of former chief justice of the Supreme Court John Marshall, former Library Committee member Levi Woodbury, and Andrew Jackson, among others. Portraits, marble and bronze busts, and framed documents also occupied the large room. Library Committee members recognized the value of these items when, in January 1840, they resolved "to make provision for the erection of a suitable building for the Library, and for the reception and preservation of such archives, records, works of art, and other books, papers, and works as Congress from time to time may order to be kept therein." Apparently in response to this resolution, architect Robert Mills sent Librarian Meehan a letter estimating the expense of "a cross gallery at the South and North ends of the Library." However, nothing ever came of this proposal.[57]

Sometimes artists sent their works to the Library hoping to receive congressional patronage for them, while in other cases the objects were simply patriotic gifts or loans. In 1830, for example, Adam Eckfeldt offered to supply the Library, at a cost of two dollars apiece, a collection of medals depicting distinguished Americans, an offer that was accepted by the Library Committee. Giuseppe Ceracchi's busts of Thomas Jefferson, Amerigo Vespucci, Christopher Columbus, and George Washington were purchased according to a Library Committee resolution of 1831 and displayed at the Library until the fire of 1851 destroyed them. The Library Committee voted on 9 January 1840 to exhibit portraits painted by Gilbert Stuart of the first five presidents and loaned to the Library by a Mr. Phelps of Boston; they were subsequently lost in the fire of 1851. Eventually the Library Committee authorized purchase of five other Stuart presidential portraits to replace them.[58]

After the fire of 1851, architect Thomas U. Walter designed a new, fireproof Library room that was even more elegant than the quarters that had been destroyed. The new Library room in itself became a work of art lavishly praised by the press and by visitors. The redesigned space of three galleries encircling twelve alcoves included an impressive array of ornamentation, as a letter from Walter to the secretary of the interior makes abundantly clear:

> All the plain surfaces of the ceiling . . . to be gilded in three shades of gold leaf, so disposed as to give depth and effect to the panels. All the ornamen-

tal moldings, pendants, and drops of the ceiling to be furnished in gold bronze, and the prominent parts to be tipped with gold, burnished, so as to produce a decided sparkling effect against the dead gold surfaces. The large consoles to be painted in light bronze green, tipped with gold bronze and burnished gold, for the purpose of giving relief to the fruits and foliage. All the cases, the railings, and the remaining iron work to be finished with light gold bronze, tipped on all the parts which receive the strongest light with burnished gold.[59]

When the room was in the final stages of construction, Meehan confided to Pearce that "I think the workmen have been a little too liberal in the use of gold leaf."[60]

The elaborate ornamentation of the new Library room, which seems inconsistent with the traditional frugality of Congress in patronizing the arts, makes sense within the context of the Library's long-standing functions as gathering place and art gallery. The Library may have been primarily a workshop for legislators, but it was also a social space and a symbol of the state of American art. A certain amount of artwork around the Capitol, decorously displayed to exemplify the progress of the arts in the United States, could be justified even by the most antiaesthetic ideologues. Congress needed a place to meet and room to store its books; the idea that these areas should be judiciously decorated according to patriotic themes did not meet with significant resistance (though individual works of art in the Capitol were often ridiculed or criticized). One architectural scholar refers to this sensibility as "a merger of American functionalism and cosmopolitan eclecticism."[61] The conception among its administrators that the Library constituted an ideologically neutral retreat for members of Congress, a cultured space existing above the sphere of partisan debates over public policy, might also have contributed to congressional acquiescence to such elaborately designed space. It will be recalled that Library Committee chairman Pearce tried to exclude partisan books from the Library to allow it to preserve an air of political neutrality.

Members of the press and public were delighted with the new Library. In April 1853 a writer in the *National Intelligencer* predicted that "this beautiful public work will doubtless be the chief scene of attraction for visitors next winter," describing the room at greater length, and somewhat breathlessly, in August: "At first view of this enchanting room thousands will experience, as we did, a glow of rapturous delight, not unmixed with something of a selfish sentiment of congratulation that as citizens of Washington we are endowed with so great a privilege as this library affords."[62] Other newspapers printed similarly enthusiastic reviews.[63] Meehan reported to Pearce that when geologist Sir Charles Lyell visited the Library in the company of President Pierce, just before it opened to the public, he [Lyell] proclaimed it "the most beautiful room in the world."[64]

Once the elegant new room was opened to the public, the Library more than ever became a tourist attraction. The *Intelligencer* reported that the public had had its first access to the new room and that Meehan, "the courteous Librarian, was present yesterday, and greeted with his well-known cordiality and *bonhomme* [sic] many of the former visiters [sic] of the hall."[65] Despite these reports, the throng of visitors somewhat annoyed Meehan. Echoing his predecessor Watterston, Meehan wrote to Pearce: "We are interrupted in the Library, today, almost as much as we were yesterday—owing, I suppose, to the many notices of it given by letter writers. I hope that the curiosity will soon be over." Less than a week later, Meehan complained that "we are very much pressed by visitors in the Library. . . . Their visits are getting to be oppressive, as they drive us from our work."[66] Meehan's complaints remind us that though the Library was open to the public as a symbol of American art and architecture, the Librarian and administrators still held a guarded conception of the public function of the Library. Library Committee chairman Pearce believed that a government library could not serve simultaneously as a public library and administered the Library accordingly in the 1850s. Thus the Library was a splendid contribution to the artwork of the Capitol, but despite the visitors it was otherwise no closer than it had been before the fire to becoming a national library in a wider sense.

While Meehan sometimes chafed at playing host to anonymous members of the public, other visitors were more cordially received. Letters Meehan wrote to Pearce later in the decade provide a sense of the social aspect of the Library. On 25 October, 1856, Meehan described visits from "the Hon. Mr. Robertson, of Virginia, and his daughter, to see the Library." John Robertson of Virginia was a former Whig member of the House of Representatives who had served with Pearce in Congress. On the same day, Meehan reported that "Mrs. J. C. Calhoun, widow of the Hon. Senator, was in the Library, this morning some time, accompanied by her daughter and a few young friends." In 1859 he reported to Pearce

visits from "the Hon. Mr. Conrad, of Louisiana, who came to read, and
. . . the Hon. Washington Hunt, of New York, and his wife and son. He
. . . is in fine health and spirits." Charles Magill Conrad was a former
Whig senator and representative and secretary of war under President
Fillmore; Hunt was a Whig turned Democratic member of the House of
Representatives from 1843 to 1849. The next year, Meehan informed
Pearce in a friendly letter that "we had the pleasure, last week, of seeing
Mrs. Pearce and one of your daughters in the Library, and [were] very
much gratified to see her in fine spirits, and apparently improved
health."[67] Just as Watterston had reported the Library filled with male
and female friends and acquaintances of congressmen in the 1820s, the
Library in the 1850s continued to serve an important social function for a
segment of Washington society, a role that was enhanced by the perception of the new rooms as a work of art worthy of admiration and comment. Its social and aesthetic functions probably account to a large extent
for the willingness of Congress to devote ample resources—ninety-three
thousand dollars for the room and eighty-five thousand dollars for the
books—to rebuilding and restocking the Library after the fire.

Activities of the Joint Library Committee

The Joint Committee on the Library in the 1840s and 1850s had responsibilities beyond administration of the Library itself. An examination of
the range of these activities illustrates the principles on which Congress
was willing to support artistic, literary, and scientific ventures. During
the years that James Alfred Pearce chaired the committee, he maintained
oversight of twelve separate funds which fell under the committee's
jurisdiction and which often far superseded in appropriations the budget
for the Library itself. There were funds for purchasing or publishing the
papers of Alexander Hamilton, John Adams, Thomas Jefferson, and
James Madison; funds for a greenhouse and a botanical garden; and
funds that were more closely related to the Library itself, including one
for the Law Library and one for printing the catalog of the Library of
Congress according to Jewett's stereotyping plan. The Library Committee also had jurisdiction over the funds used to purchase artworks for the
Capitol, so it received countless offers of work by artists both well known
and obscure. Because almost any purchase inspired the aesthetic or fiscal
criticism of some members of Congress, however, such patronage requests were granted cautiously. Among the notable artists patronized by

the Library Committee in the 1840s and 1850s were Thomas Crawford, authorized to execute an equestrian statue of George Washington for the western front of the Capitol for $20,000; Hiram Powers, who was employed to make numerous busts for the decoration of the Capitol; and Horatio Stone, who sold Congress a sculpture of John Hancock for $5,500.[68]

The largest fund by far was the one that controlled publication of the results of Captain Charles Wilkes's exploring expedition. Setting out in 1838 and returning in 1842, the Wilkes expedition circumnavigated the globe, confirmed the existence of Antarctica, and charted islands and harbors around the world, in addition to making maps of the disputed Oregon Territory.[69] It also brought back to America thousands of natural history specimens that eventually found their way into the Smithsonian Institution. Under the direction of the Joint Committee on the Library, Congress supported publication of the twenty-four-volume report of the expedition (which itself had cost about $1 million) and between 1844 and 1874 appropriated over $350,000 for these publications.[70] By contrast, a typical annual budget for the Library of Congress in the 1840s (before the fire of 1851, which necessitated increased appropriations) allotted only $8,600 for all expenses, including book purchases, salaries of the librarian and assistants, and incidentals.[71]

Publication of the *Narrative of the Exploring Expedition* provides an instructive example of how government publication of books and maps could serve specific political ends. The exploring expedition had reached Oregon while ownership of the territory was still in dispute between the United States and Great Britain. Upon its return, publication of the first volumes of Wilkes's account of the expedition in 1844 increased public interest in the area.[72] Though Great Britain had wished to make the Columbia River the boundary between the United States and Canada, Wilkes's narrative and charts helped to convince Americans (and their congressmen) that this would not give the United States a sufficient harbor. When a treaty was drawn up in 1846, the resolution of the forty-ninth parallel as a boundary was due in part to the expedition's publications.[73] Moreover, the maps and navigational charts drawn up by the expedition and published in the same year were subsequently used by other American explorers in the West and by American whalers in the Pacific, while the information on geology proved useful to the mining industry.

When the advantages to be drawn from publication advanced purely scientific as opposed to more concretely defined political and commercial interests, Congress was less enthusiastic about money spent on the *Narrative*. Congress sponsored initial publication of only one hundred copies of the account, an edition size considered wholly insufficient by the scientific community. As costs mounted into the hundreds of thousands of dollars for the venture in the 1840s and 1850s, congressmen protested having wasted so much money "for printing pictures of bugs, reptiles, etc." and suggested that the rest of the publication be thrown into the Potomac. Volumes on ornithology, botany, ichthyology, and conchology, though of interest to some of the scientific laymen in Congress, could be seen as providing little in the way of practical benefits to the United States. Library Committee chairman Pearce tried unsuccessfully to bring the project to completion in the mid-1850s by curtailing or abandoning certain of the proposed volumes. Owing to Wilkes's persistence, appropriations continued sporadically into the 1870s.[74]

The appropriations made through the Joint Committee on the Library show that Congress was willing to support artistic and publishing ventures as long as they did not exceed the bounds of ideological education or utilitarian interest. Publication of the papers of the former presidents was supposed to diffuse knowledge of the republican principles on which the country had been founded, while the artistic works ornamenting the Capitol building, including the ones in the Library room, depicted important scenes in American history or otherwise embodied appropriately patriotic themes.[75] As often as not, Congress refused to fund literary or scholarly endeavors even when they did directly involve the history of the United States and its government. Numerous petitions were made to Congress to support transcription of documents related to American history that were preserved in the British Museum, for example, but none succeeded.[76] The same spirit of frugality and utilitarianism that had kept appropriations limited to five thousand dollars per year for the Library in the antebellum era was manifested in the limited support given to other projects that placed Congress in the role of publisher or patron of the arts and sciences.

The Library of Congress had a role to play in most of the major political decisions of the 1840s and 1850s. It figured significantly in the expansion of American influence to the West, as congressmen relied on their Library for information regarding the far-flung territories to which Americans were migrating; book acquisition and land acquisition were not only parallel but also interrelated developments. The Library was consulted by congressmen on other foreign and domestic political issues of the period, including slavery, trade pacts and tariffs, the European revolutions of 1848, and new or developing technologies. Its utility to legislators in making practical political decisions continued to be the primary function of the Library, as reflected in the purchasing priorities of the 1840s and 1850s, which centered on law, politics, economics, history, geography, and technology. Meanwhile, the Library Committee disseminated American political ideology through publication of statesmen's papers, extended a limited amount of patronage to American artists, and promoted American scientific, industrial, and political interests by publishing the findings of the Wilkes exploring expedition.

The Library of Congress served entertainment, social, and aesthetic functions in the antebellum period. Its catalog chapters devoted to literature show how the Library of Congress reflected the remarkably varied, voluminous literary culture of the day. Friends and family members of Congress used the Library for access to an international world of printed works, including lavishly illustrated volumes that had no discernible practical value to legislators. By decorating it with paintings, medals, and busts, Congress turned the Library into an art gallery, and members of the public who visited the Library as a tourist destination were encouraged to take pride in its architecture as a symbol of the advancement of American art. The public's role in the Library was ultimately limited to a vicarious enjoyment of its increasingly extensive printed collections, however, by the conservative vision of the Library's administrators. Had the attitudes of James Alfred Pearce and his colleagues continued to hold sway, the Library of Congress might never have developed into the national library with comprehensive collections open to the public which was so much coveted by scholars and writers in the nineteenth century. It would take a new generation of congressional administrators and an especially dynamic Librarian to guide the Library of Congress toward a broadened role in the years following the Civil War, a role that was not implicit in the Library's antebellum history.

CONCLUSION

The Library before and
after the Civil War

After the Civil War, the Library of Congress entered a period of unprecedented growth under the leadership of Ainsworth Rand Spofford, who joined the institution in 1861 as Assistant Librarian, became Librarian of Congress in 1864, and continued in that position until 1897. By virtue of his encyclopedic knowledge of books and dynamic personality, Spofford usurped many of the functions that had previously been duties of the chairman of the Joint Committee on the Library, such as guiding purchases and formulating the rules of the Library. Unlike his predecessor, John Silva Meehan, Spofford was an experienced book dealer, writer, and bibliophile who harbored ambitious plans to turn the Library of Congress into a national library, comprehensive in its acquisitions of American books, useful to scholars across disciplines, and available to the general public. Spofford was inspired largely by the example of European institutions such as the Bibliothèque Nationale and particularly the British Museum Library, where Antonio Panizzi had pressed for more effective copyright deposit, through which he had expanded that library's collections to half a million volumes by the 1850s.[1]

Spofford presided over dramatic changes in acquisitions and the physical plant of the Library. He orchestrated the removal of the Smithsonian collections to the Library of Congress in 1866 and purchase of the Peter Force collection of Americana in 1867, and he lobbied Congress to centralize copyright deposits at the Library of Congress in 1870, a law that made additional space for the Library a pressing need. A twenty-six-year campaign by Spofford resulted in the completion in 1897 of a new building for the Library, the structure now known as the Jefferson Building, across the east plaza from the Capitol. These developments made it possible for the Library of Congress to become physically, institutionally, and intellectually a modern national library.[2] The shift in orientation of the Library of Congress is evident in the architecture of the building for which Spofford campaigned. Spofford insisted in the 1870s that design submissions for the new Library building include a circular reading room one hundred feet in diameter, an architectural feature modeled on the British Museum Library which presupposed public use of the collections as a principal function of the Library. The architectural beauty of the Library in the antebellum era had been strictly symbolic and intended for visual consumption; the architecture of the Library that Spofford oversaw retained and magnified this symbolism but was also designed for public use.

These post–Civil War developments were in sharp contrast to the limited functions the Library of Congress had served in its first six decades of existence. The history of the Library in this period shows a consistent pattern of congressional resistance to the idea that it was responsible for creating a national library or intervening in any other material way to further the cause of letters in America. Many individual members of the Joint Library Committee, including New Englanders Edward Everett and Rufus Choate and South Carolinian William C. Preston, as well as Smithsonian librarian Charles Coffin Jewett, agreed with culturally nationalistic critics that a Library of Congress expanded on the model of European national libraries could become both a practical aid to American writers and a potent symbol of the country's devotion to culture. But political trends generally made such views impractical; opposition could always be mounted on ideological grounds. In the era of the early Republic, the ideology of classical republicanism meant that a national library faced charges of luxury, charges that retained their potency in the atmosphere of populist anti-intellectualism associated with Jacksonian democracy. The example of European national libraries was mostly lost on legislators who brought to Washington attitudes of ambivalence toward European cultural riches and distrust of an activist federal government.

Despite these limitations on its growth, the Library nonetheless provided important services to government officials. The most significant of these functions, of course, was providing legislators with the books and maps they needed to govern effectively. Encoded in the early book lists and catalogs of the Library, therefore, is a record of the primary intellectual sources from which late-eighteenth- and early-nineteenth-century lawmakers derived their knowledge and authority. This record shows that in carrying out their official duties, statesmen of this period relied chiefly on books on the subjects of the law of nature and nations, political and economic theory, history, and geography. The titles most prominently featured in the personal correspondence and public writings of statesmen of the founding era were also the ones most highly valued at the Library. In keeping with the value placed on books by an ideology of classical republicanism, the Library held few volumes whose purchase could not be justified by utility. Comparing the early catalogs with those of social libraries of the same period, one finds that books on theology and the belles lettres, which often dominated the collections of social libraries, were only minimally represented at the Library. Beginning with the purchase of the Jefferson library in 1815, these limited collections priorities slowly expanded in the direction of the eclectic holdings of the antebellum years.

Just as the early catalogs reflect key aspects of the print culture in which eighteenth- and early-nineteenth-century statesmen were immersed, catalogs from closer to the Civil War provide a record of the more varied and voluminous print culture of the mid–nineteenth century. The links between the Library and print culture become especially clear in the catalogs of 1839, 1849, and 1861. Such trends as the development of a profession of authorship in America and the growing participation of women in the literary marketplace of the day are evident in the extensive holdings of such popular writers as Cooper, Irving, Simms, Sedgwick, and Gilman. The international flavor of the antebellum literary world can also be gleaned from these catalogs. American authors jostled for shelf space with British and French counterparts, including Bulwer, Dickens, Hugo, and Sand. The Library Committee maximized its purchasing ability by taking advantage of the lack of an international copyright agreement to acquire pirated editions of popular foreign books. Assuming that the Library Committee did not waste its limited budget on books that would merely sit on the shelves, these catalogs can be seen as snapshots of the literary demands of a class of relatively well educated readers. That these were not the same demands that would have been made by working-class readers is suggested by the absence of certain radical writers whose virulent social satire seems not to have been appreciated by members of the Library Committee.

It is not only in literary holdings that the Library is a reflection of the print culture of the era. Because of the relationship between political, social, and historical developments, on the one hand, and Library acquisitions, on the other, the Library can be seen as a site where the major themes of nineteenth-century American history found expression. Books and maps on the West provide a case study in this relationship. As Americans moved west and the ideology of manifest destiny took hold, books of history, geography, and fiction with the West as a subject became increasingly popular with American readers. This popularity was reflected in acquisitions decisions at the Library, where these texts served a need that went well beyond leisure reading. The Library Committee made a special effort to acquire the latest books on western subjects during the 1840s, as Congress debated and fashioned United States foreign policy in regard to the much-desired territories of Texas, Oregon, and Mexico. In this way, the Library was a crucial agent in the development of American imperialist politics.

The utility of the Library to congressmen as they negotiated the politics of manifest destiny effectively illustrates the continuity of the American conception of a legislative library between 1782 and 1861. As a member of the Second Continental Congress, James Madison had envisioned in the 1780s a library that would collect Americana in order to define and protect the nation's borders. Congressmen used the Library of Congress to exactly this purpose in the 1840s. In other subject areas, books on legal theory and Constitutional law, the law of nations, and economics had been among the accessions most coveted by legislators in the era of the early Republic, so much so that titles were purchased in the 1790s even before a Library of Congress had been created. In the 1850s the Joint Committee on the Library continued to seek out information on precisely the same subjects, sometimes acquiring the most recent editions of texts that had been useful to their forebears two generations earlier.

Other functions performed by the Library for congressmen and their acquaintances had certainly not been envisioned by its founders, but they became more important as acquisitions multiplied and the Library rooms expanded. In its earliest years, as the relatively small collection of books moved from one site to another, the Library as a physical space for unofficial activities seems hardly to have been conceived. Over time, however, the families and friends of members of Congress came to rely on the Library quarters in the Capitol for social and entertainment purposes, a function described in the novels of Librarian George Watterston. This custom led to some complaints, as the proximity of women to a collection of books that embodied the intellectual authority of the American government seemed a threat to the ideology of separate spheres. Women and men with connections to congressmen continued to visit the Library both to read and to socialize throughout the antebellum period, however, even if the Library Committee patronized its female visitors by setting aside illustrated works and light reading considered proper for female consumption. The illustrated works in particular seem to have been regarded more as conversation pieces than as literature, props that facilitated the social interactions that came to characterize the Library space. With the construction of an elegant, gold-leafed main room after the fire of 1851, the Library became a showplace for American artwork and a tourist attraction. Members of the public who visited were encouraged to appreciate the Library's visual magnificence, but they were not otherwise considered a constituency that the Library was designed to serve.

In catering to a limited group of government officials and an otherwise socially elite clientele, the Library of the antebellum years was a throwback to the social libraries of the eighteenth century on which it had originally been modeled. When the Library was legislated into existence in 1800 as a modified version of the proprietary library, Americans generally embraced a hierarchical view of society in which certain spheres of knowledge, represented by exactly the kind of books that would soon be shelved at the Library, were reserved to a limited number of socially well positioned readers. This changed in the course of the nineteenth century, as political, cultural, and technological developments conspired to open up new means of information to ever expanding classes of readers. Owing to the stunning growth of the American printing and publishing industries in the three or four decades preceding the Civil War, books in the middle of the nineteenth century were widely available consumer goods providing increasingly democratized access even to formerly unavailable fields of knowledge.

Americans of the antebellum period also cultivated their access to books through a proliferation of libraries in new institutional forms. Mercantile libraries and mechanics' libraries were only two of the institutional structures that brought books to new groups of readers. Administrators of the Library of Congress, however, remained generally unresponsive to these important trends. While the founders of the Boston Public Library managed in 1854 to circulate books to residents of the city who could not afford to patronize social or circulating libraries, James Alfred Pearce was paring down Library functions and impeding implementation of the library plan at the Smithsonian. The most important development in American library history of the nineteenth century, the spread of the institution known at the time as the free public library, had no impact on the Library of Congress until well after the Civil War.

In the period between the Revolution and the Civil War, Americans largely held the domain of arts and letters to be the responsibility of private individuals and corporations. When the government chose to promote literary or artistic affairs, it did so under relatively consistent principles. Congress appropriated limited amounts of money to fund projects and institutions that demonstrated clear utilitarian benefits or in some way reinforced the ideological principles on which the country had been founded. Beyond this, the legislature displayed little ambition to stimulate literary excellence or broaden access to literary materials among Americans, the arguments of cultural nationalists and the trend toward increased access to information notwithstanding. The Library of Congress that developed after the Civil War was an emblem of new, progressive ideas about the government's relationship to the public and the world of letters and in many ways, therefore, was an institution fundamentally different from its antebellum precursor.

APPENDIX

TABLE I.

Selected Subject Holdings in the 1812 Library of Congress
and Six Contemporary Social Libraries,
by Number of Titles and Percentage of Catalog

	HISTORY[1]		LAW[2]		GEOGRAPHY[3]		POLITICS AND ECONOMICS[4]		LITERATURE[5]		THEOLOGY[6]	
	#	%	#	%	#	%	#	%	#	%	#	%
Library of Congress, 1812	248	26.4	170	18.1	159	16.9	96	10.2	43	4.6	11	1.2
Burlington, 1807	204	19.3	46	4.4	101	9.6	—	—	129	12.2	191	18.0
Baltimore, 1809	625	16.9	87	2.3	334	9.0	300	8.1	643	17.4	316	8.5
Charleston, 1811	411	13.8	176	5.9	279	9.3	—	—	585	19.6	247	8.3
New York, 1813	688	15.0	—	—	374	8.1	371	8.1	828	18.0	610	13.3
Alexandria, 1815	—	—	75	7.5	—	—	—	—	326	32.7	103	10.3
Hartford, 1818	—	—	14	1.2	—	—	—	—	191	16.6	255	22.2

[1]Each library had a unique classification scheme. To follow is a list of the subject classifications at each library that were included in the table under "History." Multiple classifications corresponding to the subject of history are separated by semicolons.

Library of Congress: Civil history, including chronology, biography, antiquities.

Burlington: Biography (79); history (125).

Baltimore: Antiquities, chronology and mythology (77); biography (197); history (351).

Charleston: Biography and history, ancient and modern.

New York: Civil and military history, antiquities, mythology, chronology, biography and memoirs.

Alexandria: One classification encompasses civil history, voyages and travels, geography, antiquities, and biography (320 titles). No attempt has been made to separate out the history books from the rest of the classification, which explains the absence of figures in this column.

Hartford: As in Alexandria, history, voyages, and travels were classified together in one large category (245 titles) and therefore have been omitted from the table. The biography category has an additional 120 titles.

[2]Law books were classified in the different libraries as follows:

Library of Congress: Law.

Burlington: Law.

Baltimore: Law.

Charleston: Law and politics. These books are listed under law in the table, but obviously the proportion of law books is actually smaller than the figure in the table indicates.

New York: No classification corresponds exactly to law books. The books in the classification covering politics, legislation, political economy, commerce, and revenue are included in the table under "Politics."

Alexandria: Law, politics, political economy, agriculture, commerce. Because law is the principal classifier, these books are listed under "Law" in the table. The table therefore overestimates to some extent the proportion of law books.

Hartford: Law.

[3]Geography books were classified in the different libraries as follows:

Library of Congress: Geography and topography, voyages and travels.

Burlington: Geography (12); topography (16); voyages and travels (73).

Baltimore: Geography (58); voyages and travels (276).

Charleston: Voyages and travels.

New York: Geography, topography, voyages, and travels.

Alexandria: Geography and history books were classified together at this library; therefore, figures have been omitted entirely from the table.

Hartford: Figures omitted because classification makes it impossible to separate the geography books from the history books.

[4]Books on politics were classified in the various libraries as follows:

Library of Congress: General and local politics, political economy (70); trade and commerce (26).

Burlington: No classification at this library corresponds to the subjects of politics and economics.

Baltimore: Political (230); political economy (70).

Charleston: Books in the classification labeled "Law and Politics" are included in the table under "Law."

New York: Politics, legislation, political economy, commerce, revenue.

Alexandria: Books in the classification labeled "Law, Politics, Political Economy, Agriculture, Commerce" are included in the table under "Law."

Hartford: No classification in this library corresponds to the subjects of politics and economics.

[5]Works of literature were classified in each library as follows:

Library of Congress: Poetry, drama, works of fiction, wit.
Burlington: Literature, belles lettres, dictionaries, grammars (94); novels (35).
Baltimore: Belles lettres and criticism (139); novels (336); poetry and the drama (307).
Charleston: Poetry and plays (202); novels and romances (383).
New York: Poetry and drama (279); fictitious writings, novels, romances and fables (67); novels (482).
Alexandria: Poetry, the drama, belles lettres, and criticism (165); novels and romances (161).
Hartford: Novels and romances (124); poetry (67).

[6]Books on theology were classified in the various libraries as follows:

Library of Congress: Sacred history (1); ecclesiastical history (2). Eight titles that clearly had to do with theology were included from a classification labeled "Ethics, or the Moral System in General, Theology and Mythology."
Burlington: Theology.
Baltimore: Theology.
Charleston: Ecclesiastical history and theology.
New York: Theology, ecclesiastical history, sacred criticism, religious controversy.
Alexandria: Ecclesiastical history, theology, essays moral and religious, moral philosophy and metaphysics.
Hartford: Divinity, theology, and moral philosophy.

TABLE 2.

Analysis of the 1815, 1839, and 1849 Library of Congress (LC) Catalogs and the 1850 New York Society Library (NYSL) Catalog, by Percentage of Catalog

	LC, 1815 %	LC, 1839 %	LC, 1849 %	NYSL, 1850 %[1]
Politics[2]	13.4	11.2	11.2	6.7
Geography[3]	8.9	14.7	14.9	11.9
History[4]	15.5	17.2	17.9	23.2
Law[5]	15.1	14.8	14.4	2.8
Math, science, and technology[6]	17.2	15.2	17.5	12.8
Belles lettres[7]	16.7	14.1	11.7	21.4
Religion[8]	5.6	4.7	4.5	10.1
Fine arts[9]	2.2	2.7	2.7	1.7
Miscellaneous[10]	5.4	5.4	5.0	9.4

[1]In some categories, the New York Society Library classification scheme corresponded precisely to the entries in this table. The NYSL catalog had single chapters devoted to religion, law, and geography. Politics and fine arts were also classified separately,

though into classifications labeled "Political Science I and II" and "Fine Arts I and II." In other cases, classifications had to be combined to arrive at the figures in the table. The history holdings are a combination of titles from the history and biography classifications. The belles lettres holdings combine the NYSL classifications of belles lettres and novels. The math, science, and technology holdings derive from combining classifications labeled "Universal Science," "Exact Science (I and II)," "Natural Science (I–IV)," "Mathematical Arts," "Natural Arts," and "Transactions." Books in the "Miscellaneous" category in this table come from NYSL classifications of "Metaphysics," "Education," "Games," "Polygraphy," and "Catalogs."

[2]LC catalog chapter 24, "Politics."

[3]LC catalog chapter 29, "Geography."

[4]LC catalog chapters 1–5: "Ancient History," "Modern Foreign History," "Modern British History," "Modern American History," "Ecclesiastical History."

[5]LC catalog chapters 16.2 on law of nature and nations, and 18–23, on various branches of jurisprudence.

[6]LC catalog chapters 6–15 and 25–28, on various pure and applied sciences.

[7]LC catalog chapters 33–43, on various forms of poetry, drama, fiction, rhetoric, and criticism.

[8]LC catalog chapter 17, "Religion."

[9]LC catalog chapters 30–32; on architecture; gardening, painting, sculpture; and music.

[10]LC catalog chapters 16.1 on moral philosophy; 44 on polygraphical (authors who wrote on a variety of subjects); and chapter 45, which was added to the 1845 catalog and lists newspapers.

NOTES

INTRODUCTION

1. Robert Darnton, "What Is the History of Books?" in *Books and Society in History*, ed. Kenneth E. Carpenter (New York: R. R. Bowker, 1983), 3.

2. John P. Feather, "The Book in History and the History of the Book," in *Libraries, Books, and Culture: Proceedings of Library History Seminar VII*, ed. Donald G. Davis (Austin: Graduate School of Library and Information Science, University of Texas at Austin, 1986), 24.

3. Wayne Wiegand, "The Literature of American Library History, 1985–1986," *Libraries and Culture* 23, 3 (1988): 332.

4. Wayne Wiegand, *Irrepressible Reformer: A Biography of Melvil Dewey* (Chicago: American Library Association, 1996); Alistair Black, *A New History of the English Public Library: Social and Intellectual Contexts, 1850–1914* (London: Leicester University Press, 1996); Jane Aikin Rosenberg, *The Nation's Great Library: Herbert Putnam and the Library of Congress, 1899–1939* (Urbana: University of Illinois Press, 1993); Charles Goodrum and Helen Dalrymple, *The Library of Congress* (Boulder, Col.: Westview, 1982). Numerous works by John Y. Cole are relevant and are cited in the following chapters, but representative of his exemplary contributions to Library of Congress history is *For Congress and the Nation: A Chronological History of the Library of Congress* (Washington, D.C.: Library of Congress, 1979).

CHAPTER ONE

1. Alan Bisbort and Linda Barrett Osborne, *The Nation's Library: The Library of Congress, Washington, D.C.* (Washington, D.C.: Library of Congress, 2000), 19.

2. That is, as long as the Library lives up to its mission. Nicholson Baker's controversial book, which takes the Library to task for failing to preserve printed items in favor of microformats, makes for an instructive contrast with the Library's own promotional publications, such as the Bisbort and Osborne title cited above. See Baker, *Double Fold: Libraries and the Assault on Paper* (New York: Random House, 2001).

3. Both William Dawson Johnston (*History of the Library of Congress, Volume 1, 1800–1864* [Washington, D.C.: GPO, 1904]) and David Mearns (*The Story up to Now: The Library of Congress, 1800–1946* [Washington, D.C.: Library of Congress, 1947]) begin their narratives of the history of the Library of Congress with Elbridge Gerry's proposal for a library in 1789. In 1948, however, Fulmer Mood corrected the historical record by pointing out that Theodorick Bland made the first motion for a congressional library during the Second Continental Congress in November 1782; Madison chaired the committee that took Bland's motion under advisement and recommended in favor of a library ("The Continental Congress and the Plan for a Library of Congress in 1782–1783," *Pennsylvania Magazine of History and Biography* 72, [1948]: 3–24). Adrienne Koch opines that Madison "was without doubt and without significant aid from others the first sponsor of the idea of a library for Congress" ("James Madison and the Library of Congress," *Quarterly Journal of the Library of Congress* 37, 2 [1980]: 159). In "The Library List of 1783" (Ph.D. diss., Claremont Graduate School, 1969), Loren E. Smith discusses Madison's predominant role in authorship of the 1783 list of books recommended for the use of Congress.

4. Mood, "Continental Congress," 11–12.

5. *Journals of the Continental Congress, 1774–1789*, ed. Worthington C. Ford et al. (Washington, D.C.: GPO, 1904–37), 25: 858–59.

6. Smith, "Library List," 31.

7. H. Trevor Colbourn, *The Lamp of Experience: Whig History and the Intellectual Origins of the American Revolution* (Chapel Hill: University of North Carolina Press, 1965), 4.

8. *Journals of the Continental Congress* 24 (1783): 83–92.

9. Mark Olsen and Louis-Georges Harvey, "Reading in Revolutionary Times: Book Borrowing from the Harvard College Library, 1773–1782," *Harvard Library Bulletin*, n.s., 4, 3 (1993–94): 60.

10. Larry E. Sullivan, "The Reading Habits of the Nineteenth-Century Baltimore Bourgeoisie: A Cross-Cultural Analysis," *Journal of Library History* 16, 2 (1981): 230.

11. Tom Glynn and Craig C. Hagensick, "Books for the Use of the United States in Congress Assembled, 1783 and 1800," *Libraries and Culture* 37, 2 (2002): 111. Thanks to Tom Glynn for allowing me to read a draft of his essay before it appeared in print.

12. In the notes that follow (through n. 22), I have listed the editions of the works that were consulted in preparing this overview of the contents of works on Madison's list. The editions available often were not the first editions, which accounts for the discrepancy in publication dates between the text, which lists date of first publication, and the notes. Also included in the notes are secondary works that were consulted in

assessing the distinctive contribution of each work. Jonathan Carver, *Three Years Travels through the Interior Parts of North America* (Philadelphia: Joseph Cruckshank and Robert Bell, 1784). This edition of the work does not have the two maps that were present in the 1778 first edition. Daniel E. Williams, "Jonathan Carver," in *Dictionary of Literary Biography*, vol. 31, *American Colonial Writers, 1735–1781*, ed. Emory Elliott (Detroit: Gale Research, 1984), 53–59.

13. William Robertson, *The History of America* (New York: Samuel Campbell, 1798); Jeffrey Smitten, "William Robertson," in *Dictionary of Literary Biography*, vol. 104, [henceforth abbreviated *DLB* 104], *British Prose Writers, 1660–1800, Second Series*, ed. Donald T. Siebert (Detroit: Gale Research, 1991), 260–68; Abbé Raynal, *A Philosophical and Political History of the Settlements and Trade of the Europeans in the East and West Indies*, 6 vols., trans. J. O. Justamond, F.R.S. (London: J. Mundell & Co., 1798; rpt., New York: Negro Universities Press, 1969); William Doyle, "Raynal, Guillaume Thomas François," in *The Blackwell Dictionary of Historians*, ed. John Cannon (New York: Basil Blackwell, 1998), 352.

14. Bernard Bailyn, *The Ideological Origins of the American Revolution* (Cambridge: Harvard University Press, 1967), 41.

15. David Hume, *The History of England*, abridged and with an intro. by Rodney W. Kilcup (Chicago: University of Chicago Press, 1975); Donald Livingston, "David Hume," in *DLB* 104, 154–80; *The Annual Register, or a View of the History, Politics, and Literature for the Year 1781* (London: J. Dodsley, 1782).

16. Edward Gibbon, *The History of the Decline and Fall of the Roman Empire*, 2 vols. (Chicago: Encyclopaedia Britannica, 1990); Patricia B. Craddock, "Edward Gibbon," in *DLB* 104, 88–105; Plutarch, *Lives*, trans. John Langhorne, D.D., and William Langhorne, A.M. (Cincinnati: Applegate, Pounsford, & Co., 1870); Frances B. Titchener, "Plutarch," in *Dictionary of Literary Biography*, vol. 176, *Ancient Greek Authors*, ed. Ward W. Briggs (Detroit: Gale Research, 1997), 322–29. Information on references to Plutarch in *The Federalist Papers* is from Robert A. Rutland, *"Well Acquainted with Books": The Founding Framers of 1787* (Washington, D.C.: Library of Congress, 1987), 20–21.

17. Donald Lutz, "The Relative Influence of European Writers on Late-Eighteenth-Century American Political Thought," *American Political Science Review* 78, 1 (1984): 193.

18. Rutland, *"Well Acquainted with Books,"* 19; Charles de Secondat, baron de Montesquieu, *The Spirit of the Laws*, trans. Anne M. Cohler, Basia C. Miller, and Harold Stone (Cambridge, England: Cambridge University Press, 1989).

19. A review of differing opinion on Locke's influence on American political thought in the founding era can be found in Barbara Arneil, *John Locke and America: The Defence of English Colonialism* (Oxford: Oxford University Press, 1996), 11–14. In chapter 7, "Locke, Jefferson, and the Amerindian," Arneil advances the argument that Locke's theory of labor and property ownership was biased toward agrarian societies and therefore used to justify appropriating land from the native inhabitants of North America. John Locke, *Two Treatises of Government* (Cambridge, England: Cambridge University Press, 1960).

20. Algernan Sidney, *Discourses concerning Government*, 2 vols. (Philadelphia: C. P. Wayne, 1805); Caroline Robbins, "Algernon Sidney's *Discourses concerning Government*: Textbook of Revolution," *William and Mary Quarterly*, 3d ser., 4, 3 (1947): 267–96.

21. Sir James Steuart, *An Inquiry into the Principles of Political Economy*, 2 vols. (Chicago: University of Chicago Press, 1966); Adam Smith, *The Essential Adam Smith*, ed. Robert Heilbroner (New York: W. W. Norton, 1986, 149–320; Walter Eltis, "Sir James Steuart," in *The New Palgrave: A Dictionary of Economics*, ed. John Eatwell, Murray Milgate, and Peter Newman (London: Macmillan Press Limited, 1987), 494–97.

22. On the uneasy accommodation that the colonists reached between English common law and the law of nature, see Gordon S. Wood, *The Creation of the American Republic, 1776–1787* (Chapel Hill: University of North Carolina Press, 1969), 9–10.

23. "The Colonist's Advocate 1" and "The Colonist's Advocate 6," in *The Papers of Benjamin Franklin*, vol. 17, ed. William B. Willcox (New Haven: Yale University Press, 1973), 6 and 47–48, respectively; Franklin to William Franklin, 3 November 1772, in *The Papers of Benjamin Franklin*, vol. 19, ed. William B. Willcox (New Haven: Yale University Press, 1975), 361.

24. "Notes on the History of North and South America," in *The Papers of Alexander Hamilton*, ed. Harold C. Syrett, 27 vols. (New York: Columbia University Press, 1961–87), 3:702–15. The quoted passage is on 703.

25. John Adams, "II. To the Boston Gazette," in *Papers of John Adams*, vol. 1, ed. Robert J. Taylor (Cambridge: Harvard University Press, Belknap Press, 1977), 261–67.

26. "The Farmer Refuted," in *Papers of Alexander Hamilton*, 1:81–142; "The Federalist no. 12" and "The Federalist no. 84," in *Papers of Alexander Hamilton*, 4:346–52 and 704–5, respectively; "The Defence no. XVII," in *Papers of Alexander Hamilton*, 6: 279–94.

27. "Report on a National Bank," Introductory Note, and "Report on the Establishment of a Mint," Introductory Note, both in *Papers of Alexander Hamilton*, 7:236–56 and 462–72, respectively; "Report on the Subject of Manufactures," Introductory Note, in *Papers of Alexander Hamilton* 10:1–15.

28. The correspondence between books valued by Jefferson and books proposed to Congress by Madison is more than coincidence; some scholars believe that Jefferson and Madison may have collaborated in selection of the proposed library. Rutland, *"Well Acquainted with Books,"* 29.

29. Information on when Jefferson acquired certain books or which editions he owned comes from Millicent Sowerby, *Catalogue of the Library of Thomas Jefferson*, 5 vols. (Washington, D.C.: Library of Congress, 1952–59).

30. William Bradford to Madison, 17 October 1774, in *The Papers of James Madison*, vol. 1, ed. William T. Hutchinson and William M. E. Rachal (Chicago: University of Chicago Press, 1962), 126; Edmund Randolph to Madison, 30 August 1782, in *Papers of James Madison*, vol. 5, ed. William T. Hutchinson and William M. E. Rachal (Chicago: University of Chicago Press, 1967), 91–92.

31. Franklin to Dumas, 9 December 1775, in *Papers of Benjamin Franklin*, vol. 22, ed. William B. Willcox (New Haven: Yale University Press, 1982), 287; Franklin to Count Andreas Peter von Bernstorff, 22 December 1779, *Papers of Benjamin Franklin*, vol. 31, ed. Barbara B. Oberg (New Haven: Yale University Press, 1995), 263–64.

32. John Jay to Washington, 28 August 1790, and Alexander Hamilton to Washington, 15 September 1790, *The Papers of George Washington*, Presidential Series, vol. 6, ed. Mark A. Mastromarino (Charlottesville: University Press of Virginia, 1996), 353, 440–45.

33. "Opinion on the Treaty with France," *The Papers of Thomas Jefferson*, vol. 25, ed. John Catanzariti (Princeton: Princeton University Press, 1992), 608–19.

34. *Journals of the Continental Congress* 25 (1783): 859.

35. Mood, "Continental Congress," 13.

36. Edwin Wolf II, *"At the Instance of Benjamin Franklin": A Brief History of the Library Company of Philadelphia, 1731–1976* (Philadelphia: Library Company of Philadelphia, 1976), 13.

37. Johnston, *History of the Library of Congress*, 17–18.

38. Directors of social libraries may have had other reasons for encouraging legislative use of the collections. The use of the New York Society Library was apparently tendered to congressmen with some hope that New York would become the permanent capital of the nation. Austin Baxter Keep, *History of the New York Society Library* (New York: New York Society Library, 1908), 208.

39. Robert A. Rutland, "Madison's Bookish Habits," *Quarterly Journal of the Library of Congress* 37, 2 (1980): 188.

40. Johnston, *History of the Library of Congress*, 19.

41. U.S. House of Representatives, Select Committee on a Congressional Library, *Report on a Catalogue of Books Necessary for the Use of Congress Together with the Expenses Thereof*, 1st Cong., 2d sess., 23 June, 1790. Located in *Transcribed Reports of the Committee of the U.S. House of Representatives, 1789–1841*, microfilm no. 10, *Transcribed Reports of Select Committees, 1st Congress, 1st session through 4th Congress, 1st session (1769–1796)*, 61, National Archives.

42. It is erroneously claimed in an article in *Libraries and Culture* that "there is no surviving record of [Gerry's] list of recommended titles." Glynn and Hagensick, "Books for the Use of the United States in Congress Assembled," 114.

43. Smith, "Library List," 48.

44. *Report on a Catalogue of Books*, 61–65.

45. George Athan Billias, *Elbridge Gerry: Founding Father and Republican Statesman* (New York: McGraw-Hill, 1976), 8.

46. Olsen and Harvey, "Reading in Revolutionary Times," 66.

47. Quotations here and in following paragraph from Mearns, *Story up to Now*, 3; Mearns's emphasis.

48. This leaves aside college libraries, which were also, obviously, private ventures and mainly available to the faculty and students of the institution.

49. David Kaser, *A Book for a Sixpence: The Circulating Library in America* (Pittsburgh: Beta Phi Mu, 1980), 52–55.

50. In the seventeenth century, Robert Keayne had left to the city of Boston a collection of books, and in the eighteenth century, English clergyman Thomas Bray had helped establish libraries throughout the colonies that became wards of colonial legislatures. In both these cases, although the libraries were maintained by governmental agencies, the libraries were not initially founded by the governments involved. The idea of municipally supported libraries did not achieve widespread acceptance until the mid–nineteenth century. Jesse H. Shera, *Foundations of the Public Library* (Chicago: University of Chicago Press, 1949), 19–20 (on Keayne), 26–29 (Bray). Shera's book is one of the standard works of American library history. The literature of American library history is surveyed in several bibliographic sources, of which the following are recommended: Michael H. Harris and Donald G. Davis Jr., *American Library History: A Bibliography* (Austin: University of Texas Press, 1978); Arthur P. Young and Michael H. Harris, *American Library History: A Bibliography of Dissertations and Theses* (Metuchen, N.J.: Scarecrow Press, 1988); Donald G. Davis, Mark Tucker, and Michael H. Harris, *American Library History: A Comprehensive Guide to the Literature* (Santa Barbara, Calif.: ABC-CLIO, 1989). The journal *Libraries and Culture* publishes biennial reviews of the literature, the latest of which is by Edward A. Goedeken, "The Literature of American Library History, 1999–2000," *Libraries and Culture* 37, 2 (2002): 138–74.

51. Henry May, *The Enlightenment in America* (New York: Oxford University Press, 1976), 109.

52. John Viscount Morley, *Diderot and the Encyclopedists*, 2 vols. (1923; reprint, Ann Arbor: Plutarch Press, 1971), 1:187.

53. Douglas L. Wilson, "Thomas Jefferson's Library and the Skipwith List," *Harvard Library Bulletin*, n.s., 3, 4 (1992–93): 63.

54. Edwin Wolf II, "Franklin and His Friends Choose Their Books," *Pennsylvania Magazine of History and Biography* 80, 1 (1956): 15.

55. Richard Beale Davis, *Intellectual Life in the Colonial South, 1585–1763*, 3 vols. (Knoxville: University of Tennessee Press, 1978), 2:493.

56. Rutland, "Madison's Bookish Habits," 176.

57. Arthur Bestor, "Thomas Jefferson and the Freedom of Books," in *Three Presidents and Their Books* (Urbana: University of Illinois Press, 1955), 5–6. Bestor says that for Jefferson, "in the last analysis, books were tools, designed to assist men in the most serious and difficult of their labors" (8).

58. Ibid., 8.

59. Benjamin W. Rudd, "Notable Dates in American Copyright, 1783–1969," *Quarterly Journal of the Library of Congress* 28, 2 (1971): 137.

60. Jane C. Ginsburg, "A Tale of Two Copyrights: Literary Property in Revolutionary France and America," in *Publishing and Readership in Revolutionary France and America*, ed. Carol Armbruster (Westport, Conn.: Greenwood, 1993), 102.

61. John Y. Cole, *Copyright in the Library of Congress* (Washington, D.C.: Library of Congress, 1995), 3.

62. The three books that together posit what historians refer to as the "republican synthesis" are Bailyn, *Ideological Origins;* Wood, *Creation of the American Republic;* and

J. G. A. Pocock, *The Machiavellian Moment: Florentine Political Thought and the Atlantic Republican Tradition* (Princeton: Princeton University Press, 1975). Some historians contend that the hegemony of classical republican ideology has been overstated. For an overview of the debate, see Robert E. Shalhope, "Republicanism and Early American Historiography," *William and Mary Quarterly* 39, 2 (1982): 334–56. The leading critic of the republican synthesis is Joyce Appleby, whose arguments can be found in *Liberalism and Republicanism in the Historical Imagination* (Cambridge: Harvard University Press, 1992). Appleby believes that the Jeffersonian agenda included a liberal embrace of individual economic opportunity and a rejection of political models of the past, ideas that were at odds with classical republican thought.

63. John Sekora, *Luxury: The Concept in Western Thought, Eden to Smollett* (Baltimore: Johns Hopkins University Press, 1977).

64. Wood, *Creation of the American Republic*, 64.

65. Neil Harris, *The Artist in American Society: The Formative Years, 1790–1860* (New York: George Braziller, 1966), 35, 33.

66. Wood, *Creation of the American Republic*, 105.

67. *The Adams-Jefferson Letters*, ed. Lester J. Cappon (Chapel Hill: North Carolina University Press, 1959), 2:502–3.

68. *American Museum* 1 (1787): 66, 115.

69. William Hill Brown, *The Power of Sympathy*, ed. William S. Kable (Columbus: Ohio State University Press, 1969), unpaginated; Susanna Rowson, *Charlotte Temple: A Tale of Truth* (New York: Twayne, 1964), 35–36.

70. Larzer Ziff, *Writing in the New Nation* (New Haven: Yale University Press, 1991), 137.

71. Ibid., 133–34.

72. *Works of Fisher Ames*, ed. W. B. Allen (Indianapolis: Liberty Classics, 1983), 24, 35.

73. Richard Hofstadter, *Anti-intellectualism in American Life* (New York: Alfred A. Knopf, 1963), 146.

74. Quoted in ibid., 149.

75. Quoted in Mearns, *Story Up to Now*, 3; Mearns's emphasis.

76. Michael Warner, *The Letters of the Republic: Publication and the Public Sphere in Eighteenth-Century America* (Cambridge: Harvard University Press, 1990), 123.

77. Merrill D. Peterson, *Thomas Jefferson and the New Nation* (New York: Oxford University Press, 1970), 145.

78. *The Papers of Thomas Jefferson*, vol. 10, ed. Julian P. Boyd (Princeton: Princeton University Press, 1954), 244.

79. *The Writings of Thomas Jefferson*, memorial ed., vol. 12, ed. Andrew A. Lipscomb (Washington, D.C.: Thomas Jefferson Memorial Association, 1904), 282–83.

80. *American Museum* 3 (1788): 271, and 4 (1788): signature A.

81. Warner discusses the relationship between republicanism and print culture in *The Letters of the Republic*. Other books on the subject include Philip Davidson, *Propaganda and the American Revolution, 1763–1783* (1941; reprint, New York: Norton, 1973);

Bailyn, *Ideological Origins*; and Bernard Bailyn and John Hench, eds., *The Press and the American Revolution* (Worcester, Mass.: American Antiquarian Society, 1980).

82. Bailyn, *Ideological Origins*, 8.

83. Warner, *Letters of the Republic*, 32.

84. Richard B. Kielbowicz, *News in the Mail: The Press, Post Office, and Public Information, 1700–1860s* (Westport, Conn.: Greenwood, 1989), 132.

85. William Manning, *The Key of Liberty: The Life and Democratic Writings of William Manning, "A Laborer,"* ed. Michael Merrill and Sean Wilentz (Cambridge: Harvard University Press, 1993), 140, 161.

86. David Paul Nord, "A Republican Literature: A Study of Magazine Reading and Readers in Late-Eighteenth-Century New York," *American Quarterly* 40, 1 (1988): 57.

87. Looker-On [pseud.], "Thoughts on American Newspapers," *Monthly Magazine and American Review* 3, 4 (1800): 262.

88. R. [pseud.] "On Almanacks," *Monthly Magazine and American Review* 1, 2 (1799): 86, 87–88. Almanac author and publisher Robert B. Thomas of Boston shared this belief that almanacs could do a better job of disseminating useful information. In his publication *The Farmer's Almanack*, Thomas "gradually replaced astrological signs and weather predictions with advice about imbuing children with book knowledge and school learning." David Jaffee, "The Village Enlightenment in New England, 1760–1820," *William and Mary Quarterly* 47, 3 (1990): 332.

CHAPTER TWO

1. William Dawson Johnston, *History of the Library of Congress, Volume 1, 1800–1864* (Washington, D.C.: GPO, 1904), 19–20. Johnston notes that the purchase of Blackstone's *Commentaries* was ordered by the Senate on 10 March 1794 but offers no provenance for the other volumes.

2. Ibid., 23.

3. David Mearns, *The Story up to Now: The Library of Congress, 1800–1946* (Washington, D.C.: Library of Congress, 1947), 8.

4. Johnston, *History of the Library of Congress*, 29.

5. Ibid., 33.

6. Jesse H. Shera, *Foundations of the Public Library* (Chicago: University of Chicago Press, 1949); see chapter 5, "The Circulating Library." David Kaser, *A Book for a Sixpence: The Circulating Library in America* (Pittsburgh: Beta Phi Mu, 1980).

7. Shera, *Foundations*, 59. In *History of the New York Society Library* (New York: New York Society Library, 1908), Austin Baxter Keep reports that membership in the New York Society Library totaled a mere 239 people in 1789; cost of a share in the institution was five pounds. In a few years, though, despite a rise in the cost of a share to fifteen dollars, membership reached nearly 900 before declining again as the library fell into debt (248). The character of the library is revealed to some extent by Keep's descriptions of its members, including Brockholst Livingston, who would become a Supreme Court justice; Matthew Clarkson, president of the Bank of New York; and "merchant prince" Henry Remsen (206). Analyzing the iconography of

bookplates used by social libraries in England and the colonies in the eighteenth century, including the New York Library Society, James Raven concludes that "libraries [were] to offer public statements of beneficence but also to be closed institutions, books locked away, the consultation of books to be left for the inner sanctum of the subscription or society library or for the private library of the gentleman" ("The Representation of Philanthropy and Reading in the Eighteenth-Century Library," *Libraries and Culture* 31, 2 [1996]: 502).

8. Mearns, *Story Up to Now*, 8.

9. C. Seymour Thompson, *Evolution of the American Public Library, 1653–1876* (Washington, D.C.: Scarecrow Press, 1952), 38.

10. Anne-Imelda Radice, *The Original Library of Congress: The History (1800–1814) of the Library of Congress in the United States Capitol* (Washington, D.C.: GPO, 1981), 30, 31, in John Y. Cole, *The Library of Congress: A Documentary History* (Bethesda, Md.: CIS Academic Editions, 1987), microfiche 4-1-1.

11. Quoted in Herman R. Friis, "Baron Alexander von Humboldt's Visit to Washington, D.C., June 1 through June 13, 1804," *Records of the Columbia Historical Society* 44 (1960–1962): 16.

12. Dana J. Pratt, foreword to "The First Booklist of the Library of Congress: A Facsimile," in *The Library of Congress*, ed. John Y. Cole, microfiche 1-4-1.

13. Tom Glynn and Craig C. Hagensick, "Books for the Use of the United States in Congress Assembled, 1783 and 1800," *Libraries and Culture* 37, 2 (2002): 117, 118.

14. *Catalogue of the Books, Maps, and Charts Belonging to the Library of the Two Houses of Congress* (Washington, D.C.: William Duane, 1802).

15. George H. Nash, *Books and the Founding Fathers* (Washington, D.C.: Library of Congress, 1989), 9, and Robert A. Rutland, *"Well Acquainted with Books": The Founding Framers of 1787* (Washington, D.C.: Library of Congress, 1987), 12.

16. The position of Librarian of Congress presupposed no particular knowledge of books. Jefferson, in fact, passed over an applicant who was perhaps better qualified than Beckley to superintend a library; petitioner John McDonald managed a circulating library in Philadelphia. Johnston, *History of the Library of Congress*, 34. But librarianship was not yet a profession, and for the most part the position of librarian in a social library was merely custodial in this period.

17. Edmund Berkeley and Dorothy Smith Berkeley, "The First Librarian of Congress: John Beckley," in *Librarians of Congress, 1802–1974* (Washington, D.C.: Library of Congress, 1977), 3–37. See also their full-length biography of Beckley, *John Beckley: Zealous Partisan in a Nation Divided* (Philadelphia: American Philosophical Society, 1973).

18. Berkeley and Berkeley, "First Librarian of Congress," 7.

19. John Beckley to James Monroe, Philadelphia, 26 August 1800, in *Justifying Jefferson: The Political Writings of John James Beckley*, ed. Gerald W. Gawalt (Washington, D.C.: Library of Congress, 1995), 191.

20. The advice to Jefferson, letter to Rush, and article in the *National Intelligencer* of 11 April 1806 are all described in Berkeley and Berkeley, "First Librarian of Congress," 15–16.

21. Martin K. Gordon, "Patrick Magruder: Citizen, Congressman, Librarian of Congress," in Berkeley and Berkeley, *Librarians of Congress*, 44.

22. The 1806 report is quoted in Johnston, *History of the Library of Congress*, 46. John Quincy Adams's memoirs confirm Mitchill's authorship of the report; see *Memoirs of John Quincy Adams*, vol. 1, ed. Charles Francis Adams (Philadelphia: J. B. Lippincott & Co., 1874), 478. For additional information on Mitchill see Lyman C. Newell's entry in the *Dictionary of American Biography*, vol. 7, ed. Dumas Malone (New York: Charles Scribner's Sons, 1934), 69–71.

23. *Memoirs of John Quincy Adams*, 424.

24. Johnston, *History of the Library of Congress*, 26, 26–27.

25. Quoted in Russell Kirk, *John Randolph of Roanoke: A Study in American Politics* (Chicago: Henry Regnery Company, 1964), 16.

26. Hugh B. Grigsby, "The Randolph Library," *Southern Literary Messenger* 20, 2 (1854): 76, 78.

27. Nathan Sargent, *Public Men and Events* (Philadelphia: J. B. Lippincott & Co., 1875), 125.

28. David A. Carson, "That Ground Called Quiddism: John Randolph's War with the Jefferson Administration," *Journal of American Studies* 20 (1986): 74, 73.

29. *National Intelligencer*, 4 January 1802, and Johnston, *History of the Library of Congress*, 29–30.

30. Carson, "That Ground Called Quiddism," 74.

31. Johnston, *History of the Library of Congress*, 50. Samuel C. Williams repeats this claim in his entry on Tatham in the *Dictionary of American Biography*, as does George Herndon in his biography. See Williams, "William Tatham," in *Dictionary of American Biography* vol. 9, ed. Dumas Malone (New York: Charles Scribner's Sons, 1964), 309, and Herndon, *William Tatham, 1752–1819: American Versatile* (Johnson City: East Tennessee State University Press, 1973), 204.

32. Herndon, *William Tatham*, 24.

33. Tatham to the Speaker of the House of Representatives, 10 February 1806, *American State Papers*, 10, *Miscellaneous* 1: 457.

34. Ibid., 456.

35. Ibid., 457.

36. Herndon, *William Tatham*, 79; Tatham's emphasis.

37. *American State Papers*, 458.

38. Cathy Davidson, *Revolution and the Word: The Rise of the Novel in America* (New York: Oxford University Press, 1986), 40–41. See in particular chapter 3, "Ideology and Genre."

39. *American State Papers*, 460.

40. *National Intelligencer*, 6 November 1813; Tatham's emphasis.

41. Herndon, *William Tatham*, 281.

42. *The 1812 Catalogue of the Library of Congress: A Facsimile* (Washington, D.C.: Library of Congress, 1982), 94.

43. Robert A. Rutland, introduction to *1812 Catalogue of the Library of Congress*, xi.

44. Leo E. LaMontagne, *American Library Classification, with Special Reference to the Library of Congress* (Hamden, Conn.: Shoestring Press, 1961), 45; Francis Miksa, *The Development of Classification at the Library of Congress*, University of Illinois Graduate School of Library and Information Science Occasional Papers no. 164 (Champagne: USGLIS, 1984), 5.

45. *Catalogue of Books, Maps, and Charts Belonging to the Library of the Two Houses of Congress* (Washington, D.C., 1804).

46. *Catalogue of the Books, Maps, and Charts Belonging to the Library Established in the Capitol at the City of Washington, for the Two Houses of Congress* (Washington, D.C.: A. & C. Way, 1808).

47. It is true that the Department of State, which had authority over foreign relations, had a library of its own to consult. However, the Senate was responsible for ratifying treaties (such as the Louisiana Purchase), so it was necessary for Congress to have current information on United States boundaries with foreign empires.

48. Rutland, introduction, xx, xvii.

49. *Catalogue of Books Belonging to the Library Company of Burlington* (Burlington: S. C. Ustick, 1807); *Catalogue of the Books, &c. Belonging to the Library Company of Baltimore* (Baltimore: Edes and Leaken, 1809); *A Catalogue of Books Belonging to the Charleston Library Society* (Charleston: W. P. Young, 1811); *A Catalogue of the Books Belonging to the New York Society Library* (New York: C. S. Van Winkle, 1813); *A Catalogue of Books, Belonging to the Alexandria Library Company* (Alexandria: John A. Stewart, 1815); *Catalogue of Books Belonging to the Hartford Library Company* (Hartford: Hamlen & Newton, 1818).

50. For example, Vattel's *Law of Nations* was classed under "Law and Politics" at the Charleston Library Society and under "Law, Politics, Political Economy, Agriculture, Commerce, Etc." at the Alexandria Library Company.

51. It was only at Burlington and Hartford, where Politics and Political Economy classifications did not exist, that *Wealth of Nations* and *Discourses concerning Government* were classified more generally under Dissertations and Essays (Burlington) and Miscellanies (Hartford).

52. The only books whose classification substantially differed were classical literature. Such volumes were sometimes placed in a category on Greek and Roman authors (as at the Charleston Library Society) and sometimes classified according to subject matter (which was the practice at the Library of Congress). But these differences in classification of classical literature do not affect conclusions to be drawn about collection priorities at the Library of Congress, where Greek and Roman authors were not particularly stressed.

53. *Journal of the Assembly of the State of New-York at Their Forty-Second Session* (Albany: J. Buel, 1819), 148–52.

54. Johnston reprints the legislation pursuant to Library of Congress privileges in *History of the Library of Congress*, 55–56.

CHAPTER THREE

1. His recommendations suggest that in the early years of the Library, Jefferson, despite his own passion for books, supported a utilitarian conception of its role. In a letter to Joint Library Committee chairman Abraham Baldwin dated 14 April 1802, Jefferson wrote that, "in conformity" with Baldwin's ideas about the scope of a legislative library, he had compiled a catalog excluding "books of entertainment" and "confined ... to those branches of science which belong to the deliberations of the members as statesmen," omitting "those classical books, ancient and modern, which gentlemen generally have in their private libraries, but which can not properly claim a place in a collection made merely for the purpose of reference." Quoted in William Dawson Johnston, *History of the Library of Congress, Volume 1, 1800–1864* (Washington, D.C.: GPO, 1904), 36.

2. Douglas L. Wilson, "Thomas Jefferson and the Legacy of a National Library," *Wilson Library Bulletin* 64, 1 (1990): 40.

3. Quoted in Johnston, *History of the Library of Congress*, 87; *New York Evening Post*, 31 January 1815.

4. Quoted in Johnston, *History of the Library of Congress*, 86. King chose not to acknowledge that the Library that had been destroyed had two complete sets of the works of Voltaire.

5. Neil Harris, "Public Funding for Rarity: Some American Debates," *Libraries and Culture* 31, 1 (1996): 40. The most thorough account of the politicians in favor of and opposed to the purchase is found in David Mearns, *The Story up to Now: The Library of Congress, 1800–1946* (Washington, D.C.: Library of Congress, 1947), 18–25. Mearns lists the votes of individual members and breaks down the vote by region of the country; Federalist New England generally opposed the sale, and the Republican South and West favored it.

6. *The Debates and Proceedings of the Congress of the United States* (Washington, D.C.: Gales and Seaton, 1854), 10 October 1814. Hereafter cited as *Debates and Proceedings*.

7. *Debates and Proceedings*, 17 October 1814, and *National Intelligencer*, 27 January 1815. William E. Ames writes of the very close relationship between this paper and the Jefferson and Madison administrations in *A History of the "National Intelligencer"* (Chapel Hill: North Carolina University Press, 1972).

8. *Catalogue of the Library of the United States* (Washington, D.C.: Jonathan Elliot, 1815).

9. Articles on the purchase of Jefferson's library appeared in the *Boston Gazette, Petersburg Courier, New York Evening Post, Niles' Weekly Register, Walsh's American Register, Essex Register, Richmond Daily Compiler, Georgetown Daily Federal Republican*, and in Washington's *National Intelligencer* and *Weekly Gazette*.

10. The article originally published in *Walsh's American Register* was reprinted in the *National Intelligencer*, 14 July 1817, from which these quotes are taken. Emphasis is in the original.

11. Ibid.

12. Loren Smith points out, rightly, that Madison's library list of 1783 was broader of scope than Gerry's and entailed a more liberal conception of the value of a government library. Smith goes on to argue, however, that Madison planted "the seeds of a national archive" in 1783, seeds that sprouted with the acquisition of the Jefferson collection. Given the limited justifications that Madison offered for the library he proposed and the complete exclusion of some categories of works (such as fine arts) from Madison's list, I think Smith overstates the line of development from the Madison proposal to the Jefferson library. Loren E. Smith, "The Library List of 1783" (Ph.D. diss., Claremont Graduate School, 1969), 65.

13. The Papers of George Watterston, Library of Congress; Johnston, *History of the Library of Congress*, 111.

14. Henri Petter, *The Early American Novel* (Columbus: Ohio State University Press, 1971), 327. On the subject of cultural opposition to fiction, see Nina Baym, *Novels, Readers, and Reviewers: Responses to Fiction in Antebellum America* (Ithaca: Cornell University Press, 1984).

15. William Matheson, "George Watterston, Advocate of the National Library," in *Librarians of Congress, 1802–1974* (Washington, D.C.: Library of Congress, 1977), 58.

16. Julia Kennedy proposes another reason for Watterston's anonymity, at least in the case of *The L. . . . Family*: he might have anticipated that acquaintances would be displeased with his satirical treatment of Washington society. Julia E. Kennedy, "George Watterston: Novelist, 'Metropolitan Author,' and Critic" (Ph.D. diss., Catholic University of America, 1933), 31.

17. Johnston, *History of the Library of Congress*, 116.

18. Watterston to Everett, 10 January 1828 and 30 May 1828, Watterston Papers.

19. Relevant letters from Watterston to Everett are dated 3 January 1832, 15 February 1832, 7 July 1832, 13 December 1832, 7 January 1833, 11 March 1834, and 11 December 1834, in ibid.

20. The *Intelligencer* was the natural choice for Watterston to use in describing or proposing policies concerning the Library of Congress because of the newspaper's close relationship with the government. During the Madison and Monroe administrations, the *Intelligencer* continued to serve as the semiofficial organ of the administrative branch of the government, and newspaper editors from across the country copied accounts of congressional debates as they were reported in the *Intelligencer*. Ames, *History of the "National Intelligencer."* As I will discuss, however, Watterston's opinions about the Library did not necessarily accord with those of the paper's editors, Gales and Seaton.

21. James Gilreath and Douglas Wilson, introduction to *Thomas Jefferson's Library: A Catalog with the Entries in His Own Order*, ed. Gilreath and Wilson (Washington, D.C.: Library of Congress, 1989), 4.

22. Quoted in Leo E. LaMontagne, *American Library Classification, with Special Reference to the Library of Congress* (Hamden, Conn.: Shoestring Press, 1961), 35. The information on Jefferson's cataloging innovations in this paragraph comes from LaMontagne's book and from Francis Miksa, *The Development of Classification at the*

Library of Congress, University of Illinois Graduate School of Library and Information Science Occasional Papers no. 164 (Champaign: USGLIS, 1984).

23. *Catalogue of the Library.*

24. Johnston, *History of the Library of Congress*, 155. The biographical information on Fromentin comes from the *Biographical Directory of the American Congress, 1774–1996*, ed. Joel D. Treese (Alexandria, Va: CQ Staff Directories, 1997), 1062.

25. Frederick R. Goff discovered in the Rare Book Division of the Library of Congress at least two volumes that were in the original Library. He writes that the fate of the original Library has "never been satisfactorily explained" but believes that "the destruction of the Library must have been virtually complete." See Goff, "Early Library of Congress Bookplates," *Quarterly Journal of the Library of Congress* 26, 1 (1969): 55.

26. *In Senate of the United States. January 26th, 1816*, U.S. Cong., 1815–17, 4. Extracts from this report are also reprinted in Johnston, *History of the Library of Congress*, 151–53.

27. This comes from Johnston's reprint of the 1817 report in *History of the Library of Congress*, 157.

28. Ibid., 158.

29. Eugene Edgar Doll, "American History as Interpreted by German Historians from 1770 to 1815," *Transactions of the American Philosophical Society*, n.s., 38, 5 (1948): 478. As far as I know, Adams's interest in the Ebeling library for the Library of Congress has not been noticed by previous Library of Congress historians.

30. Adams to A. H. Everett, 29 October 1817, *Writings of John Quincy Adams*, vol. 6, ed. Worthington Chauncey Ford (New York: Macmillan, 1916; reprint, New York: Greenwood, 1968), 227.

31. Ibid., 23 November 1817, 264.

32. Adams to Joseph Hopkinson, 1 June 1818, in ibid., 345–46.

33. There is no explanation in this report as to why the Ways and Means Committee assumed the authority to push for increased appropriations for the Library, a duty that normally was reserved for the Joint Library Committee. I would speculate that members of the Joint Committee might have chosen to work through the Ways and Means Committee, hoping that its recommendation would be more persuasive to members.

34. This report is reproduced in Johnston, *History of the Library of Congress*, 161–62.

35. Paul A. Varg, *Edward Everett: The Intellectual in the Turmoil of Politics* (Selinsgrove: Susquehanna University Press, 1992), 27, quotation on 36.

36. See, for example, Everett to Watterston, 16 and 17 October 1826, Watterston Papers.

37. Ibid., 31 October 1826.

38. *The Microfilm Edition of the Edward Everett Papers*, ed. Frederick S. Allis Jr. (Boston: Massachusetts Historical Society, 1972). Entries are dated rather than paginated.

39. Three years later, on 13 March 1830, Everett succeeded in persuading a new

Joint Committee to purchase this work. Journal of the Committee on the Library, 1829–1861, 9, Library of Congress Archives, Library of Congress.

40. Matheson, "George Watterston," 70.

41. Everett to Watterston, 31 October 1826, and Watterston to Everett, 13 December 1826; Everett to Watterston, 31 October 1826; all in Watterston Papers.

42. Watterston to Everett, 12 July 1825, in ibid.

43. *The Life and Writings of Jared Sparks*, vol. 1, ed. Herbert B. Adams (Boston: Houghton, Mifflin and Company, 1893), 461–62.

44. Library Committee report of 19 December 1820, reproduced in Johnston, *History of the Library of Congress*, 127–28.

45. Ibid., 124.

46. *National Intelligencer*, 25 March 1817. The article is printed over the signature "W," indicating Watterston's authorship. *Washington Gazette*, 8 December 1817.

47. Elmer D. Johnson, *History of Libraries in the Western World* (Metuchen, N.J.: Scarecrow Press, 1970), 166.

48. George Watterston, *The L . . . Family at Washington; or, A Winter in the Metropolis* (Washington, D.C.: Davis and Force, 1822), 35, 37.

49. Descriptions of the rooms constructed by Bulfinch are quoted from the *Columbian Star* newspaper in Johnston, *History of the Library of Congress*, 129–30. Johnston describes the medals and busts on pages 131–32.

50. George Watterston, *Wanderer in Washington* (Washington, D.C.: Jonathan Elliot, jr., 1827), 55, 218, 220.

51. Milligan to Jefferson, 24 September 1814, quoted in Johnston, *History of the Library of Congress*, 79.

52. *National Intelligencer*, 15 September 1815.

53. *National Intelligencer*, 14 July 1817.

54. *National Intelligencer*, 28 August 1823.

55. For example, Everett noted in his diary on 8 June 1832 seeing Washington Irving using the Library collections. Allis, *Edward Everett Papers*.

56. Members of Congress sometimes authorized family members or friends to withdraw books on their behalf. Margaret Bayard Smith, author, prominent Washington hostess, and wife of publisher Samuel Harrison Smith, wrote to her sister in 1828, "The library of the Dept. of State, is close to us, and the city library and I count on access to the Congress Library as in times of old, when as Mary Ann may recollect I used to have members names signed on blanks for me to fill out at my pleasure." Smith, *The First Forty Years of Washington Society*, ed. Gaillard Hunt (New York: Charles Scribner's Sons, 1906), 241. Smith was very well connected socially, but in this letter she implicitly recognized the possibility that her access to the Library might be revoked. She "counts on" access as in times of old, probably (given her husband's support of the Republican Party) the Madison and Monroe administrations, but a change of political administrations might affect that access.

57. Watterston to Edward Everett, 5 March 1828, Watterston Papers.

58. *United States Telegraph*, 12 June 1829, and *National Journal*, 15 June 1829. Both articles are reprinted in full in Johnston, *History of the Library of Congress*, 192–95.

59. Johnston, *History of the Library of Congress*, 177.

60. Ibid., 190.

61. Gordon S. Wood, "The Democratization of Mind in the American Revolution," in *The Moral Foundations of the American Republic*, ed. Robert H. Horwitz (Charlottesville: University Press of Virginia, 1977), 102–28; Cathy Davidson, *Revolution and the Word: The Rise of the Novel in America* (New York: Oxford University Press, 1986), vii; Richard D. Brown, *Knowledge Is Power: The Diffusion of Information in Early America, 1700–1865* (New York: Oxford University Press, 1989), 218; William J. Gilmore, *Reading Becomes a Necessity of Life: Material and Cultural Life in Rural New England, 1780–1835* (Knoxville: University of Tennessee Press, 1989), 6, 274–75.

62. Jesse H. Shera, *Foundations of the Public Library: The Origins of the Public Library Movement in New England, 1629–1855* (Chicago: University of Chicago Press, 1949), 69; C. Seymour Thompson, *Evolution of the American Public Library, 1653–1876* (Washington, D.C.: Scarecrow Press, 1952), 80–94. See also Sidney Ditzion, "Mechanics' and Mercantile Libraries," *Library Quarterly* 10 (1940): 192–219.

63. David Kaser, *A Book for a Sixpence: The Circulating Library in America* (Pittsburgh: Beta Phi Mu, 1980), 121.

64. *Catalogue of Books Belonging to the Washington Library* (Washington, D.C.: 1815).

65. "Washington Library," in *Manual of Public Libraries, Institutions, and Societies in the United States and British Provinces of North America*, ed. William J. Rhees (Philadelphia: J. B. Lippincott & Co., 1859); rpt., Champaign: University of Illinois Graduate School of Library Science, 1967), 521–22.

66. Walter Channing, "Reflections on the Literary Delinquency of America," *North American Review* 2 (1815): 33–43.

67. John T. Kirkland, "Literary Institutions—University—Library," *North American Review* 9 (1819):191–200.

68. Paulding received his first government appointment with the navy after Madison read his sketches of American naval victories and heroes in the *Analectic Magazine*. Paulding was given a cabinet post in 1838 as secretary of the navy by President Van Buren as a reward for services rendered to the party through journalistic contributions to the *New York Evening Post*. Larry J. Reynolds, *James Kirke Paulding* (Boston: Twayne Publishers, 1984), 10–15. Interestingly, Watterston wrote to Paulding in 1817 apparently to ask for advice or help in getting pieces published in the *Analectic Magazine*. Paulding replied that he had no influence over editorial decisions with the magazine, but as a reader he would be glad to see Watterston's work in the periodical. Paulding to Watterston, 25 January 1817, Watterston Papers.

69. Johnston reprints the Joint Committee's request for deposit copies of some books in *History of the Library of Congress*, 158; the summary of appropriations is on page 159. John Y. Cole points out that annual appropriations for books and maps increased to two thousand dollars in 1820 in *For Congress and the Nation: A Chronological History of the Library of Congress* (Washington, D.C.: Library of Congress, 1979), 12.

CHAPTER FOUR

1. William Dawson Johnston, *History of the Library of Congress, Volume 1, 1800–1864* (Washington, D.C.: GPO, 1904), 214; John McDonough, "John Silva Meehan: A Gentleman of Amiable Manners," in *Librarians of Congress, 1802–1974* (Washington, D.C.: Library of Congress, 1977), 79.

2. *The Papers of Henry Clay*, vol. 8, ed. Robert Seager II (Lexington: University Press of Kentucky, 1984), 79; William Matheson, "George Watterston: Advocate of the National Library," in *Librarians of Congress*, 67. Journalist Anne Royall claimed that Watterston distributed religious pamphlets in the Library and used his franking privilege to distribute anti-Jackson campaign propaganda. But there is no evidence that these charges directly influenced Jackson's decision to replace him. See Alice S. Maxwell and Marion B. Dunlevy, *Virago! The Story of Anne Newport Royall (1769–1854)* (Jefferson, N.C.: McFarland & Company, 1985), 130; Bessie Rowland James, *Anne Royall's U.S.A.* (New Brunswick. N.J.: Rutgers University Press, 1972), 251; Anne Royall, *The Black Book; or, Continuation of Travels in the United States*, vol. 3 (Washington, D.C.: Printed for the Author, 1829), 211.

3. Richard Hofstadter, *Anti-intellectualism in American Life* (New York: Alfred A. Knopf, 1963), 159–60.

4. *United States Telegraph*, 9, 12, and 16 June 1829; *National Journal*, 9, 11, and 15 June 1829. On 16 June 1829 the *National Intelligencer* reprinted some of Watterston's side of the argument and defended his performance as Librarian.

5. *Petersburg Intelligencer*, copied in the *National Journal*, 15 June 1829; *New England Palladium*, reprinted in the *National Intelligencer*, 22 June 1829.

6. Johnston, *History of the Library of Congress*, 201; *United States Telegraph*, 12 June 1829, quoted in ibid., 193.

7. McDonough, "John Silva Meehan," 83.

8. *National Intelligencer*, 11 December 1834. See also articles of 5 December 1834 and 5 January 1835.

9. The articles are discussed later in this chapter and are documented in notes 52 to 55.

10. Journal of the Committee on the Library, 1829–1861, 1 March 1831, Library of Congress Archives, Library of Congress.

11. Johnston, *History of the Library of Congress*, 229.

12. See, for example, Journal of the Committee on the Library, 21 May 1830, 1 March 1831, 26 May 1832, 12 February 1833, and 21 June 1834.

13. Ibid., 9 January 1830, 20 March 1830, 17 March 1832, 12 February 1833, 27 January 1835, and 9 July 1838.

14. Ibid., 9 January 1830, 17 January 1832, and 10 March 1832.

15. Ibid., 9 January 1830, 7 March 1830, 3 January 1834, 6 February 1830, 28 February 1831, and 22 January 1838.

16. For example, a quorum failed to attend on three consecutive scheduled meetings: 26 January, 2 February, and 9 February 1833. Such entries are common in

the minutes of the committee. A particularly inactive committee was that of the second session of the Twenty-fourth Congress which met infrequently in 1837.

17. *The Microfilm Edition of the Edward Everett Papers*, ed. Frederick S. Allis Jr. (Boston: Massachusetts Historical Society, 1972), 26 February 1834.

18. Ibid., 8 January 1835. This motion is recorded in the Journal of the Committee on the Library on the same day.

19. Wilde's letter was printed in the *National Intelligencer*, 9 February 1836.

20. Reprinted in the *National Intelligencer*, 19 February 1836.

21. George W. Greene, "Art. VI," *North American Review* 45 (1837): 146–47.

22. Greene argued for "the enlargement of the library of Congress upon those broad principles" that were followed in the national libraries of Europe, including liberal expenditures for books to meet the needs of American scholars. Ibid., 140.

23. Neil Harris, "Public Funding for Rarity: Some American Debates," *Libraries and Culture* 31, 1 (1996): 41.

24. John R. Van Atta, "William Campbell Preston," in *American National Biography*, vol. 17, ed. John A. Garraty and Mark C. Carnes (New York: Oxford University Press, 1999), 851–53. See also J. G. deR. Hamilton, "William Campbell Preston," in *Dictionary of American Biography*, vol. 15, ed. Dumas Malone (New York: Charles Scribner's Sons, 1935), 207–8.

25. *Report of the Library Committee*, 24th Cong., 1st sess., 1836, S. Rept. 242.

26. Johnston, *History of the Library of Congress*, 243.

27. Ibid., 100.

28. Journal of the Committee on the Library, 9 January 1830, 17 March 1832, and 9 January 1840.

29. The entire statute is reprinted in Johnston, *History of the Library of Congress*, 249–50.

30. Nancy E. Gwinn, "The Origins and Development of International Publication Exchange in Nineteenth-Century America" (Ph.D. diss., George Washington University, 1996), 92.

31. Robert D. Stevens, *The Role of the Library of Congress in the International Exchange of Official Publications* (Washington, D.C.: Library of Congress, 1953), 3; *Report on the Memorial of Mr. Alexandre Vattemare*, 26th Cong., 1st sess. 1840, S. Doc. 521.

32. *Southern Literary Messenger* 9 (1843): 757. See also "National Exchanges," *Literary World* 3 (1848): 389–91, and "Monsieur Vattemare," *Holden's Dollar Magazine* 3 (1849): 125–26.

33. *Report on the Memorial of Mr. Alexandre Vattemare*.

34. *Report of the Library Committee*, 30th Cong., 1st sess., 1848, H. Rept. 590. This report was made by Henry C. Murphy of New York on behalf of the Joint Committee on the Library. In it he stated that "the extent to which the federal government can co-operate in this great and ennobling plan for the fraternization of Europe and America is, in the opinion of the committee, confined to the distribution of such publications, documents, and laws, as are printed by its authority, or for its use in the discharge of its constitutional functions."

35. The letter is reprinted in Stevens, *Role of the Library of Congress*, 8.

36. McDonough, "John Silva Meehan," 94, and Stevens, *Role of the Library of Congress*, 8.

37. Meehan to James Alfred Pearce, 26 November 1849 and 28 February 1850, Librarian's Letterbooks, 1843–1899, Library of Congress Archives, Library of Congress.

38. In a letter written to Pearce after the exchange provisions had been repealed by Congress, Meehan complained that "the Parliament of France would not offer so great an indignity to Congress or be so wanting in self-respect, as to send us, in *exchange* for our complete sets of documents, well bound, a few of the loose papers published for their daily use. Mr. Vattemare knows this well." He also described some of the books received by the Library as "evidently the refuse of a French library." Librarian's Letterbooks, 6 September 1854.

39. *Report on the Memorial of Mr. Alexandre Vattemare.*

40. *Catalogue of the Library of Congress in the Capitol* (Washington, D.C.: By Order of Congress, 1840). The estimate of thirty thousand volumes is Johnston's (*History of the Library of Congress*, 515).

41. Journal of the Committee on the Library, 7 March and 17 April 1830.

42. Ibid., 24 March 1840.

43. *U.S. Statutes at Large* 4 (1831): 436–39.

44. Quoted in James J. Barnes, *Authors, Publishers, and Politicians: The Quest for an Anglo-American Copyright Agreement, 1815–1854* (Columbus: Ohio State University Press, 1974), 51.

45. Ezra Greenspan, *George Palmer Putnam: Representative American Publisher* (University Park: Pennsylvania State University Press, 2000), 87.

46. Barnes, *Authors, Publishers, and Politicians*, 71.

47. *Report with Senate Bill no. 233*, 24th Cong., 2d sess., 1837, S. Doc. 179.

48. *Report to Accompany Senate Bill no. 32*, 25th Cong., 2d session, S. Doc. 494.

49. Aubert J. Clark, "The Movement for International Copyright in Nineteenth-Century America" (Ph.D. diss., Catholic University, 1960), 48.

50. *Report to Accompany Senate Bill no. 32.*

51. In one of their petitions to the United States Congress on the matter of international copyright, British authors maintained that an "equitable remuneration" from American publishers who had pirated Scott's work "might have saved his life, and would, at least, have relieved its closing years from the burden of debts and destructive toils." *Petition of Thomas Moore, and Other Authors of Great Britain*, 24th Cong., 2d sess., 1837, S. Doc. 134.

52. *National Intelligencer*, 8 January 1834; David Mearns, *The Story up to Now: The Library of Congress, 1800–1946* (Washington, D.C.: Library of Congress, 1947), 42.

53. Quoted in Johnston, *History of the Library of Congress*, 228–29.

54. "Art. VI," 140; Charles Bowen "Public Libraries," in *The American Almanac and Repository of Useful Knowledge for the Year 1837* (Boston: Charles Bowen, 1836), 82.

55. "Art. VI," 134–35, 138.

56. *National Intelligencer*, 5 December 1834, 3 January 1844.

57. Quoted in Johnson, *History of the Library of Congress*, 177.

58. John Y. Cole, *For Congress and the Nation: A Chronological History of the Library of Congress* (Washington, D.C.: Library of Congress, 1979), 15. The Joint Committee had approved this extension of privileges on 30 December 1829 (Journal of the Committee on the Library).

59. *Everett Papers*, 4 April 1832; Journal of the Committee on the Library, 27 March 1834, 31 March 1832, 3 January 1834.

60. Ibid., 3 February 1832, 12 February 1833, 30 May 1834, and 8 May 1844.

61. George Watterston, *The L.... Family at Washington; or, A Winter in the Metropolis* (Washington, D.C.: Davis and Force, 1822), 85; George Watterston, *Wanderer in Washington* (Washington, D.C.: Jonathan Elliot, Jr., 1827), 218, 222.

62. *National Intelligencer*, 30 March 1832, 5 December 1834.

63. Reprinted in Johnston, *History of the Library of Congress*, 380, 381.

64. Harriet Martineau, *Retrospect of Western Travel* (New York: Harper and Brothers, 1838), 180.

65. Anne Firor Scott, *Natural Allies: Women's Associations in American History* (Urbana: University of Illinois Press, 1991), esp. chap. 1, "To Cast Our Mite on the Altar of Benevolence: Women Begin to Organize," 11–36. The first women's antislavery society was founded in 1832 in Salem, Massachusetts, soon to be followed by organizations in Boston (1833), Philadelphia (1833), and New York (1835). By 1837 many members of these organizations supported the notion of women lecturing to "promiscuous" (male and female) audiences, considered at the time a radical breach of propriety, as English reformer Fanny Wright had discovered in 1836 when she was driven from a lecture platform in New York by an outraged mob. Mary P. Ryan describes Fanny Wright's "aggressive assault" on "the masculine border of the public sphere" and the angry reaction she provoked in *Women in Public: Between Banners and Ballots, 1825–1880* (Baltimore: Johns Hopkins University Press, 1990), 134. South Carolina–born abolitionist Angelina Grimké lectured to an audience of over six hundred men and women on 21 June 1837 at a hall in Lynn, Massachusetts. Thereafter, she and her sister, Sarah, frequently lectured to mixed audiences. Ruth Bogin and Jean Fagan Yellin, introduction to *The Abolitionist Sisterhood: Women's Political Culture in Antebellum America*, ed. Yellin and John C. Van Horne (Ithaca: Cornell University Press, 1994), 15.

66. Debra Gold Hansen, "The Boston Female Anti-Slavery Society and the Limits of Gender Politics," in Yellin and Van Horne, *Abolitionist Sisterhood*, 50.

67. On this organization, see Carroll Smith-Rosenberg, "Beauty, the Beast, and the Militant Woman: A Case Study in Sex Roles and Social Stress in Jacksonian America," *American Quarterly* 23, 4 (1971): 562–84. Ryan also discusses the activities of the New York Female Moral Reform Society in chapter 3 of *Women in Public*, "Political Space: Of Prostitutes and Politicians," 95–129.

68. Carroll Smith-Rosenberg, *Disorderly Conduct: Visions of Gender in Victorian America* (New York: Alfred A. Knopf, 1985), 86.

69. Quoted in Deborah Bingham Van Broekhoven, "'Let Your Names Be En-rolled': Method and Ideology in Women's Antislavery Petitioning," in Yellin and Van Horne, *Abolitionist Sisterhood*, 187–88.

70. Ibid., 187.

71. Journal of the Committee on the Library, 1 March 1843 (Reynolds) and 10 April 1844 (Duhamel du Monceau).

72. Nina Baym, *Woman's Fiction: A Guide to Novels by and about Women in America, 1820–1870* (Ithaca: Cornell University Press, 1978), chap. 3 "Catharine Sedg-wick and Other Early Novelists," 51–85; Jacqueline Gray, "Lady Charlotte Bury," in *DLB*, vol. 116, *British Romantic Novelists, 1789–1832*, ed. Bradford K. Mudge (Detroit: Gale Research, 1992), 56.

73. Nina Baym, *Novels, Readers, and Reviewers: Responses to Fiction in Antebellum America* (Ithaca: Cornell University Press, 1984), 255.

74. David Kaser, *A Book for a Sixpence: The Circulating Library in America* (Pitts-burgh: Beta Phi Mu, 1980), 77–78.

75. While it is true that circulating libraries catered more than other library types to female clientele, the architecture of Robinson's library nonetheless sent equivocal messages to women about their relationship to literary culture. Cathy Davidson discusses the role of circulating libraries in bringing books to female readers in *Revolution and the Word: The Rise of the Novel in America* (New York: Oxford University Press, 1986), 27–29.

76. C. Seymour Thompson, *Evolution of the American Public Library, 1653–1876* (Washington, D.C.: Scarecrow Press, 1952), 89.

77. William J. Rhees, ed., *Manual of Public Libraries, Institutions, and Societies in the United States and British Provinces of North America* (Philadelphia: J. B. Lip-pincott & Co., 1859; rpt., Champaign: University of Illinois Graduate School of Library Science, 1967), 378. The Mercantile Library Association of New York re-ported in 1857 that a ladies' reading room was "the result of a most pleasing necessity, influenced by a large increase in the list of our lady subscribers" (287). And at the Town Library of New Hampshire in 1857, women had difficulty competing with men for access to books: "The eagerness with which books are called for, in the hours when the library is open, prevents many females from mingling in the crowd, and complaint is made by them that they cannot obtain books, as they would, if better facility was afforded" (208). Administrators of the library planned to remedy the problem by appointing one hour per week for the exclusive purpose of deliver-ing books to women.

78. Abigail A. Van Slyck, *Free to All: Carnegie Libraries and American Culture, 1890–1920* (Chicago: University of Chicago Press, 1995), 16.

79. Abigail A. Van Slyck, "The Lady and the Library Loafer," *Winterthur Port-folio* 31, 4 (1996): 241.

80. Anne M. Boylan, *Sunday School: The Formation of an American Institution, 1790–1880* (New Haven: Yale University Press, 1988), 50.

81. David Paul Nord, "The Evangelical Origins of Mass Media in America, 1815–1835," *Journalism Monographs* no. 88 (May 1984): 21. The ATS printed five million

tracts annually during these years, while the ABS printed about a quarter of a million Bibles per year (19).

82. Carl Bode, *The American Lyceum: Town Meeting of the Mind* (New York: Oxford University Press, 1956), 7, 24.

83. Jesse H. Shera, *Foundations of the Public Library: The Origins of the Public Library Movement in New England, 1629–1855* (Chicago: University of Chicago Press, 1949), 123.

84. A good example of the growth of such libraries is the Apprentices Library of New York City, which grew from its foundation in 1820 to become the primary wing of the General Society of Mechanics and Tradesmen of that city and in 1842 opened its doors to use by people other than members upon payment of an annual subscription. Tom Glynn, "Books for a Reformed Republic: The Apprentices Library of New York City, 1820–1865," *Libraries and Culture* 34, 4 (1999): 356.

85. Sidney Ditzion, "Mechanics' and Mercantile Libraries," *Library Quarterly* 10 (1940): 213.

86. Joseph Lawrence Yeatman, "Literary Culture and the Role of Libraries in Democratic America: Baltimore, 1815–1840," *Journal of Library History* 20, 4 (1985): 345; Thompson, *Evolution of the American Public Library*, 145.

87. Henry Wadsworth Longfellow to Stephen Longfellow, 10 March 1829, *The Letters of Henry Wadsworth Longfellow*, ed. Andrew Hilen (Cambridge: Harvard University Press, 1966), 302–3; Longfellow's emphasis. On the Portland Library Society (which had been established in 1765) merging with the Portland Athenaeum, see Thompson, *Evolution of the American Public Library*, 73–74.

88. Frederick M. Binder, *The Age of the Common School, 1800–1865* (New York: John Wiley and Sons, 1974). The material throughout this paragraph comes from Binder's work.

89. New York passed legislation in 1835 giving school districts the authority to tax themselves for the purpose of founding libraries intended to serve both students and adults; Massachusetts passed a similar law in 1837. And Michigan's constitution, adopted in 1835, encouraged establishment of district-school libraries funded by penal fines and money paid in substitute for military service as part of the state educational system. Sidney Ditzion, "The District-School Library, 1835–55," *Library Quarterly* 10 (1940): 545–77.

90. Ibid., 576.

91. Ralph Waldo Emerson, "The American Scholar," in *Ralph Waldo Emerson*, ed. Richard Poirier (New York: Oxford University Press, 1990), 37.

92. Timothy Flint, "Obstacles to American Literature," *Knickerbocker* 2, 3 (1833): 21; John L. O'Sullivan, "Introduction," *United States Magazine and Democratic Review* 1, 1 (1837): 14. Flint complained that "our national and state governments do little or nothing for literature by furnishing example, premiums, excitement, money" ("Obstacles," 21). George W. Greene held the federal government responsible for cultivating library resources in America ("Art. VI," 140).

93. O'Sullivan wrote, "In the spirit of her literature we can never hope to rival

England . . . but we should not follow in her wake; a radiant path invites us forward in another direction" ("Introduction," 14).

94. Ray W. Frantz Jr., "A Re-Examination of the Influence of Literary Nationalism on the Public Library," *Journal of Library History* 1 (1966): 183.

CHAPTER FIVE

1. Rodney P. Carlisle, "James Alfred Pearce," in *American National Biography*, vol. 17, ed. John A. Garraty and Mark C. Carnes (New York: Oxford University Press, 1999), 205–6.

2. *Congressional Globe*, 37th Cong., 3d sess., 1863, 293.

3. This comment from Emerson's journal is quoted in John Y. Cole, *For Congress and the Nation: A Chronological History of the Library of Congress* (Washington, D.C.: Library of Congress, 1979), 28.

4. Report of the Librarian to the Joint Committee on the Library, 7 January 1863, Library of Congress Archives, Library of Congress.

5. *Congressional Globe*, 28th Cong., 2d sess., 1845, 116.

6. *Joint Resolution to Grant Judges and Solicitor of Court of Claims Use of Congressional Library*, 35th Cong., 1st sess., 1858, S. Rpt. 328.

7. Ibid.

8. William J. Rhees, ed., *The Smithsonian Institution: Documents Relative to Its Origin and History* (Washington, D.C.: Smithsonian Institution, 1879), 144, 5.

9. See, for example, the *Southern Literary Messenger* 6 (1840): 25–34 and 7 (1841): 277–79. In the *American Whig Review*, it was proposed that the new institution be merged with the National Institute (a private Washington organization devoted to scientific research), a suggestion that was debated for a time in Congress. F. W. Ingersoll, "National Institute," *American Whig Review* 2 (1845): 235–55.

10. Rhees, *Smithsonian Institution*, 160–61.

11. The entire letter is reprinted by William Dawson Johnston, *History of the Library of Congress*, vol. 1, *1800–1864* (Washington, D.C.: GPO, 1904), 243–44.

12. *Library of Durazzo Family, at Genoa, Memorial of Amherst College and Illinois College for Purchase*, 28th Cong., 1st sess., 1844, H. Rpt. 553.

13. Rhees, *Smithsonian Institution*, 419.

14. Jean V. Matthews, "Libraries, Books, and the Nature of America: The Creation of the Smithsonian Institution," *Journal of Library History* 16, 1 (1981): 154; David Lowenthal, *George Perkins Marsh: Versatile Vermonter* (New York: Columbia University Press, 1958), 82.

15. Rhees, *Smithsonian Institution*, 268.

16. Nancy E. Gwinn, "The Origins and Development of International Publication Exchange in Nineteenth-Century America" (Ph.D. diss., George Washington University, 1995), 179.

17. Rhees, *Smithsonian Institution*, 313.

18. Ibid., 314, 318.

19. Ibid., 317, 318.

20. Ibid., 319–20, 322.

21. Richard William Leopold, *Robert Dale Owen: A Biography* (Cambridge: Harvard University Press, 1940), 190, 221.

22. Rhees, *Smithsonian Institution*, 374–75, 377.

23. Rhees, *Smithsonian Institution*, 415, 418, 419.

24. Joseph A. Borome, *Charles Coffin Jewett* (Chicago: American Library Association, 1951), 22.

25. C. Hale, "The Smithsonian Institution," *North American Review* 79 (1854): 447.

26. Matthews, "Libraries, Books," 158.

27. The catalog, published in 1843, was divided into two parts. The first "listed all the works in the library alphabetically by author. Beneath each author's name appeared, first, his complete works, then single titles alphabetically, and, lastly, biographies written by others. . . . The second part . . . was a very full subject index—alphabetical and classified—with many cross references." At the time this catalog appeared, previous printed college library catalogs had simply listed a title per line, arranged by subject. Borome, *Jewett*, 11–12.

28. *Report of the Board of Regents of the Smithsonian Institution*, 30th Cong., 1st sess., 1848, S. Misc. Doc. 23, 191.

29. Borome describes the plan in chapter 4, "The Grand Scheme: Its Origin," in *Jewett*, 43–51. The plan was eventually tested on the catalog of the Library of Congress, with some success, until it was learned that the clay blocks Jewett was using for plates shrank during baking and became useless. Borome, *Jewett*, 98.

30. *Third Annual Report of the Board of Regents of the Smithsonian Institution*, 30th Cong., 2d sess., 1849, H. Misc. Doc. 48, 40–42; *Eighth Annual Report of the Board of Regents of the Smithsonian Institution*, 33d Cong., 1st sess., 1854, H. Misc. Doc. 97, 216. The eighth annual report reprinted excerpts of earlier reports in order to present the history of the library controversy and to justify the dismissal of Jewett.

31. Borome, *Jewett*, 82–84.

32. Ibid., 36.

33. *Fifth Annual Report of the Board of Regents of the Smithsonian Institution*, 32d Cong., special sess., 1851, S. Misc. Doc. 1, 31.

34. Borome, *Jewett*, 66.

35. *Eighth Annual Report*, 31.

36. Rhees, *Smithsonian Institution*, 325.

37. *Eighth Annual Report*, 83, 85, 91; Pearce's emphases.

38. Meacham's report can be found in the *Eighth Annual Report* of the Smithsonian Institution that was submitted to the House of Representatives, 292. The shorter report submitted to the Senate does not include Meacham's dissenting opinion.

39. Hale, "Smithsonian Institution," 460.

40. Two items in Pearce's correspondence relate to his authorship of the report, including a letter from A. G. Brown of Mississippi dated 25 June 1854 (written from Washington), and one from Asa Gray dated 4 August 1855. Brown, in fact, thanks Pearce for having sent him a copy of the report, strong evidence that Pearce was

indeed the primary author. James Alfred Pearce Papers, Maryland Historical Society, Baltimore.

41. Gray to Pearce, 4 August 1855, Pearce Papers.

42. Pearce to Henry, 12 March 1851, Joseph Henry Papers, Smithsonian Institution Archives, Smithsonian Institution, Washington, D.C.

43. Cf. letters from Henry to Pearce reprinted in Bernard Steiner, "James Alfred Pearce," *Maryland Historical Magazine* 18 (1923): 42–45.

44. Reprinted in ibid., 42. Witte was an author of one of the congressional reports into Rufus Choate's resignation and his charges that the Smithsonian fund was being managed contrary to the intent of Congress. Witte took the position that Henry was justified in firing Jewett and also suggested that the Library of Congress was already serving scholars as a national library. *Report of Select Committee on Management of Smithsonian Institution*, 33d Cong., 2d sess., 1855, H. Rpt. 141.

45. Steiner, "Pearce," 45.

46. Borome, *Jewett*, 172–73.

47. *Eighth Annual Report*, 86, 285.

48. John Y. Cole, *Copyright in the Library of Congress* (Washington, D.C.: Library of Congress, 1995), 5.

49. David Mearns, *The Story Up to Now: The Library of Congress, 1800–1946* (Washington, D.C.: Library of Congress, 1947), 57.

50. *Fourth Annual Report of the Board of Regents*, 31st Cong., 1st sess., 1850, S. Misc. Doc. 120, 35.

51. Meehan to Rich, 14 April 1849, Librarian's Letterbooks, 1843–1899, Library of Congress Archives, Library of Congress. Meehan had made similar comments about lack of shelf space in letters to Rich, 21 August 1848, and to Pearce, 17 September 1849.

52. Meehan to Pearce, 23 March 1847, Librarian's Letterbooks; Meehan's emphasis.

53. Benjamin Perley Poore, *Reminiscences of Sixty Years in the National Metropolis* (Philadelphia: Hubbard Brothers, 1886), 176; Frank Luther Mott, *A History of American Magazines*, vol. 2, *1850–1865* (Cambridge: Harvard University Press, 1967), 500.

54. *Fourth Annual Report*, 35.

55. *Catalogue of the Library of Congress* (Washington, D.C.: Lemuel Towers, 1861).

56. Mott, *American Magazines*, 131–32.

57. Richard D. Brown, *Knowledge Is Power: The Diffusion of Information in Early America, 1700–1865* (New York: Oxford University Press, 1989), 243–44.

58. Rhees, *Smithsonian Institution*, 418.

59. Charles Coffin Jewett, "Report of the Assistant Secretary," in *Fifth Annual Report*, 31.

60. Brown, *Knowledge Is Power*, 243.

61. Hale, "Smithsonian Institution," 441–64; W. H. Hurlbutt, "The Smithsonian Institution," *Christian Examiner* 57 (1854): 385–95; "Smithson's Bequest: Its Objects and Issues," *Southern Literary Messenger* 21 (1855): 457–71 (unsigned); and T. M. Brewer, "The Smithsonian Institution," *Putnam's Monthly* 4 (1854): 121–31.

62. Hale, "Smithsonian Institution," 454, 456, 462.

63. Hurlbutt, "Smithsonian Institution," 393, 395.

64. Brewer, "Smithsonian Institution," 130.

65. "Smithson's Bequest," 462.

66. Matthews, "Libraries, Books," 162.

67. Ibid., 161.

68. Gwinn, "International Publication Exchange," 206.

69. Quoted in Johnston, *History of the Library of Congress*, 281.

70. Congress appropriated $10,000 for books on 13 January 1852 and $75,000 more on 31 August of that year. The first estimate for rebuilding the Library room was for $72,500, appropriated on 19 March 1852. Architect Walter requested an additional $20,500 in December and received it in February 1853. Apparently, the additional money for the building was the only appropriation that received opposition, and only because the legislators were critical of Walter for exceeding his original estimate. Ibid., 291–308.

71. Meehan to Pearce, 9 April 1852, Librarian's Letterbooks; Journal of the Committee on the Library, 1829–1861, 18 August 1852 and 3 March 1853, Library of Congress Archives, Library of Congress; Johnston, *History of the Library of Congress*, 309; *New York Daily Tribune*, 31 May 1852.

72. Johnston, *History of the Library of Congress*, 301–2; Journal of the Committee on the Library, 3 March 1853.

73. Meehan to Pearce, 4 May 1853, and Meehan to Cass, 29 July 1853, Librarian's Letterbooks.

74. Meehan to Rich Brothers, 28 February 1856, and Meehan to Pearce, 18 April 1856, Librarian's Letterbooks.

75. *Statutes at Large* 4 (1828): 321; *Statutes at Large* 11 (1857): 253.

76. Cole, *Copyright in the Library of Congress*, 10.

77. Jesse H. Shera, *Foundations of the Public Library* (Chicago: University of Chicago Press, 1949), 175.

78. Quoted in C. Seymour Thompson, *Evolution of the American Public Library, 1653–1876* (Washington, D.C.: Scarecrow Press, 1952), 180, and *Report of the Trustees of the Public Library of the City of Boston* (Boston: J. H. Eastburn, City Printer), 15. The standard history of the institution is by Walter Muir Whitehill, *Boston Public Library: A Centennial History* (Cambridge: Harvard University Press, 1956).

79. Quoted in Michael H. Harris and Gerard Spiegler, "Everett, Ticknor, and the Common Man: The Fear of Societal Instability as the Motivation for the Founding of the Boston Public Library," *Libri* 24 (1974): 256.

80. *National Intelligencer*, 25 May 1853.

81. The quoted phrase is from Ezra Greenspan, *Walt Whitman and the American Reader* (Cambridge: Cambridge University Press, 1990), 23. Other statistics in this paragraph come from John Tebbel and Mary Ellen Zuckerman, *The Magazine in America, 1741–1990* (New York: Oxford University Press, 1991), 18, and Frank Luther Mott, *American Journalism* (New York: Macmillan, 1959), 11.

82. John Tebbel, *A History of Book Publishing in the United States*, vol. 1, *The Creation of an Industry, 1630–1865* (New York: R. R. Bowker, 1972), 221, 245; Donald Sheehan, *This Was Publishing: A Chronicle of the Book Trade in the Gilded Age* (Bloomington: Indiana University Press, 1952), 19.

83. Ronald J. Zboray, *A Fictive People: Antebellum Economic Development and the American Reading Public* (New York: Oxford University Press, 1993), 11.

CHAPTER SIX

1. *Catalogue of the Library of Congress* (Washington, D.C.: Library of Congress, 1849).

2. In the citations that follow, I have included the full name of the author when I could identify it, a short title, and the year of publication. For books that were located in the catalog, the publication year indicates the edition the Library had. In some cases the long title of the work is included to convey a more accurate sense of the book's content. The Library Committee could not possibly record in its minutes the titles of every book it wished to acquire for the Library. The titles listed in the paragraphs that follow were therefore of particular interest to the committee, an interest also signified by the orders for multiple titles of certain works.

3. Journal of the Committee on the Library, 1829–1861, 26 February 1845, 1 March 1851, and 19 January 1858, Library of Congress Archives, Library of Congress.

4. Ibid., 11 February 1840, 2 June 1840, 17 January 1846, 5 June 1846, and 6 April 1854.

5. Ibid., 18 February 1840, 24 December 1841, 21 January 1842, 27 March 1844, 10 March 1846, 28 January 1848, and 18 February 1848.

6. Ibid., 11 February 1840, 17 January 1846, and 6 April 1854.

7. Ibid., 8 July 1842, 10 March 1846, 13 and 20 June 1846, and 1 August 1846.

8. Meehan to Rich, 8 March 1845, Librarian's Letterbooks, 1843–1899, Library of Congress Archives, Library of Congress.

9. Quoted in William Dawson Johnston, *History of the Library of Congress, Volume I, 1800–1864* (Washington, D.C.: 1904), 328. Congress did eventually vote to acquire the manuscript, but by the time this decision was made it had already been sold to James Lenox of New York (340).

10. Journal of the Committee on the Library, 16 June 1840, 8 January 1846.

11. James D. Dana to Asa Gray, 16 March 1846, quoted in Harry Miller Lydenberg, introduction to Daniel C. Haskell, *The United States Exploring Expedition, 1838–1842, and Its Publications, 1844–1874* (New York: Greenwood Press, 1968), 11.

12. Journal of the Committee on the Library, 23 January 1849.

13. Meehan to Pearce, 3 December 1852, Librarian's Letterbooks.

14. Journal of the Committee on the Library, 13 February 1850; Meehan to Rich Brothers, 18 February 1850, Librarian's Letterbooks.

15. Journal of the Committee on the Library, 11 March 1842, 18 April 1846. Southern states, incidentally, were often strongly represented among Library Committee personnel. The committee of the second session of the Twenty-seventh

Congress (1846–47), for example, included Pearce of Maryland, Joseph W. Chalmers of Mississippi, Dixon H. Lewis of Alabama, all from the Senate, and Representative James McDowell of Virginia. Senator Jefferson Davis was also a sometime member of the committee.

16. *Catalogue of the Library of Congress* (Washington, D.C.: Lemuel Towers, 1861).

17. A letter from Meehan to Philadelphia bookseller Thomas DeSilver indicates that the Library was still trying to find a copy of Foote's *Texas and the Texans* in mid-1848. Meehan to DeSilver, 24 June 1848, Librarian's Letterbooks.

18. Library of Congress Invoice Book, 1841–1862, 61, 77–78, Library of Congress Archives, Library of Congress.

19. Washington Irving, *The Adventures of Captain Bonneville*, U.S.A. (Norman: University of Oklahoma Press, 1961), 377. See also Irving, *Astoria* (Norman: University of Oklahoma Press, 1964).

20. Journal of the Committee on the Library, 3 March 1840; Marcus B. Simpson Jr., "John Kirk Townsend," in *American National Biography*, vol. 21, ed. John A. Garraty and Mark C. Carnes (New York: Oxford University Press, 1999), 787–88. Information on Jason Lee is from Ray Allen Billington, *The Far Western Frontier, 1830–1860* (New York: Harper and Row, 1956), 84.

21. Journal of the Committee on the Library, 18 December 1844; Gordon B. Dodds, "Robert Greenhow," in *American National Biography*, vol. 9 ed. John A. Garraty and Mark C. Carnes (New York: Oxford University Press, 1999), 538–39.

22. Journal of the Committee on the Library, 31 January and 14 February 1846. Although the committee elected to purchase Robertson's *Oregon: Our Right and Title*, for some reason it had not been acquired by 1849.

23. Frederick Merk, *History of the Westward Movement* (New York: Alfred A. Knopf, 1978), 325.

24. John Charles Frémont, *The Expeditions of John Charles Frémont*, ed. Donald Jackson and Mary Lee Spence (Urbana: University of Illinois Press, 1970).

25. Journal of the Committee on the Library, 30 May 1846; Billington, *Far Western Frontier*, 169–70.

26. Meehan to Bruff, 28 May 1847, Librarian's Letterbooks; Journal of the Committee on the Library, 11 February and 10 March 1848.

27. Ray Allen Billington and Martin Ridge, *Western Expansion: A History of the American Frontier*, 5th ed. (New York: Macmillan, 1982), 502.

28. All the acquisitions listed to this point in the paragraph are recorded in the Library of Congress Invoice Book, 1841–1862, 123–25, 160–61.

29. Journal of the Committee on the Library, 14 January 1848; Meehan to Black, 18 September 1848, Librarian's Letterbooks.

30. Billington and Ridge, *Westward Expansion*, 502.

31. In 1852, Meehan had written to the Library's London bookseller that "all or nearly all our chapters containing Voyages, Travels, Geographies, Gazetteers, Atlases, etc. were destroyed. Even Lord Kingsborough's *Antiquities of Mexico*, which

we received from you only a few weeks before the meeting of Congress, was burnt." Meehan to Rich Brothers, 11 February 1852, and Meehan to Borland, 20 April 1853, Librarian's Letterbooks. Borland had been appointed minister to Central America on 18 April 1853.

32. Rodney P. Carlisle, "James Alfred Pearce," in *American National Biography*, vol. 17, ed. John A. Garraty and Mark C. Carnes (New York: Oxford University Press, 1999), 205–6.

33. Information on U.S. interest in Central America comes from Robert E. May, *The Southern Dream of a Caribbean Empire, 1854–1861* (Baton Rouge: Louisiana State University Press, 1973).

34. Meehan to Rich Brothers, 28 February 1856, Librarian's Letterbooks.

35. See Ezra Greenspan, *George Palmer Putnam: Representative American Publisher* (University Park: Pennsylvania State University Press, 2000).

36. By 1849, Poe had published *The Narrative of Arthur Gordon Pym* (1838), *Tales of the Grotesque and Arabesque* (1839), and *Tales* (1845), all with major New York and Philadelphia literary publishers.

37. The characterization of *Recollections of a Southern Matron* is from Nina Baym, *Woman's Fiction: A Guide to Novels by and about Women in America, 1820–1870* (Ithaca: Cornell University Press, 1978), 70. Gilman's commitment to domesticity is described by Madeline B. Stern, "Caroline Gilman," in *Dictionary of Literary Biography*, vol. 3, *Antebellum Writers of New York and the South*, ed. Joel Myerson (Detroit: Gale Research, 1979), 119.

38. D. C. Woodcox, "Marguerite, Countess of Blessington (Margaret Power Farmer Gardiner)," in *Dictionary of Literary Biography*, vol. 166, *British Travel Writers, 1837–1875*, ed. Barbara Brothers and Julia Gergits (Detroit: Gale Research, 1996), 50–54.

39. Receipt Book F, 1849–1851, 355, Library of Congress Archives, Library of Congress. All receipt books mentioned in subsequent citations are from the Library of Congress Archives.

40. Elisa E. Beshero-Bondar, "Eliza Leslie," in *Dictionary of Literary Biography*, vol. 202, *Nineteenth-Century American Fiction Writers*, ed. Kent P. Ljungquist (Detroit: Gale Research 1999), 166–72.

41. Caruthers's novels *The Kentuckian in New-York* and *The Cavaliers of Virginia* were both published by Harper of New York in the 1830s. Ingraham's books of the period include *Burton; or, The Sieges* (1838), *Captain Kyd* (1839), and *The Quadroone; or, St. Michael's Day* (1841), all three also published by Harper.

42. McIntosh's novels of the 1840s include *Conquest and Self-Conquest* (1843), *Woman an Enigma* (1843), and *Two Lives* (1846), the former two published by Harper and the latter by D. Appleton of New York. Stephens published, among other works, *Alice Copley: A Tale of Queen Mary* (1844), *The Tradesman's Boast* (1846), and *Henry Longford; or, The Forged Will* (1847).

43. The characterization of radical democrat fiction is from David S. Reynolds, *Beneath the American Renaissance: The Subversive Imagination in the Age of Emerson*

and Melville (New York: Alfred A. Knopf, 1988), 198. The sales figures for Lippard's *Quaker City* come from ibid., 207.

44. David A. Rawson, "Nathaniel Beverly Tucker," in *Dictionary of Literary Biography*, vol. 248, *Antebellum Writers in the South, Second Series*, ed. Kent Ljungquist (Detroit: Gale Research, 2001), 402; William Crisman, "Thomas Dunn English," in *Dictionary of Literary Biography*, 202:102.

45. David B. Kesterson, "Johnson Jones Hooper," in *Dictionary of Literary Biography*, 248:163.

46. For a summary of *The Planter's Northern Bride*, see Baym, *Women's Fiction*, 136.

47. Meehan to Pearce, 2 November 1855, Librarian's Letterbooks.

48. Meehan to Eli French, 29 December 1851, ibid.

49. Journal of the Committee on the Library, 14 February 1846 (Catlin), 16 June 1848 (Sibthorp), and 20 February 1850 (Boydell).

50. Ibid., 10 January 1853.

51. Receipt Book F, 1849–51, 97; Receipt Book G, 1851–53, 166.

52. Receipt Book F, 328 (Frémont), 227 (Webster).

53. Receipt Book F, 96; Receipt Book G, 345, and Receipt Book H, 1853–55, 288 (Davis); Receipt Book G, 262, and Receipt Book H, 236 (Houston).

54. Receipt Book F, 355 (Crittenden), and 182 (Douglas); Receipt Book G, 338 (Benton).

55. Librarian Meehan sometimes had to write to friends of former members of Congress to retrieve books that had been circulated from the Library. For example, Meehan wrote to A. McMakin of Philadelphia to inform him that his late partner had charged several books from the Library on the account of an unnamed member of Congress from the state of Massachusetts. And he wrote to attorney B. F. Brewster of Philadelphia, apparently a personal friend of Meehan's, that several books had been taken from the Library by Brewster's sister, on the account of a member of Congress, but had since found their way back to the Library. Meehan to McMakin, 16 April 1846, and Meehan to Brewster, 17 June 1853, Librarian's Letterbooks.

56. Harriet Martineau, *Retrospect of Western Travel* (New York: Harper and Brothers, 1838), 164.

57. Journal of the Committee on the Library, 21 January and 4 February 1840.

58. Ibid., 7 May 1830, 9 February 1831, 9 January 1840, and 6 April 1854; Beverly Elson, "The Library of Congress: A Merger of American Functionalism and Cosmopolitan Eclecticism" (Ph.D. diss., University of Maryland, 1981), 42.

59. *Estimates of Additional Appropriations for Congressional Library*, 32d Cong. 2d sess., 1852, H. Exec. Doc. 18.

60. Meehan to Pearce, 8 June 1853, Librarian's Letterbooks.

61. Elson, "Library of Congress."

62. *National Intelligencer*, 23 April and 15 August 1853.

63. Johnston, *History of the Library of Congress*, 298 n. 5, reports that there were notices in the *Washington News* (16 April 1853), *Washington Star* (23 August 1853), and *Washington Union* (28 August 1853).

64. Meehan to Pearce, 6 July 1853, Librarian's Letterbooks.

65. *National Intelligencer*, 24 August 1853.

66. Meehan to Pearce, 24 and 29 August 1853, Librarian's Letterbooks.

67. Ibid., 25 October 1856, 3 October 1859, and 15 October 1860.

68. Journal of the Committee on the Library, 12 February 1845 (in regard to Crawford and Powers) and 30 January 1857. On the subject of federal government patronage of artists, see Alan Howard Levy, *Government and the Arts: Debates over Federal Support of the Arts in America from George Washington to Jesse Helms* (Lanham, Md.: University Press of America, 1997).

69. See Donald Dale Jackson, "Around the World in 1,392 Days with the Navy's Wilkes—and His 'Scientifics,'" *Smithsonian* 16 (November 1985): 49–62, and Herman J. Viola, "The Wilkes Expedition on the Pacific Coast," *Pacific Northwest Quarterly* 80 (1989): 21–31.

70. Lydenberg, introduction, 16.

71. Meehan to Thomas L. Smith, United States Treasury Department, 21 October 1844, Librarian's Letterbook. Meehan's letter estimated expenses for the Library for the upcoming fiscal year. Expenditures for publication of the Wilkes volumes are found in the account books titled Wilkes Exploring Expedition Funds, vol. 1, 1842–50, and vol. 2, 1851–64, in the Library of Congress Archives, Library of Congress.

72. According to Viola, "The most immediate benefit of the expedition's visit to the Pacific Northwest was its map of the Oregon territory. Published in 1844, it was the most detailed map of the region north of the Sacramento River up to that time and gave Americans a new image of that vast and important area" ("Wilkes Expedition," 29).

73. Viola writes that "the expedition not only persuaded a doubting Congress that Puget Sound was essential to the nation's future welfare, but it also helped convince the British that continued insistence on the Columbia River as the boundary between the United States and Canada would be fruitless" (ibid., 31).

74. The congressional debate is summarized in Lydenberg, introduction, 23.

75. See Charles Fairman, *Art and Artists of the Capitol of the United States of America* (Washington, D.C.: 1927), and Vivien Green Fryd, *Art and Empire: The Politics of Ethnicity in the United States Capitol, 1815–1860* (New Haven: Yale University Press, 1992).

76. Johnston, *History of the Library of Congress*, 314, which states that Edward Everett introduced a resolution in 1827 "providing that copies of all papers in the archives of Great Britain relating to the history of the American colonies be secured and placed in the Library of Congress." In 1831 the Library Committee received a letter from one S. Converse, who intended to transcribe from British archives important documents regarding the history of the American colonies (315). And in 1860, W. Noel Sainsbury proposed to edit a calendar of documents in England relating to the American colonies (318). None of these proposals was accepted.

CONCLUSION

1. John Y. Cole, "Cross-Currents: BL and LC in Historical Perspective," *Library Review* 23 4 (1983): 247–58.

2. John Y. Cole, *Ainsworth Rand Spofford: Bookman and Librarian* (Littleton, Col.: Libraries Unlimited, 1975).

INDEX

Boston Female Anti-Slavery Society, 134
Boston Public Library, 140, 148, 166, 174–
  75, 178, 214
Bowen, Charles, 130
Bradford, William, 17
Bray, Thomas, 226n. 50
Bremer, Fredrika, 137, 196
British Museum Library, 4, 31, 97, 210–11
Brontë, Charlotte, *Jane Eyre*, 196
Brown, Charles Brockden, 79, 90
Brown, Richard D., 99–100, 166
Brown, William Hill, *The Power of Sym-
  pathy*, 30
Brown University, 156
Buchanan, James, 187
Bulfinch, Charles, 91, 94, 202
Bulwer, Lady, *Chevely*, 128
Bulwer-Lytton, Edward, 124, 126, 128,
  195
Burlamaqui, Jean Jacques, 9, 14
Burr, Aaron, 64
Bury, Lady Charlotte, 136–37, 196
Buturlin library, 114–17, 130, 142, 151

Cadell and Davies, 41, 44–45, 51
Calhoun, John C., 149, 185
California, 188–91
Carey, Mathew, 30, 33, 48
Carey and Hart, 198
Carson, David, 52
Carver, Jonathan, *Travels through the In-
  terior Parts of North America*, 11
Cass, Lewis, 129–30, 172
Central America, 192–93
Channing, Walter, 101–2
Charleston Library Society, 66–70, 217–
  19
Charlotte Temple (Rowson), 30
Chase, Samuel, 64
Chesapeake-Leonard affair, 64
Chevely (Lady Bulwer), 128
China, 183
Choate, Rufus, 132, 147, 151–55, 161, 167–
  69, 188
Christian Examiner, 167–68
Circulating libraries, 24, 42, 100, 114
Clark, William, 54
Clarke, William, 132

Classical republicanism, 2, 28, 37–38, 39,
  43, 53, 57, 71, 75, 86, 104, 123, 211–12,
  227n. 62
Clay, Henry, 107–9, 112, 116, 127–28, 142,
  181, 200
Clay, Joseph, 51
Clayton-Bulwer Treaty, 193
Cogswell, Joseph G., 87, 199
Coke, Edward, *Institutes*, 14, 16, 46
Colbourn, H. Trevor, 9
Cole, John Y., 5, 173–74, 221n. 4
College libraries, 42
Commentaries on the Laws of England
  (Blackstone), 14, 16, 46
Compromise of 1850, 165
Continental Congress, 19–20
Cooper, James Fenimore, 80, 90, 124
Copyright deposit, 28, 81, 90–91, 103, 121,
  158, 162–64, 169, 173–74, 194, 199, 210
Copyright law, 27–28, 126–29, 194
Crawford, Thomas, 207
Crittenden, John J., 196, 201
Cultural nationalism, 3, 76, 101, 114–15,
  129–30, 141–42, 169–70
Cushing, Caleb, 183

Dabney, John, 24
D'Alembert, Jean Le Rond, 60, 70, 82
Dalrymple, Helen, 5
Dana, James D., 182–83
Dana, Richard Henry, *Two Years before
  the Mast*, 191
Darnton, Robert, 5
Davidson, Cathy, 57, 99
Davis, Jefferson, 147, 193, 201
Davis, Richard Beale, 26
Declaration of Independence, 101
Democratic Party, 108, 116, 146, 153, 187,
  188
Denmark, 18
Dennie, Joseph, 79
Description . . . de l'Isle Saint-Domingue
  (Saint-Méry), 63
Dickens, Charles, 124, 126, 195; *Posthu-
  mous Papers of the Pickwick Club*, 128
Dickerson, Mahlon, 110
Diderot, Denis, *Encyclopédie Méthodique*,
  14, 24–25, 60, 62, 70, 82

Born and raised in Detroit, Carl Ostrowski graduated summa cum laude from Wayne State University in 1990. He earned his M.A. in English in 1992 from the University of Tennessee and his Ph.D. in 1997 from the University of South Carolina, where he specialized in American literature and the history of the book. He has published articles on William Cullen Bryant, Nathaniel Hawthorne, and Jesuit characters in novels by Don DeLillo and Thomas Pynchon. His article "James Alfred Pearce and the Question of a National Library in Antebellum America," published in the journal *Libraries & Culture*, won the 2002 Donald G. Davis Award from the American Library Association. After teaching for two years as a member of the English Department at Cameron University in Lawton, Oklahoma, he moved to Middle Tennessee State University in Murfreesboro, where he is an assistant professor of English. He lives in Nashville, Tennessee.